"*Value of Statistical Life in India* provides a rigorous empirical assessment of how mortality and injury risks are valued in the Indian labour market. Integrating global meta-analysis with original evidence from Indian manufacturing, the book estimates the Value of Statistical Life (VSL) and the Value of Statistical Injury (VSI) while addressing heterogeneity, labour market segmentation, compensation benefits, and time preferences for health risks. Grounded in institutional realities, the analysis informs occupational safety regulation and cost-benefit appraisal under India's Labour Code on Occupational Safety, Health and Working Conditions. The volume offers an essential evidence base for scholars, policymakers, and practitioners engaged in labour regulation, risk governance, and social welfare policy".

– **Dr Venkatachalam Anbumozhi,** *Senior Research Fellow at the Economic Research Institute for ASEAN and East Asia (ERIA)*

"*Value of Statistical Life in India* advances labour economics by integrating modern econometric analysis with pressing policy questions on occupational risk and worker protection. Using hedonic wage frameworks, compensation-adjusted specifications, and mixed-effects meta-analysis, the book confronts core identification challenges – endogenous job risk, unobserved heterogeneity, and labour market segmentation. Drawing on Indian labour market evidence, it estimates robust Values of Statistical Life and Injury and examines how wages, compensation regimes, and time preferences jointly shape risk-bearing at work. The findings speak directly to regulatory design, cost-benefit analysis, and the implementation of the Labour Code on Occupational Safety, Health and Working Conditions, offering an empirically grounded basis for labour regulation in a developing-economy context".

– **Prof. Alkah Sharma,** *Director, Institute for Human Development; President, Indian Society of Labour Economics, New Delhi*

"*Value of Statistical Life in India* delivers a methodologically rigorous and policy-relevant contribution to the economics of risk valuation. Employing advanced micro-econometric techniques – including compensation-adjusted hedonic wage models, mixed-effects meta-analysis, and intertemporal discounting frameworks – the book addresses endogeneity, unobserved heterogeneity, and labour market segmentation in estimating the Value of Statistical Life (VSL) and Injury (VSI). Grounded in Indian labour market data, the analysis generates credible valuation parameters for regulatory impact assessment. By explicitly linking econometric evidence to occupational safety regulation, compensation design, and the Labour Code on Occupational Safety, Health and Working Conditions, the book provides policymakers with robust tools for evidence-based risk governance and efficient allocation of public resources".

– **Prof. Ram Singh,** *Department of Economics, Delhi School of Economics, University of Delhi*

"*Value of Statistical Life in India* integrates economic theory, formal modelling, and econometric evidence to examine how mortality and injury risks are valued in the labour market. Grounded in compensating wage differential theory, the book develops mathematical representations of wage–risk trade-offs and intertemporal health risk valuation and tests them using advanced econometric methods, including compensation-adjusted hedonic wage equations and mixed-effects meta-analysis. Drawing on Indian labour market data, it produces robust estimates of the Value of Statistical Life and Injury and uncovers systematic heterogeneity and segmentation in risk pricing. The findings inform cost-benefit analysis, occupational safety regulation, and the implementation of India's Labour Code on Occupational Safety, Health and Working Conditions".

– **Prof. K.R. Shanmugam,** *Former Director, Madras School of Economics; Adviser, Government of Tamil Nadu*

"*Value of Statistical Life in India* offers a unified labour-economics and econometric analysis of how occupational risks are priced in Indian labour markets and how such valuations should inform public policy. Combining compensation-adjusted hedonic wage models, mixed-effects meta-analysis, and intertemporal discounting frameworks, the book addresses endogeneity of job risk, unobserved heterogeneity, and labour market segmentation. Using original Indian data, it produces robust estimates of the Value of Statistical Life and Injury with direct relevance for regulatory impact assessment. By linking empirical evidence to occupational safety regulation, compensation design, and the Labour Code on Occupational Safety, Health and Working Conditions, the volume provides a rigorous foundation for evidence-based labour policy and risk governance".

– **Prof. TCA Anant,** *Former Professor, Delhi School of Economics; Former Chief Statistician of India and Secretary MOSPI, GOI; Former Member UPSC; Adjunct Professor, School of Public Policy, TISS, Hyderabad*

Value of Statistical Life in India

In an era where evidence-based policymaking defines the credibility of governance, *Value of Statistical Life in India* offers a landmark contribution to the economics of risk, labour welfare, and regulatory design. This ground-breaking volume presents one of the most rigorous empirical estimations of the Value of Statistical Life (VSL) in the Indian context, addressing a critical gap in public policy analytics.

Focusing on occupational risks within India's manufacturing sector – particularly in Gujarat – the book systematically examines compensating wage differentials (CWD), insurance mechanisms, and Occupational Safety and Health (OSH) frameworks. Through advanced econometric modelling and a global meta-analysis using mixed-effects regression techniques, the authors situate Indian VSL estimates within international standards, aligning domestic policy discourse with practices in developed economies such as the United States.

Transcending descriptive analysis, the book offers a robust analytical foundation for cost-benefit evaluation, regulatory impact assessment, environmental risk governance, and labour protection reforms. By advocating the institutional adoption of VSL as a cornerstone of policy appraisal, it provides a transformative framework for integrating economic valuation into safety and health legislation.

Scholarly, in depth, and strategic in relevance, this volume is indispensable for academics, policymakers, multilateral agencies, and regulatory authorities committed to strengthening risk governance and advancing labour welfare in emerging economies.

Agamoni Majumder is a lecturer in economics at the School of Economics, Adelaide University, whose empirical research in applied economics focuses on labour, health, and environmental issues, particularly workplace conditions, occupational and environmental health risks, and their economic implications.

S. Madheswaran is a development economist and econometrician and currently an adviser to Jain University and ICRISAT. Former RBI Chair Professor, Director of ISEC, Vice-Chancellor of GRI, Economic Adviser to Karnataka, and founder of the Karnataka Evaluation Authority, he has published 130 papers and five books with international academic publishers worldwide.

Value of Statistical Life in India

Agamoni Majumder and S. Madheswaran

Routledge
Taylor & Francis Group
LONDON AND NEW YORK

First published 2027
by Routledge
4 Park Square, Milton Park, Abingdon, Oxon OX14 4RN

and by Routledge
605 Third Avenue, New York, NY 10158

Routledge is an imprint of the Taylor & Francis Group, an informa business

British Library Cataloguing-in-Publication Data
A catalogue record for this book is available from the British Library

ISBN: 978-1-041-03925-9 (hbk)
ISBN: 978-1-041-04415-4 (pbk)
ISBN: 978-1-003-62826-2 (ebk)

DOI: 10.4324/9781003628262

Typeset in Sabon
by Apex CoVantage, LLC

Contents

Figures

Tables

Foreword

It is a pleasure to write the Foreword for this superbly presented book with a thoughtful title of 'Valuations of Statistical Life in India'. Valuing human life has long stood at the frontier of economics, ethics, and public policy. Policy decisions frequently involve implicit trade-offs between limited resources and reductions in mortality and injury risks. Decisions regarding investments in cleaner environments, safer workplaces, improved healthcare, and risk-reducing infrastructure require governments to assess the value of marginal reductions in the risk of death. The concept of the value of statistical life (VSL) provides a systematic framework for addressing these decisions. Although VSL is widely used in policy evaluation in advanced economies, credible empirical evidence from developing countries, particularly India, remains scarce. *Value of Statistical Life in India* makes a timely and important contribution by addressing this gap.

This book advances the literature by combining a comprehensive review of international VSL research with original empirical analysis grounded in the Indian labour market. It carefully examines methodological challenges in estimating VSL, synthesises evidence through a large-scale review and meta-analysis, and situates the discussion within India's institutional and regulatory context, with particular attention to occupational risks and safety standards.

A major strength of the book lies in its empirical rigour. Using a combination of secondary data on occupational fatalities and injuries and primary survey data from manufacturing workers in Ahmedabad, the study provides original estimates of compensating wage differentials, the value of statistical life and injury, and discount rates for long-term health risks. The explicit incorporation of compensation benefits and intertemporal decision-making enhances the relevance of the findings for policy design.

This volume will be valuable to researchers in labour and health economics, as well as to policymakers involved in occupational safety, environmental regulation, and public health. It offers a strong empirical foundation for evidence-based policy evaluation in India and other developing economies.

Kaliappa Kalirajan
Emeritus Professor
Arndt-Corden Department of Economics
Crawford School of Public Policy
The Australian National University
Canberra, ACT 2601, Australia.
Visiting Professor, Madras School of Economics, Chennai, India.
VKRV Chair Professor, Institute for Social and Economic Change, Bengaluru, India.

Acknowledgements

I thank my agent, publisher, editors, the book design team, and the reviewers for their support, professionalism, and constructive feedback throughout the publication process.

The author also gratefully acknowledges the journals and publishers that granted permission to reproduce and adapt previously published material, including ISEC Working Paper Series (Institute for Social and Economic Change, Bangalore), The Indian Journal of Labour Economics (Springer), and Social Indicators Research (Springer Nature); full credit and permission statements are provided alongside the relevant material and in the credits section.

Abbreviations

Abbreviation	*Full form*
2SLS	2 Stage Least Squares
ASI	Annual Survey of Industries
BLS	Bureau of Labour Statistics
BTM	Benefit Transfer Method
CBA	Cost Benefit Analysis
CFOI	Census of Fata Occupational Injuries
CPS	Current Population Survey
CSO	Central Statistical Organization
CVM	Contingent Valuation Method
CWD	Compensating Wage Differential
DEYL	Discounted Expected Life Years Approach
DGFASLI	Directorate General Factory Advice Service & Labour Institutes
DISH	Directorate of Industrial Safety and Health
EPA	Environment Protection Agency
ESI	Employees' State Insurance
GDP	Gross Domestic Product
GSDP	Gross State Domestic Product
GSVA	Gross State Value Added
GVA	Gross Value Added
HCA	Human Capital Approach
ILO	International Labour Organization
INR	Indian Rupees
MOSPI	Ministry of Statistics and Programme Implementation
NBER	National Bureau of Economic Research
NCIB	National Crime Investigation Bureau
NIC	National Industrial Classification
NIOSH	National Institute of Occupational Safety and Health
NVA	Net Value Added
OLS	Ordinary Least Squares
OSH	Occupational Safety and Health
OSHA	Occupational Safety and Health Administration
OWS	Occupational Wage Survey
PSID	Panel Study of Income Dynamics
QES	Quality of Employment Survey
RPM	Revealed Preference Method

(*Continued*)

(Continued)

Abbreviation	*Full form*
SARS	Severe Acute Respiratory Syndrome
SEARO	South-East Asia Region
SOA	Society of Actuaries
SWC	Survey of Working Conditions
UK	United Kingdom
USA	United States of America
USAF	United States Air Force
USD	United States Dollars
VAC	Value of Asthma Control
VMR	Value of Mortality Risk
VSI	Value of Statistical Injury
VSL	Value of Statistical Life
VSLY	Value of Statistical Life Year
WLS	Weighted Least Squares
WTP	Willingness to Pay

1 Introduction

Vignette: Perils of work – The Price of Red Hands

I met Ramesh (name changed) in a small industrial town in Gujarat, where the air itself seemed tinged with colour. A migrant from Bihar, he had been working in a dye-producing chemical factory for a few years – long enough for the factory's red dye to seep into his life. It stained his fingernails, clung to his hands, and even left a faint hue on his teeth. The walls, floors, and every surface around him were painted the same relentless shade of red.

Ramesh worked in slippers and everyday clothes, without gloves, boots, or any protective gear. All day, he stood over vats of corrosive liquids, breathing in acrid fumes in the stifling heat. When I asked about the dangers, he smiled – shyly, almost dismissively – and spoke of his wife and two children waiting for him back in Bihar. His wages were just enough to keep them in school, but there was no promise he would come home safe at the end of each day.

Ramesh's story is not unique. Across the chemical and textile factories I visited, workers faced similar hazards with little protection, no health insurance, and minimal bargaining power. Many accepted dangerous jobs for low pay simply because they had no better option. But how do we measure the value of the risks they take each day? This book delves deeper to answer this and many other pressing questions, such as: What is the occupational health and safety scenario in Indian industries? Are workers in the Indian manufacturing sector adequately compensated for the risks they take on the job? Are these compensations truly justified? Do workers anticipate the long-term health consequences of bearing such risks? How does prolonged exposure to risk shape their preference for present versus future health?

DOI: 10.4324/9781003628262-1

1.1 Background – The importance of valuing mortality risks

In the era of pandemics, extreme weather events, and rapid changes in the occupation and lifestyle of people across the world, the need for health and life risk reduction policies has never been more pressing. Evidence-based policymaking drives the government efforts to sustain the health and productivity of citizens. Government interventions in sectors like transportation, health and sanitation, energy and industry are devised to reduce the risk of death and injury related to traffic accidents, risks of fire accidents, health risks from air pollution and other environmental health risks, fatal risk reduction from natural disasters, et cetera. However, government policies that aim at reducing health and life risks impose substantial costs to society. The costs are compared with the benefits of risk reduction to determine whether these projects are socially desirable. Thus, a government must engage in a risk-money trade-off while making policy decisions.

Life is priceless, and any attempt to monetise would be unjustified from an individual perspective. But from the perspective of policymakers, this is a necessary exercise if they want to design policy interventions that save lives or reduce the risk of death. Weighing the costs against the benefits of such life-saving policies is an essential exercise to determine their worth and to ensure efficient allocation of society's resources. Thus, the benefits – in the form of lives saved – must be valued in monetary terms. The Value of Statistical Life (VSL) quantifies the benefit of avoided deaths. It reflects the value a population places on reducing the risk of death for an unidentified individual or a statistical life. The concept of statistical or unidentified life is crucial to understand the meaning of the term VSL. For example, an identified life is saved when a group of people contribute money for an expensive surgery required to save the life of an ill person. On the other hand, suppose there is a government regulation on air pollution that aims at reducing the risk of premature death of citizens of a country by one in one million. If this policy were implemented, on average, it would save the life of any one random person out of one million citizens. Therefore, the regulation would save a statistical life and not an identified life. Since the probability of death would be reduced for each person in the population by a small amount, each of them is likely to assign a value to this reduction. If each person is willing to pay INR 50 for the reduction in his/her death risk, then a million citizens are jointly willing to pay INR 50 million on average to save one statistical life (Majumder & Madheswaran, 2020). VSL indicates how much money people are collectively willing to pay for small reductions in death risks. This payment reduces the risk by a minuscule amount and doesn't ensure the death risks will be completely avoided (Viscusi, 2011). Thus, VSL is based on the trade-off between money and the reduction of small health risks.

1.2 Willingness to pay for risk reduction

The willingness to pay (WTP) approach has been widely used to obtain the risk-money trade-off. The amount a society is willing to pay for obtaining the benefits of a risk reduction policy reflects its economic value (Viscusi, 2008). Thus, the amount that all the individuals in a society are willing to pay for a small change in the level of risk can be appropriately used as a point of reference for measuring the benefits of risk reduction policies. Economic literature has been consistently assessing the benefits of risk reduction policies using the trade-off between risk and money. "Thus, the emphasis for fatality risks has been on the ex-ante valuation of statistical lives because at the time of a decision the lives that will be saved are only known probabilistically" (Viscusi, 2014, p. 386). Individuals also engage in a trade-off between income and risks while making day-to-day decisions. Any type of risk reduction policy intervention by the government relies on the "understanding of the value that individuals place on changes in risk levels for threats to life and health" (Bosworth et al., 2017, p. 5). Therefore, it is very important to understand these trade-offs to understand the value of life-saving public policies.

The risk-money trade-offs are popularly measured using two approaches: stated and revealed preference methods. The stated preference approach is used to directly obtain the responses on WTP from concerned individuals (who will be the beneficiaries of the government's health risk reduction project). The revealed preference approach obtains the trade-offs that are implicitly inferred from the observed labour market decisions. In this approach, the hedonic property of a job plays an important role in determining the risk-money trade-off. Studies based on labour market data mainly rely on the theory of compensating wage differentials, a concept introduced by Adam Smith in 1776 (Majumder & Madheswaran, 2016). This theory says that workers would require higher wages to accept jobs with unpleasant or unattractive characteristics, such as a higher risk of job injury or fatality. Thus, controlling other job characteristics, employees must pay compensating wage differentials to motivate workers to take up risky jobs (Majumder & Madheswaran, 2022). In this context, wages reflect a trade-off with job risks. The revealed preference approach is widely used by researchers since information on job risks and wages can be obtained from the labour market, and the wage–risk trade-off can be estimated. The estimated VSL can then be used for assessing various environmental, health, and safety projects of the government.

1.3 The story – How VSL became a popular policy tool?

The term "Value of Statistical Life" was first used by Thomas Schelling (1968) in his essay titled "The Life You Save May Be Your Own". However, the advent of VSL in policymaking happened when a dispute arose between the RAND Corporation and US Air Force (USAF) (Majumder & Madheswaran, 2016). The USAF assigned the RAND Corporation the task of designing the first aerial attack on the Soviets in 1949. The RAND Corporation had to estimate the optimum combination of atom bombs and fighter jet pilots so that maximum damage could be caused to the Soviets, given the constraint on budget and quantity of fissile material available with the USAF. The RAND Corporation minimised the cost by suggesting the USAF use low-cost propeller aeroplanes, which in turn led to huge fatalities. Since the RAND Corporation couldn't assess the lives of the bomber crew, a massive debate emerged on the valuation of lives (Banzhaf, 2014). Thus, this incident emphasised the need for evaluation of lives, and researchers began using VSL for such evaluations.

1.4 VSL – An essential tool for OSH and risk policy evaluation

In 1982, an analysis of a proposed policy on hazard communication was undertaken by the US government. The Occupational Safety and Health Administration (OSHA) used the human capital approach for analysis of the regulation. The policy was rejected since the costs associated with the policy surpassed the benefits. Even though this was a very important legislation intended at saving numerous lives by putting warning labels on hazardous chemical substances at the workplace, this regulation failed to pass. Therefore, a re-valuation of this regulation became necessary. Ultimately, the regulation was accepted after VSL was used to value the benefits of this regulation, which indicated that the benefits of the regulation surpassed its cost (Viscusi, 2011). This event was a game changer in the context of application of VSL in policy decisions by the US government. The government of other countries followed suit and began using VSL for the evaluation of regulations that involved the reduction of fatality risks (Majumder & Madheswaran, 2016).

1.5 Alternative approaches to valuing mortality risk reduction

Before VSL was widely adopted, early mortality risk reduction studies and policy decisions relied on the human capital and benefit transfer approaches. However, research shows that human capital approach undermines the amount that people themselves would pay for small changes in risk. Viscusi (1993) found the estimates of WTP for risk reduction using the CWD approach to be 8–23 times higher than the value obtained using the human capital approach. Another alternative to the human capital approach is the benefit transfer methodology (BTM). It is used by policymakers to estimate VSL for developing countries without undertaking original studies for such countries. This is done by extrapolating the VSL estimates from the developed countries to developing countries. In doing so, BTM assumes that job risk preferences of individuals in the two countries are identical and income elasticity of WTP for risk reduction equals to one. However, job risk preferences vary across countries, and the income elasticity of WTP for risk reduction is less than one in developing countries. In this context, transferring VSL estimates from developed to developing countries would underestimate the VSL of developing countries (Majumder & Madheswaran, 2018). Thus, without conducting independent studies on VSL in developing countries, such assumptions are difficult to validate (Simon et al., 1999).

In most developing countries, the occupational health and safety concerns are left either unaddressed or under-addressed, while the workers pay the price of unsafe workplaces with their limbs or lives. New occupational hazards emerge as countries grow, and these necessitate devising policies and regulations that not only address physical safety at the workplace but also mental well-being of workers. This book presents a VSL study from the Indian labour market. Given that India is currently the most populous country and a major emerging market economy in the world, this study contributes to the small pool of VSL literature from developing countries.

Most VSL studies in India (Shanmugam, 2000, 2001, 2006, 2011; Madheswaran, 2007; Shanmugam & Madheswaran, 2011) are based on labour market data from the 1990s–2001 and provide crude estimates without fully considering how changes in insurance, compensation benefits, or life expectancy affect VSL. To address these gaps, this book presents a comprehensive VSL study for India and answers three key questions:

- Do workers receive adequate wage compensation for taking on risky jobs, and what does this suggest about the value placed on life in India's labour market?
- How do insurance and compensation benefits shape both workers' wages and the estimated VSL?
- What discount rates do workers place on deferred health risks from the job, and what do these preferences imply for workplace safety and policy design?

In doing so, it provides robust, policy-relevant evidence to better protect workers and strengthen health and safety regulations in India and other developing countries.

This book has seven chapters. This chapter, which is Chapter 1, began with a series of questions that will be explored throughout the book. It explains the need for valuing mortality risks and introduces the idea of VSL – its relevance for mortality risk reduction and its use as a tool for cost-benefit analysis of life-saving policies. Chapter 2 explores the issues associated with VSL estimates and the challenges it creates for policymaking. It goes further and deeper into exploring the issues by undertaking a systematic review and meta-analysis of VSL studies from developing and developed countries. Over 100 VSL studies have been reviewed in this context, and the full list of studies along with a summary of them is available in the chapter appendix. The book then situates the study within India's labour market and institutional setting. Chapter 3 highlights the issues and challenges related to occupational risk and mishap data in developing countries like India, followed by a discussion on the OSH regulations in India. The core analysis of VSL unfolds across three chapters: estimating wage–risk trade-offs and VSL – Chapter 4; examining how insurance and compensation benefits shape VSL estimates – Chapter 5; and calculating discount rates for deferred health risks – Chapter 6. The findings are translated into policy recommendations for worker safety and regulation, with Chapter 7 concluding the book by consolidating insights and highlighting future research directions.

Reference list

Banzhaf, S. H. (2014). The cold-war origins of value of a statistical life. *Journal of Economic Perspectives*, *28*, 213–226. https://doi.org/10.1257/jep.28.4.213

Bosworth, R. C., Hunter, A., & Kibria, A. (2017). *The value of a statistical life: Economics and politics*. STRATA. https://share.google/OkEcX1qaKD5rQOLKG

Madheswaran, S. (2007). Measuring the value of statistical life: Estimating compensating wage differentials among workers in India. *Social Indicators Research*, *84*(1), 83–96. http://www.jstor.org/stable/20734507

Majumder, A., & Madheswaran, S. (2016). *Value of statistical life: A meta-analysis with mixed effects regression model* (ISEC Working Paper No. 362). https://www.isec.ac.in/wp-content/uploads/2023/07/WP-362-Agamoni-Majumder-Final.pdf

Majumder, A., & Madheswaran, S. (2018). *Role of worker's compensation benefit in estimating value of statistical life* (ISEC Working Paper No. 407). https://www.isec.ac.in/wp-content/uploads/2023/07/WP-407-Agamoni-Majumder-and-Madheswaran-Final.pdf

Majumder, A., & Madheswaran, S. (2020). Compensation for occupational risk and valuation of statistical life. *Social Indicators Research*, *149*, 967–989. Retrieved October 31, 2024, from https://doi.org/10.1007/s11205-020-02269-z

Majumder, A., & Madheswaran, S. (2022). Discounting long-term job-related health risks in the context of Indian workers. *The Indian Journal of Labour Economics*, *65*, 1099–1120. https://doi.org/10.1007/s41027-022-00415-4

Shanmugam, K. R. (2000). Valuations of life and injury risks-empirical evidence from India. *Environmental and Resource Economics*, *16*, 379–389.

Shanmugam, K. R. (2001). Self-selection bias in the estimates of compensating wage differentials for job risks in India. *Journal of Risk and Uncertainty*, *22*(3), 263–275.

Shanmugam, K. R. (2006). Rate of time preference and the quantity adjusted value of life in India. *Environment and Development Economics*, *11*(5), 569–583.

Shanmugam, K. R. (2011). Discount rate for health benefits and the value of life in India. *Economics Research International*, *2011*, 1–5.

Shanmugam, K. R., & Madheswaran, S. (2011). The value of statistical life. In A. K. Haque, M. N. Murty, & P. Shyamsundar (Eds.), *Environmental valuation in South Asia* (pp. 413–443). Cambridge University Press.

Simon, N., Cropper, M., Alberini, A., & Arora, S. (1999). *Valuing mortality reductions in India: A study of compensating wage differentials*. World Bank.

Viscusi, W. K. (1993). The value of risks to life and health. *Journal of Economic Literature*, *31*, 1912–1946.
Viscusi, W. K. (2008). How to value a life. *Journal of Economics and Finance*, *32*, 311–323.
Viscusi, W. K. (2011). Policy challenges of the heterogeneity of the value of statistical life. *Foundations and Trends in Microeconomics*, *6*(2), 99–172.
Viscusi, W. K. (2014). The value of individual and societal risks to life and health. In M. J. Machina & W. K. Viscusi (Eds.), *Handbook of the economics of risk and uncertainty* (Vol. 1, pp. 385–452). Elsevier.

2 Unpacking the variation in VSL estimates

Insights from meta-analysis

2.1 Introduction

Valuing benefits of any mortality risk reduction policy is a challenging task, and results may vary based on the context of usage, even if a universal/standard Value of Statistical Life (VSL) estimate is used to measure it. VSL is non-uniform and varies widely depending on the method of estimation, country of study, and population characteristics such as risk preferences, age, gender, race, income, immigration status, etc. This is known as the heterogeneity issue of VSL. The presence of such variability in VSL estimates often leads to confusion regarding the best VSL estimate that can be used for policy decisions. This issue is solved by undertaking a meta-analysis of VSL studies. Meta-analysis not only helps in identifying the source of variation in VSL estimates across studies but also provides the income elasticity of VSL. With the income elasticity known, VSL estimates from one country can be adjusted/transferred for use in government policy evaluation in another country. Income elasticity also help policymakers to adjust VSL over time using income elasticity to reflect changes in income and willingness to pay (Sunstein, 2004).

The results of our meta-analysis tell a powerful story: wealthier individuals and developed countries tend to have higher VSL, contrary to expectations, risky jobs do not always command a risk premium, and safety nets like insurance and compensation shape the premium for risky jobs. These highlights set the stage for this chapter, each one unpacked in turn to show what the global evidence reveals about how societies value health and safety at work.

This chapter covers two main themes. It begins with a discussion of the heterogeneity issues in VSL estimates, explaining how they vary across factors such as risk contexts, countries, survey methods. Following this, the chapter presents the systematic meta-analysis of VSL studies. It provides a brief description of the data and studies included and then discusses the results of the meta-analysis.

DOI: 10.4324/9781003628262-2

2.2 Heterogeneity issues of VSL

It is observed that even though two studies follow the same method, the VSL estimates they yield are different and they vary considerably within as well as across populations with respect to dimensions such as individual risk preferences and personal characteristics. Such differences often reflect valid heterogeneity in the valuation of job risk (Viscusi, 2011). Therefore, more precise and accurate estimates of VSL can be obtained by incorporating the heterogeneity issues. The next few sub-sections discuss the dimensions that lead to heterogeneity in VSL estimates.

2.2.1 *Individual risk preferences and VSL*

A substantial body of research shows that individuals who display a higher willingness to accept risk in their personal decision-making are more likely to select riskier occupations. By accepting risky jobs, these workers implicitly reveal a lower concern for mortality risk and, hence, a lower implicit value of life relative to the average worker. In contrast, risk-averse individuals require larger wage compensation for risk exposure, leading to higher wage–risk trade-offs and higher VSL, while risk-tolerant workers display lower trade-offs and hence lower VSL (Majumder & Madheswaran, 2016, 2017).

However, direct measures of risk aversion are rare. Hence, most studies use observed risky behaviors of individuals to study wage-risk trade-offs. Hakes and Viscusi (2007) found that individuals with lower VSL were less likely to fasten the seatbelts in automobiles. A recent study by Parada-Contzen (2019) uses preferences over hypothetical gambles and proxies based on observed risky behaviours such as smoking, drinking, and stock investments and found that the VSL in Chile ranges between about 0.6 million and 8.7 million dollars.

The value of wage–risk trade-offs can become inflated or have an upward bias if risk aversion is not included in the calculation of these trade-offs. This is mainly because risk-averse people tend to choose less risky occupations, and risk aversion in general tends to reduce wages. (Hersch & Viscusi, 1990; Viscusi & Hersch, 2001; Eeckhoudt & Hammitt, 2004; Bonin et al., 2007; Hammitt et al., 2009; Dohmen et al., 2011; Le et al., 2011; Pollmann et al., 2013).

2.2.2 *VSL and worker's age*

The idea that VSL varies with the age of an individual had been an issue of great debate. Earlier studies had limited evidence in support of variation in VSL estimates by individual age. Later, many noteworthy studies emerged which confirmed that there exists a relation between age and VSL, but the debate on this issue still exists. Johansson (2002) showed in his study that the age pattern for WTP for fatality risk reductions over the life cycle is unclear. However, most of the studies in the last decade found an inverted-U-shaped relationship between VSL and the age of individuals over the life cycle of an individual. Aldy and Viscusi (2004) used a life-cycle model and found the VSL of a 60-year-old worker to range between $2.5 million and $3.0 million, which is less than half the VSL of workers aged between 30 and 40. Blomquist (2004) views that a multi-period model with an uncertain lifetime is more realistic and helpful in deriving an individual's WTP for changes in fatality risks at various phases of his life.

Kniesner et al. (2006) argue that policymakers generally assign a lower value to the lives of older individuals compared with younger ones. Nevertheless, programmes aimed at reducing mortality risks may generate age-specific benefits. The notion of a "senior discount" has therefore motivated further research into the relationship between age and the VSL. A common perception is that older individuals, having fewer remaining years of life, are less willing to pay for reductions in fatality risk, which would imply a lower VSL. However, theoretical considerations do not necessarily predict a lower VSL for older populations. In this context, using the Value of Statistical Life Year (VSLY) multiplied by life years saved is more appropriate and convenient to capture the phenomenon of short life expectancy (Krupnick, 2007). VSLY[1] shows a linear or discounted relationship between VSL and the remaining life year.

A recent study by Ketcham et al. (2024) found that VSL measures increase with better health, higher income and remaining life expectancy. They report mean VSLY values of approximately $70,000 in the late 60s, $40,000 in the mid-70s, and $20,000 in the early 90s.

Aldy and Viscusi undertook a study in 2008 where they used fatality risk data based on the age and industry of the workers. They found that older workers had higher VSL. However, a study by Aldy and Viscusi (2007) found that the WTP for fatality risk reduction in younger cohort depends on the lifetime income.

The recent research on age-VSL relationship is focused on exploring the presence of multiple labour market equilibria relating to worker's age. The WTP for fatality risk reduction varies among individuals of different ages. A younger worker may demand higher wage differential for a certain level of job risk compared to an otherwise equivalent older worker. The choice of wage-risk trade-offs change as a worker ages (Aldy & Viscusi, 2008). In contrast, employers may offer differentiated wages to older and younger workers that reflect age-specific differences in safety-related productivity. Since workers' trade-offs between wage and job risk evolve with age, and firms adjust their wage–risk offers accordingly, different age groups may reach distinct wage–risk equilibria in the labor market (Aldy & Viscusi, 2007).

2.2.3 VSL and gender of workers

Obtaining VSL estimates by gender of workers is a difficult task since women are less likely to take up risky jobs compared to men. Nevertheless, many studies have attempted to study the gender differences in the risk-money trade-off. Using a gender-specific sample of workers classified into five age groups, Aldy and Viscusi (2004) found an inverted-U shape relationship between VSL and age for both male and female workers. The VSL estimate peaked for both samples in the 35–44 age group. The peak VSL for females was estimated to be $6.7 million, which declined to $1.8 million for the age group 55–62. On the other hand, Costa and Kahn (2004) found that during 1940, on an average, male workers were exposed to job risks that was nearly four times larger than what their female counterparts faced, and during 1980, it was twice. This implies that over time, the gap between men and women has been decreasing in terms of the level of job risks faced by them. However, more in-depth analysis is required to come to any conclusion regarding this issue. This is a major issue that needs attentions of researchers because the participation of women in workforce has been increasing over the last few decades, and women are engaging in areas of work which were once male-dominated. There are a higher number of women engaged in construction and industrial sectors than before. Besides, it needs to be examined whether a segmented labour market arises for male and female workers.

2.2.4 VSL and cultural tradition

There has been very little work on studying the influence of cultural factors on VSL. Victor Brajer and Morteza Rahmatian (2004) attempted to examine the influence of an Iranian cultural tradition called Diye on individual preferences and willingness to pay to avoid early death. Diye is a type of financial compensation that is offered to a victim's family by the perpetrator in cases of accidental death and injury. The Diye compensation is like the value obtained from human capital approach, and it is commonly considered to be the lower bound for VSL. This study conducted a contingent valuation survey and estimated the VSL to be $66,750. The estimated VSL is nearly 50 per cent higher than the compensation value under the Diye. The estimated WTP for averting mortality risk is $100,000. The WTP value in turn yielded an income elasticity for VSL of 2.44. Therefore, they found that WTP to reduce premature death in Iran is strongly influenced by Diye (Majumder & Madheswaran, 2016, 2017).

2.2.5 VSL and union status

Labour unions contribute to workers' welfare not only by bargaining for higher wages and retirement benefits but also by advocating safer working conditions and adequate compensation for occupational injuries and fatalities. Moreover, unions help disseminate information about job-related risks, addressing the information gap faced by workers who may not be fully aware of the workplace hazards prior to employment (Majumder & Madheswaran, 2016, 2017).

Being a member of labour union can have significant influence on job risks and hence on VSL. Many studies in the US labour market indicate that union members face higher wage–risk trade-offs (Viscusi & Aldy, 2003). However, studies from other countries yield mixed results. In India, Madheswaran (2007) found that union members earn higher wages compared to non-members. Workers with an union membership faced lower fatal job risk but a higher non_fatal risk. Another notable finding of this study is that unionised workers exhibit greater awareness of job-related risks than their non-union counterparts.

2.2.6 *Impact of worker's compensation benefits on VSL*

Workers are provided with compensation if they incur an on-the-job injury or fatality. It includes medical expenses and a portion of lost wages due to injury. Compensation benefit can be given by the employer to the workers either in the form of ex-ante compensating wage differential or in the form of ex-post compensation benefits. It plays an important role in determining the wage–risk trade-off of the workers and hence affects their VSL. Many studies do not incorporate the compensation benefit in hedonic wage equation and end up with biased estimates of VSL and VSI[2] (Majumder & Madheswaran, 2016, 2017).

In the Indian context, Shanmugam and Madheswaran (2011) incorporated compensation benefits into the estimation of a hedonic wage equation. They found workers earn lower CWD if they're receive a compensation benefit for job injury and fatality. Viscusi (2003) found that Black workers were ready to accept considerably lower wages if they were provided with higher compensation benefits.

2.2.7 *Impact of wealth effects on VSL*

Previous research finds higher income levels are associated with higher VSL. Since VSL should rise with per capita income of a country, poorer developing countries tend to have lower VSL compared to developed countries (Viscusi, 2011). While supervisory jobs generally pay more, it remains unclear whether workers are compensated with higher wages for taking on riskier jobs. Hedonic wage theory has long been criticised based on this contradiction (Madheswaran, 2007). The hedonic wage framework treats employment as a set of job characteristics, with risk being a key component.

Consider two occupations: a company CEO and a factory machine operator. CEOs typically earn higher wages than machine operators. However, in terms of health and mortality risk, the machine operator faces far greater risk than the CEO. Hedonic wage theory would suggest that jobs involving higher risk should offer higher compensation. Yet, in practice, high-status jobs such as CEOs receive higher pay, pointing to a mismatch between job quality and job risk in wage determination (Majumder & Madheswaran, 2016).

Safety is generally considered a normal good, implying that demand for safety rises with income. As a result, wealthier individuals are more likely to prefer safer jobs. This also shows that the wealth of an individual affects the job risk choice of an individual (Madheswaran, 2007). Kniesner et al. (2012) found that the workers with higher income levels sort themselves into safer jobs and have higher VSL. In the Indian context, Shanmugam and Madheswaran (2011) found wealthier individuals face lower job risks.

2.2.8 *Job risks and long-term health*

Workers implicitly apply discount rates to mortality risks that occur over time. Because the loss from death is greater for younger workers than for older ones, estimating long-term health benefits or costs requires an appropriate discount rate. Since health is not traded in intertemporal markets, and capital markets are imperfect, a single social rate of time preference may not adequately reflect individual valuations. This raises the question of whether a same or different discount rate should be applied to long-term health impacts. The issue is resolved through empirical analysis. (Majumder & Madheswaran, 2017). Approaches that can be used to estimate appropriate discount rates are the Discounted Expected Life Years Approach, Life Cycle Approach, and the Markov Decision Model (Shanmugam & Madheswaran, 2011).

2.2.9 *Publication selection bias and VSL*

Another issue that has emerged in VSL literature during the last decade is the publication selection bias. Doucouliagos et al. (2014) describe publication bias to be a type of selection bias in which only those selected estimates are reported by researchers that are statistically significant and have appropriate sign as per economic theory. Therefore, studies that obtain insignificant values of compensating wage differentials hardly get published (Hwang et al., 1992, p. 855). Even if studies report unexpected VSL estimates (such as negative VSL estimates), researchers are unlikely to select a negative VSL as their preferred estimate (Viscusi, 2015b). Ashenfelter and Greenstone (2004) used various "publication rules" (rules that improve the chance of publication) to show that there is high probability that consensus estimate is considerably upward-biased because of publication bias. Stanley and Doucouliagos (2012) found that correcting the publication selection bias shrinks VSL estimates by 70–80 per cent.

2.3 Labour market segmentation

Labour market segmentation refers to the presence of distinct categories within the labour market that further differentiate and subdivide workers. As a result, different group of workers face different sets of market opportunities. Viscusi (2011) observed this phenomenon and found that it is possible that the CWD of two workers can vary even though they are exposed to the same risk level. Alternatively, different groups of workers may face different wage–risk trade-offs so that some workers face relatively low risk but receive higher wage premiums, while others are exposed to greater risk yet receive lower compensation (**see Appendix 2A for more explanation on this**) (Majumder & Madheswaran, 2016, 2017).

Segmentation of labour market has important implications on many aspects of the labour market operations and outcomes. A thorough examination of the sources of labour market segmentation is necessary prior to accounting for heterogeneity in policy evaluation. It needs to be understood that all the differences in personal attributes of workers do not create segmented labour market. For example, women workers are less likely to work in a job with fatality risk, and, therefore, obtaining a gender-specific estimation of VSL is difficult (Viscusi, 2011). There are only a handful of studies that have examined the presence of labour market segmentation, and all these studies are based in the United States. The next few sub-sections discuss the aspects which can lead to segmented labour market. While some of these aspects have been studied, many aspects are yet to be explored by researchers.

2.3.1 Segmented labour market based on colour of the worker

Numerous US-based studies identify workers' race, specifically whether individuals are White or Black, as a key dimension of differentiation. Viscusi (2003) found significant differences in the wage-risk trade-offs between the white and Black workers in the US labour market. His study showed that Black workers face higher risk of death in occupations like manufacturing, construction, transportation, wholesale, and retail trade. However, their VSL was found to be much lower than the White worker's sample. This evidence indicates that Black and White workers are confronted with distinct market offer curves (curves showing the wage-risk trade-offs or the iso-profit curves of firms) within the US labour market.

2.3.2 Segmented labour market based on personal habits of workers

Personal habits can be used as an indicator of health risk preferences for the workers since such preferences cannot be observed directly. A study by Viscusi and Hersch (2008) used cigarette smoking preferences of workers as a proxy for attitude towards risk. They found that smokers incurred a higher number of work-related injury risks, but they were paid much lower wage differentials than non-smokers. Therefore, their study indicated that the two groups of workers face segmented labour markets with different market offer curves.

2.3.3 Segmented labour market based on immigrant status of the worker

Another major factor that affects the studies undertaken in the United States is workers' origin, specifically whether an individual is an immigrant or a native-born worker. In this context, Hersch and Viscusi (2010) examined the presence of segmented labour market for immigrants in the United States. They found that the Mexican immigrants not only incurred a higher number of work-related fatality risks compared to immigrants of other nationals and native US workers but also received lower CWD for job risks. The fatality risk of Mexican immigrants was found to be much higher (about 36 per cent to 46 per cent) compared to other immigrants. Besides, they were paid CWD based on their ability to understand the English language. This clearly indicates labour market segmentation in the United States based on workers' immigrant status.

2.3.4 Segmented labour market based on caste of the worker

In a developing country context such as India, workers' caste (social class) has been found to significantly influence CWD and VSL estimates. Madheswaran (2007) reports that caste has a strong influence on worker's wages. This finding suggests that workers belonging to lower castes receive a higher wage premium than workers from other castes in blue-collar manufacturing industries. Shanmugam and Madheswaran (2011) found similar results which highlight the fact that the workers belonging to lower castes tend to earn more in risky jobs. Thus, a segmented labour market may exist in India based on worker's caste. However, this issue is yet to be explored by researchers.

2.4 VSL studies from across the globe

Developed countries have ample literature on VSL compared to the developing countries. Table 2B.2 (see Appendix 2B) summarises VSL studies in developed countries. Table 2B.1 (see Appendix 2B) presents a review of VSL studies from countries like China, Malaysia, Tunisia, Pakistan, Bangladesh, India, et cetera.

Research on VSL in developing countries, including India, is limited due to lack of fatality risk data, reliance on biased stated-preference surveys, and difficulties in explaining the concept of probability to less-educated respondents in stated preference surveys. In India, most labour market studies are based on data collected during the 1990s. Important gaps remain in the literature in the Indian context, such as how compensation affects wage–risk trade-offs and how time preferences have changed with longer life expectancy. These gaps will be explored further in the next few chapters.

2.5 VSL estimates: a meta-analysis

The heterogeneity issues of VSL that are presented in the earlier sections of this chapter indicate that VSL estimates vary across studies based on several dimensions. To examine and explain the key drivers of this variation, this section undertakes a meta-analysis of existing VSL studies. Unlike a conventional literature review, a meta-analytic approach allows for a systematic and in-depth analysis of findings across studies (Majumder & Madheswaran, 2017). Meta-analysis enables researchers to account for the dimensions of heterogeneity in VSL estimates (like variation in income levels, probability of death, and methods of estimation of VSL) and thereby provide estimates of major elasticities of VSL (Stanley & Doucouliagos, 2012). Most of the meta-analysis studies report the income elasticity of VSL, which aids in understanding the responsiveness of VSL to the changes in income level. Table 2.1 briefly summarises a few studies on meta-analyses of VSL. It must be noted that the meta-analyses differ in terms of the composition of samples, models used for estimation (i.e. different regression models), and explanatory variables.

The recent meta-analysis by Keller et al. (2021) used 120 VSL studies and estimated median VSL to be $5.7 million (USD 2019) while Banzhaf (2022) did a meta-analysis of VSL with seven meta-analyses and found the central VSL of US$8.0 million. Both studies do not provide the estimate of elasticity of VSL.

It is evident from VSL literature that methodological differences and sampling variance are possibly two major factors responsible for such variations in VSL estimates. However, there exist numerous unobserved and uncontrollable factors that considerably influence the outcome (Majumder & Madheswaran, 2018). In this study, mixed-effects regression model has been used for meta-analysis because it can account for the unobserved heterogeneity and therefore aid in examining the role of unobserved factors in causing variation in VSL estimation. The mixed-effects regression model hypothesises that estimation variance is not the only source of variation (Bellavance et al., 2009). The mixed effects regression model is given in **Appendix 2C**.

2.5.1 Description of the sample for the meta-analysis

The meta-analysis draws on 34 VSL estimates taken from 30 studies employing the hedonic wage approach. Estimation is carried out using a mixed-effects regression model, consistent with the methodology proposed by Bellavance et al. (2009). The dataset covers VSL estimates from both developed and developing economies. Because VSL estimates form the dependent variable, studies lacking sufficient information to compute VSL were excluded. The set of explanatory variables includes: fatal occupational risk measure for each study (measured as deaths per 10,000 workers), average income of samples in each study, year of publication of each study, dummy variables indicating whether each study has unionized workers, white workers only in their sample, and whether the studies include worker's compensation for injury in VSL estimation, treat job risks as endogenous and examine whether VSL varies

Table 2.1 Summary of studies on meta-analyses of VSL

Author	*Title of the study*	*Number of VSL studies used*	*Results-income elasticity of VSL/ VSL estimates*
Liu et al. (1997)	Estimated Hedonic Wage Function and Value of Statistical Life in a Developing Country	17	0.53
Miller (2000)	Variations between Countries in Values of Statistical Life	60	0.85–0.96
Bowland and Beghin (2001)	Robust Estimates of Value of Statistical Life for Developing Economies	33	Model I: 1.7 Model II: 2.3
Mrozek and Taylor's (2002)	What Determines the Value of Statistical Life? A Meta-Analysis	33	Estimate I: 0.46 Estimate II: 0.49
De Blaeij et al. (2003)	The Value of Statistical Life in Road Safety: A Meta-Analysis	30	0.19–3.98
Viscusi and Aldy (2003)	The Value of Statistical Life: A Critical Review of Market Estimates Throughout the World	100	0.50–0.60
Kluve and Schaffner (2008)	The Value of Life in Europe: A Meta-Analysis.	37	0.26
Bellavance et al. (2009)	The Value of Statistical Life: A Meta-Analysis with a Mixed-Effects Regression Model	37	0.72–0.86
Stanley and Doucouliagos (2012)	Are Estimates of the Value of Statistical Life Exaggerated?	32	0.20–0.38
Viscusi (2015b)	The Role of Publication Selection Bias in Estimates of the Value of Statistical Life	17	0.76–1.13
Viscusi and Masterman (2017a)	Anchoring Biases in International Estimates of the Value of Statistical Life	68	0.6–1.0
Viscusi (2017)	Viscusi, 2015b Bias in the Value of Statistical Life	68	0.53–0.85

Source: Author's own compilation (Majumder & Madheswaran, 2016, 2017).

with worker's age (Majumder & Madheswaran, 2017). Table 2.2 presents the description of the sample used in the meta-analysis of this study.

As observed from Table 2.2, about 41 per cent of the studies selected in this meta-analysis have included union workers in their sample, while 26 per cent of them incorporated worker's compensation benefits for job injury in estimation of VSL. Even though only 26 per cent of the studies included

Table 2.2 **Descriptive statistics of the variables used in meta-analysis**

Variable	*Mean*
Average income (in USD 2005)	25,857.4
Death risk (per 10,000 workers)	1.67
White workers only sample	9%
Unionised sample	41%
Compensation benefit provided	26%
Endogenous risk	17%
Age of the workers	26%
Square of age of the workers	15%

Source: Majumder and Madheswaran (2016, 2017).

Note: Standard deviation of income is 14389.58, and standard deviation of death risk is 1.97.

worker's age as an independent variable, only 15 per cent of them included age squared as well in their study to examine how VSL varies with worker's age. The full list of studies used in this meta-analysis along with details on variables is presented in Table 2C.1 (see **Appendix 2C for detailed list of studies**).

2.5.2 Results of meta-analysis and discussion

In the first step, VSL for each study included in the sample was re-estimated and expressed in a common monetary unit to ensure comparability. In this study, all VSL estimates were converted into US dollars, with 2005 chosen as the base year. Purchasing power parity (PPP) exchange rates from the Penn World Table version 7.1 were used to convert VSL estimates from countries other than the United States (Heston et al., 2012). On the other hand, for US-based studies, consumer price index (from Council of Economic Advisors, 2013) was used to convert the VSL and average income values. Once the conversion of values to a common currency was done, the meta-regression was run according to Equation 2.3, (see Table 2.3, Appendix 2C).

The logarithms of the re-estimated VSLs were used as the dependent variable in the meta-regression. Findings suggest that higher-income earners demonstrated a greater WTP for reductions in fatality risk. The estimated income elasticity of VSL was 0.25, as derived from the coefficient on the logarithm of average income. The income elasticity obtained from this study is in line with the estimates of earlier studies like De Blaeij et al. (2003), Kluve and Schaffner (2008), and Stanley and Doucouliagos (2012). However, it is lower than the range of income elasticity of other recent studies like Viscusi (2015b), Viscusi and Masterman (2017b), and Viscusi (2017).

Table 2.3 **Result of meta-analysis of VSL studies**

Variables	*Coefficient*	*t-value*
Constant	14.148*	8.82
Average income (Log)	0.257**	2.69
Death risk	-0.443*	-4.86
Compensation to workers	-0.662**	-1.98
White workers sample	0.888***	1.65
Union sample	0.366***	1.78
Age	-1.318**	-2.22
Age^2	1.511**	2.18
Year of Publication	0.007**	2.31
N	34	
REML estimate of between-study variance ($\hat{\Gamma}^2$)	0.89	
% residual variation due to heterogeneity (I^2_{res})	100%	
Proportion of between-study variance explained (Adjusted R^2)	65.72%	
Joint test for all covariates	8.91	
With Knapp-Hartung modification (Prob > F)	0	

Source: Majumder and Madheswaran (2016, 2017).

*, **, *** indicates statistical significance at 1%, 5%, and 10% levels, respectively.

Although theory predicts an ambiguous relationship between the VSL and the average probability of death, the results of this meta-analysis indicated a negative association between the two. A similar relationship was reported by Bellavance et al. (2009). On average, studies that incorporated measures of workers' compensation reported lower VSL estimates than those that did not. This result suggests that workers who receive compensation benefits for job-related injuries require lower risk premiums for taking up risky jobs (Majumder & Madheswaran, 2017).

White workers' only sample had higher VSL estimates than other samples; however, the estimated coefficient was not statistically significant. Therefore, there is no strong evidence of racial discrimination for the studies in the sample. This result differs from the findings of Bellavance et al. (2009). As discussed earlier, evidence on the effect of unionisation on workers' WTP for risk reduction is mixed. In this analysis, unionised samples have higher VSL, but the estimated coefficient is not statistically significant. In contrast, Bellavance et al. (2009) found a negative relationship between unionisation and VSL, although their estimates were also statistically insignificant (Majumder & Madheswaran, 2017).

Age was negatively associated with VSL, whereas its squared term was positively associated, implying a U-shaped relationship between age and VSL. In addition, the year of publication of the VSL studies included in the sample had a positive association with VSL estimates, suggesting that recent studies reported higher VSL estimates than previous studies (Majumder & Madheswaran, 2017).

The primary objective of this meta-analysis of VSL studies was to identify the sources of variation in VSL estimates across studies. The statistic I^2_{res} measures the proportion of total variation across studies that is attributable to heterogeneity rather than other factors, with values ranging between 0 and 100 per cent. A value close to zero indicates minimal heterogeneity, while higher values indicate greater heterogeneity. In this study, I^2_{res} was equal to 100 per cent, as shown in Table 2.3, indicating that all variation in VSL estimates was due to unobserved heterogeneity. The model explained 65.72 per cent of the between-study variance, while the remaining unexplained variance, represented by ($\widehat{\Gamma}^2$) was estimated at 0.89. These results suggest that unobserved heterogeneity plays a key role in explaining differences in VSL estimates across studies (Majumder & Madheswaran, 2017).

2.6 Conclusion

Recent research on the VSL has increasingly focused on emerging issues such as heterogeneity and segmented labour markets, producing more precise and less biased estimates that can inform policy. Yet many dimensions of heterogeneity remain underexplored, and the meta-analysis in this chapter suggests that unobserved heterogeneity plays a key role in explaining the variation in VSL estimates. The income elasticity of VSL is estimated at 0.25, consistent with earlier studies (De Blaeij et al., 2003; Kluve & Schaffner, 2008; Stanley & Doucouliagos, 2012).

Against this backdrop of heterogeneity, segmented labour markets, and data limitations, this chapter sets the stage for deeper inquiry. The chapters that follow address some of the most pressing questions: Are workers adequately compensated for job-related risks? Does the WTP for risk reduction vary with age? How do compensation benefits influence wage–risk trade-offs and VSL estimates? What is the implicit rate of time preference for long-term health risks? And do workers from different groups face unequal opportunities in the labour market?

Notes

1 Assuming a time-invariant VSLY each year, then

$$\mathrm{VSL} = \frac{\mathrm{VSLY}}{\mathrm{r}} - \frac{1}{(1+\mathrm{r})^{\mathrm{L}}}\left[\frac{\mathrm{VSLY}}{\mathrm{r}}\right]$$

From the above equation, VSLY is obtained as follows:

$$VSLY = \frac{rVSL}{[1 - (1+\mathrm{r})^{-\mathrm{L}}]}$$

In this expression, "r" refers to the rate of interest which is used to discount worker's years of life, and "L" is the remaining life expectancy of worker. VSLY estimates are not constant or steadily decreasing with age; rather, it increases gradually and finally taper off.

2 Compensation benefit can be included in the hedonic equation in a multiplicative form as shown in equation (2.a).

$$LnW_i = \alpha + \beta_1 p_i + \beta_2 q_i + \sum_k \gamma_k X_{ki} + \varphi_k WC_i q_i + \epsilon_i \qquad \ldots (2.a)$$

As observed from equation (2.a), workers' compensation benefit (WC_i) interacts with the injury risk variable and is incorporated in the hedonic wage equation.

Reference list

Ainy, E., Soori, H., Ganjali, M., Basirat, B., & Haddadi, M. (2016). Cost estimation of road traffic injuries among Iranian motorcyclists using the willingness to pay method. *Archives of Trauma Research*, *5*(2), e23198. Retrieved July 05, 2017, from https://doi.org/10.5812/atr.23198

Alberini, A., & Chiabai, A. (2005). Urban environmental health and sensitive populations: How much are the Italians willing to pay to reduce their risks? *Regional Science and Urban Economics*, *37*(2), 239–258. Retrieved February 02, 2017, from https://doi.org/10.1016/j.regsciurbeco.2006.08.008

Alberini, A., Krupnick, A., Cropper, M., Simon, N., & Cook, J. (2002). *The willingness to pay for mortality risk reductions: A comparison of the United States and Canada* (CESifo Working Paper, No. 668, Center for Economic Studies and ifo Institute (CESifo), Munich). Retrieved August 05, 2016, from https://hdl.handle.net/10419/76004

Aldy, J., & Viscusi, W. K. (2004). *Age variations in workers' value of statistical life* (NBER Working Paper 10199). Retrieved July 12, 2017, from https://doi.org/10.3386/w10199

Aldy, J., & Viscusi, W. K. (2007). Age differences in the value of statistical life: Revealed preference evidence. *Review of Environmental Economics and Policy*, 241–260. Retrieved April 29, 2015, from https://www.journals.uchicago.edu/doi/10.1093/reep/rem014

Aldy, J., & Viscusi, W. K. (2008). Adjusting the value of a statistical life for age and cohort effects. *The Review of Economics and Statistics*, *90*(3), 573–581. Retrieved April 29, 2015, from https://scholarship.law.vanderbilt.edu/faculty-publications/49/

Ananthapavan, J., Moodie, M., Milat, A. J., & Carter, R. (2021). Systematic review to update value of a statistical life estimates for Australia. *International Journal of Environmental Research and Public Health*, *18*, 6168. Retrieved July 12, 2025, from https://doi.org/10.3390/ijerph18116168

Arabsheibani, G. R., & Marin, A. (2000). Stability of estimates of the compensation for danger. *Journal of Risk and Uncertainty*, *20*(3), 247–269. Retrieved August 05, 2016, from https://doi.org/10.1023/A:1007819530588

Ashenfelter, O., & Greenstone, M. (2004). Using mandated speed limits to measure the value of a statistical life. *Journal of Political Economy*, *112*(S1), S226–S267. Retrieved October 07, 2015, from https://doi.org/10.1086/379932

Banzhaf, H. S. (2022). The value of statistical life: A meta-analysis of meta-analyses. *Journal of Benefit-Cost Analysis*, *13*(2), 182–197. Retrieved July 09, 2025, from https://doi.org/10.1017/bca.2022.9

Bellavance, F., Dionne, G., & Lebeau, M. (2009). The value of a statistical life: A meta-analysis with a mixed effects regression model. *Journal of Health*

Economics, *28*, 444–464. Retrieved April 25, 2015, from https://doi.org/10.1016/j.jhealeco.2008.10.013

Benkhalifa, A. (2010). *The value of mortality risk reductions in the Tunisian building and manufacturing industries* (Munich Personal RePEc Archive Paper No. 63617). Retrieved December 31, 2018/July 15, 2016, from https://mpra.ub.uni-muenchen.de/63617/

Benkhalifa, A., Lanoie, P., & Ayadi, M. (2013). Estimated hedonic wage function and value of life in an African country. *Economics Bulletin*, *33*(4), 3023–3031. Retrieved March 11, 2016, from http://www.accessecon.com/Pubs/EB/2013/Volume33/EB-13-V33-I4-P282.pdf

Bhattacharya, S., Alberini, A., & Cropper, M. L. (2007). The value of mortality risk reductions in Delhi, India. *Journal of Risk and Uncertainty*, *34*, 21–47. Retrieved July 05, 2016, https://doi.org/10.1007/s11166-006-9002-5

Blomquist, G. C. (2004). Self-protection and averting behaviour, values of statistical lives, and benefit cost analysis of environmental policy. *Review of Economics of the Household*, *2*(1), 89–110. Retrieved December 10, 2015, from https://doi.org/10.1023/B:REHO.0000018024.53114.3a

Blomquist, G. C., Dickie, M., & Conor, R. M. (2011). Willingness to pay for improving fatality risks and asthma symptoms: Values for children and adults of all ages. *Resource and Energy Economics*, *33*(2), 410–425. Retrieved December 31, 2018, from https://doi.org/10.1016/j.reseneeco.2010.05.004

Bonin, H., Dohmen, T., Falk, A., Huffman, D., & Sunde, U. (2007). Cross-sectional earnings risk and occupational sorting: The role of risk attitudes. *Labour Economics*, *14*(6), 926–937. Retrieved July 15, 2018, https://doi.org/10.1016/j.labeco.2007.06.007

Bowland, B., & Beghin, J. C. (2001). Robust estimates of value of a statistical life for developing economies. *Journal of Policy Modeling*, *23*, 385–396. Retrieved April 25, 2015, from https://doi.org/10.1016/S0161-8938(01)00072-2

Brajer, V., & Rahmatian, M. (2004). From Diye to value of statistical life: A case study for the Islamic Republic of Iran. International Waters Learning Exchange & Research Network (IW:LEARN). Retrieved December 26, 2018/July 13, 2016, from https://iwlearn.net/documents/6053

Cameron, M. P., Gibson, J., Helmers, K., Lim, S., Lim, S., & Lim, S. (2010). The value of statistical life and cost-benefit evaluations of landmine clearance in Cambodia. *Environment and Development Economics*, *15*(4), 395–416. Retrieved July 11, 2016, https://doi.org/10.1017/S1355770X10000069

Carlsson, F., Daruvala, D., & Jaldell, H. (2008). *Value of statistical life and cause of accident: A choice experiment* (Working Papers in Economics 332, Department of Economics, University of Gothenburg). Retrieved June 12, 2017.

Carlsson, F., Olof, J.-S., & Martinsson, P. (2004). Is transport safety more valuable in the air? *Journal of Risk and Uncertainty*, *28*(2), 147–163. Retrieved May 01, 2018, from https://doi.org/10.1023/B:RISK.0000016141.88127.7c

Chilton, S., Covey, J., Hopkins, L., Jones-Lee, M., Loomes, G., Pidgeon, N., & Spencer, A. (2002). Public perceptions of risk and preference-based values of safety. *Journal of Risk and Uncertainty*, *25*, 211–232. Retrieved October 13, 2017, from https://doi.org/10.1023/A:1020962104810

Chilton, S., Covey, J., Jones-Lee, M., Loomes, G., & Metcalf, H. R. (2004). *Valuation of health benefits associated with reductions in air pollution*. Retrieved August 05, 2016.

Costa, D., & Kahn, M. E. (2004). Changes in the value of life, 1940–1980. *Journal of Risk and Uncertainty*, *29*(2), 159–180.

Council of Economic Advisers. (2013). *Economic report of the president*. Government Printing Office. Retrieved January 5, 2019, from https://www.govinfo.gov/app/details/ERP-2013/context

Davis, L. W. (2004). The effect of health risk on housing values: Evidence from a cancer cluster. *American Economic Review*, *94*(5), 1693–1704. Retrieved June 12, 2017, from https://www.aeaweb.org/articles?id=10.1257/0002828043052358
De Blaeij, A., Florax, R. J. G. M., Rietveld, P., & Verhoef, E. (2003). The value of statistical life in road safety: A meta-analysis. *Accident Analysis and Prevention*, *35*, 973–986. Retrieved April 25, 2015, from https://doi.org/10.1016/S0001-4575(02)00105-7
de Wit, R. A. C., Helsloot, I., & Koetse, M. J. (2024). The value of a statistical life in reducing fire risk: A choice experiment among Dutch citizens. *Safety Science*, *169*, Article 106322. Retrieved July 15, 2025, from https://doi.org/10.1016/j.ssci.2023.106322
DeLeire, T., Khan, S., & Timmins, C. (2013). Roy model sorting and nonrandom selection in the valuation of a statistical life. *International Economic Review*, *54*(1), 279–306. Retrieved June 19, 2015, from http://www.jstor.org/stable/23352326
Dohmen, T., Falk, A., Huffman, D., Sunde, U., Schupp, J., & Wagner, G. G. (2011). Individual risk attitudes: Measurement, determinants, and behavioral consequences. *Journal of the European Economic Association*, *9*, 522–550. Retrieved July 15, 2018, from https://doi.org/10.1111/j.1542-4774.2011.01015.x
Doucouliagos, H., Stanley, D. T., & Viscusi, W. K. (2014). Publication selection and the income elasticity of the value of a statistical life. *Journal of Health Economics*, *33*, 67–75. Retrieved October 23, 2015, from https://doi.org/10.1016/j.jhealeco.2013.10.010
Eeckhoudt, L. R., & Hammitt, J. K. (2004). Does risk aversion increase the value of mortality risk? *Journal of Environmental Economics and Management*, *47*(1), 13–29. Retrieved October 05, 2017, from https://doi.org/10.1016/S0095-0696(03)00076-7
Evans, M. F., & Schaur, G. (2010). A quantile estimation approach to identify income and age variation in the value of a statistical life. *Journal of Environmental Economics and Management*, *59*(3), 260–270. Retrieved December 31, 2018, from https://doi.org/10.1016/j.jeem.2009.11.004
Gentry, E. P., & Viscusi, W. K. (2016). The fatality and morbidity components of the value of statistical life. *Journal of Health Economics*, *46*, 90–99. Retrieved February 11, 2018, from https://doi.org/10.1016/j.jhealeco.2016.01.011
Ghani, N., & Yusoff, M. Z. (2003). *Value of life of Malaysian motorists: Estimates from a nationwide survey*. Retrieved July 05, 2016, from https://easts.info/2003journal/papers/3031.pdf
Giergiczny, M. (2008). Value of a statistical life – The case of Poland. *Environmental and Resource Economics*, *41*(2), 209–221. Retrieved October 13, 2017, from https://doi.org/10.1007/s10640-007-9188-2
Greenstone, M., & Nigam, V. (2020, March 30). *Does social distancing matter*? (University of Chicago, Becker Friedman Institute for Economics Working Paper No. 2020–26). Retrieved July 12, 2025, from https://doi.org/10.2139/ssrn.3561244
Haddak, M. M. (2016). Estimating the willingness-to-pay for road safety improvement. *Transportation Research Procedia*, *14*, 293–302. Retrieved June 19, 2015, from https://doi.org/10.1016/j.trpro.2016.05.084
Hakes, J. K., & Viscusi, W. K. (2007). Automobile seatbelt usage and the value of statistical life. *Southern Economic Journal*, *73*(3), 659–676. Retrieved June 14, 2016, from Wiley Online Library.
Hammitt, J., & Haninger, K. (2010). Valuing fatal risks to children and adults: Effects of disease, latency, and risk aversion. *Journal of Risk and Uncertainty*, *40*(1), 57–83. Retrieved December 31, 2018, from https://doi.org/10.1007/s11166-009-9086-9
Hammitt, J., & Liu, J.-T. (2004). Effects of disease type and latency on the value of mortality risk. *Journal of Risk and Uncertainty*, *28*(1), 73–95. Retrieved May 01, 2018, from https://doi.org/10.1023/B:RISK.0000009437.24783.e1

Hammitt, J. K., Haninger, K., & Treich, N. (2009). Effects of health and longevity on financial risk tolerance. *Geneva Risk and Insurance Review*, *34*(2), 117–139. Retrieved July 15, 2018, from https://doi.org/10.1057/grir.2009.6

Hammitt, J. K., & Zhou, Y. (2006). The economic value of air-pollution-related health risks in China: A contingent valuation study. *Environmental and Resource Economics*, *33*(3), 399–423. Retrieved July 05, 2016, https://doi.org/10.1007/s10640-005-3606-0

Hendryx, M., & Ahern, M. M. (2009). Mortality in Appalachian coal mining regions: The value of statistical life lost. *Public Health Reports*, *124*(4), 541–550. Retrieved June 12, 2017, from https://doi.org/10.1177/003335490912400

Hersch, J., & Viscusi, W. K. (1990). Cigarette smoking, seatbelt use, and differences in wage-risk tradeoffs. *Journal of Human Resources, University of Wisconsin Press*, *25*(2), 202–227. Retrieved March 12, 2016, from https://doi.org/10.2307/145754

Hersch, J., & Viscusi, W. K. (2010). Immigrant status and the value of statistical life. *Journal of Human Resources*, *45*(3), 749–771. Retrieved May 10, 2016, from http://www.jstor.org/stable/25703475

Heston, A., Summers, R., & Aten, B. (2012). Penn world table version 7.1. Center for International Comparisons of Production, Income and Prices at University of Pennsylvania. Retrieved March 12, 2016, from BibSonomy

Hintermann, B., Alberini, A., & Markandya, A. (2006). *Estimating the value of safety with labor market data: Are the results trustworthy*? (Fondazione Eni Enrico Mattei (FEEM) Working paper No. 119). Retrieved July 8, 2018/May 01, 2018, from https://papers.ssrn.com/sol3/papers.cfm?abstract_id=932510

Hoffmann, S., Qin, P., Krupnick, A., Badrakh, B., Batbaatar, S., Altangerel, E., & Sereeter, L. (2012). The willingness to pay for mortality risk reductions in Mongolia. *Resource and Energy Economics*, *34*(4), 493–513. Retrieved March 11, 2016, from https://doi.org/10.1016/j.reseneeco.2012.04.005

Hua Wang, J. H. (2014). Estimating the economic value of statistical life in China: A study of the willingness to pay for cancer prevention. *Frontiers of Economics in China*, *9*(2), 183–215. Retrieved March 11, 2016, from https://ideas.repec.org/a/fec/journl/v9y2014i2p183-215.html

Huang, D., Andersson, H., & Zhang, S. (2017). Willingness to pay to reduce health risks related to air quality: Evidence from a choice experiment survey in Beijing. *Journal of Environmental Planning and Management, Taylor & Francis Journals*, *61*(12), 2207–2229. Retrieved November 24, 2017, from https://doi.org/10.1080/09640568.2017.1389701

Hwang, H.-S., Reed, W. R., & Hubbard, C. (1992). Compensating wage differentials and unobserved productivity. *Journal of Political Economy*, *100*, 835–858. Retrieved August 05, 2016, from http://www.jstor.org/stable/2138690

Itaoka, K., Krupnick, A., Makoto, A., Alberini, A., Maureen, C., & Simon, N. (2007). Age, health, and the willingness to pay for mortality risk reductions: A contingent valuation survey of Shizuoka, Japan, residents. *Environmental Economics and Policy Studies*, *8*(3), 211–237. Retrieved February 02, 2017, from https://doi.org/10.1007/BF03353958

Johansson, P. O. (2002). On the definition and age-dependency of the value of a statistical life. *Journal of Risk and Uncertainty*, *25*(3), 251–263. Retrieved October 11, 2015, from https://doi.org/10.1023/A:1020975905719

Keller, E., Newman, J. E., Ortmann, A., Jorm, L. R., & Chambers, G. M. (2021). How much is a human life worth? A systematic review. *Value in Health*, *24*(10), 1531–1541. ISSN 1098–3015. Retrieved July 09, 2025, from https://doi.org/10.1016/j.jval.2021.04.003

Ketcham, J. D., Kuminoff, N. V., & Saha, N. (2024, November). *The value of statistical life for seniors* (NBER Working Paper No. 33165). National Bureau of

Economic Research. Retrieved February 09, 2016, from https://doi.org/10.3386/w33165

Kluve, J., & Schaffner, S. (2008). The value of life in Europe – A meta-analysis. *Sozialer Fortschritt*, *57*(10–11), 279–287. Retrieved August 05, 2016.

Kniesner, T., J., & Kip Viscusi, W. (2005). Value of a statistical life: Relative position vs. relative age. *American Economic Review*, *95*(2), 142–146. Retrieved February 02, 2017, from American Economic Association.

Kniesner, T. J., Viscusi, W. K., Woock, C., & Ziliak, J. P. (2012). The value of a statistical life: Evidence from panel data. *Review of Economics and Statistics*, *94*(1), 74–87. Retrieved April 13, 2016, from https://doi.org/10.1162/REST_a_00229

Kniesner, T. J., Viscusi, W. K., & Ziliak, J. P. (2006). Life-cycle consumption and the age-adjusted value of life. *Journal of Economic Analysis and Policy: Contributions to Economic Analysis and Policy*, *5*(1), 1–34. Retrieved December 08, 2015, from https://doi.org/10.1515/1538-0645.1524

Kochi, I. (2011). Endogeneity and estimates of the value of a statistical life. *Environmental Economics*, *2*(4), 17–31. Retrieved April 13, 2016, from https://doi.org/10.1016/j.jhealeco.2008.10.013

Krupnick, A. (2007). Mortality-risk valuation and age: Stated preference evidence. *Review of Environmental Economics and Policy*, *1*(2), 261–282. Retrieved February 09, 2016, from https://doi.org/10.1093/reep/rem014

Kuhn, A., & Ruf, O. (2013). The value of a statistical injury: New evidence from the Swiss labor market. *Swiss Journal of Economics and Statistics*, *149*(1), 57–86. Retrieved June 19, 2015, from https://doi.org/10.1007/BF03399381

Lavettiy, K. (2017). The estimation of compensating wage differentials: Lessons from the deadliest catch. *Journal of Business and Economics Statistics*. Retrieved February 11, 2018, from https://www.tandfonline.com/doi/full/10.1080/07350015.2018.1470000

Le, A. T., Miller, P. W., Slutske, W. S., & Martin, N. G. (2011). Attitudes towards economic risk and the gender pay gap. *Labour Economics*, *18*(4), 555–561. Retrieved March 12, 2016, from https://doi.org/10.1016/j.labeco.2010.12.007

Lee, G., Lee, Y., Lee, H., Hong, J., & Yang, J. (2015). Value of a statistical life estimation of carcinogenic chemicals for socioeconomic analysis in Korea. *Environmental Health and Toxicology*, *30*. Retrieved December 31, 2018, from https://www.eeht.org/journal/view.php?doi=10.5620/eht.s2015005

Lee, J. M., & Taylor, L. O. (2017). *Randomized safety inspections and risk exposure on the job: Quasi-experimental estimates of the value of a statistical life*. Center for Environmental and Resource Economic Policy (Working Paper Series: No. 17–016). US Census Bureau. Retrieved December 31, 2018/February 11/2018, from https://cenrep.ncsu.edu/cenrep/wp-content/uploads/2017/08/WP-2017-016-1.pdf

León, G., & Miguel, E. (2017). Risky transportation choices and the value of a statistical life. *American Economic Journal: Applied Economics*, *9*(1), 202–228. Retrieved November 24, 2017, from http://www.jstor.org/stable/26156213

Liu, J., Hammitt, J. K., & Liu, J. L. (1997). Estimated hedonic wage function and value of a statistical life in a developing country. *Economics Letters*, *57*(3), 353–358. Retrieved October 07, 2015, from https://doi.org/10.1016/S0165-1765(97)00238-3

Liu, J.-T., Hammitt, J. K., Wang, J.-D., & Tsou, M.-W. (2003). *Valuation of the risk of SARS in Taiwan. National Bureau of Economic Research* (Working Paper No.10011). Retrieved August 05, 2016, from http://www.nber.org/papers/w1001

Madheswaran, S. (2007). Measuring the value of statistical life: Estimating compensating wage differentials among workers in India. *Social Indicators Research*, *84*(1), 83–96. Retrieved October 11, 2015, from https://doi.org/10.1007/s11205-006-9076-0

Mahmud, M. (2005). *Measuring trust and the value of statistical lives: Evidence from Bangladesh. Economic Studies No. 145* (Ph.D. thesis, Department of Economics, School of Economics and Commercial Law, Goteborg University). Retrieved July 05, 2016, from http://hdl.handle.net/2077/2920

Majumder, A. (2019). *Valuation of statistical life: A study on compensating wage differential* (Doctoral dissertation, University of Mysore).

Majumder, A., & Madheswaran, S. (2016). *Value of statistical life: A meta-analysis with mixed effects regression model* (ISEC Working Paper No. 362). Retrieved October 11, 2017, from https://www.isec.ac.in/wp-content/uploads/2023/07/WP-362-Agamoni-Majumder-Final.pdf

Majumder, A., & Madheswaran, S. (2017). Compensating wage differential and value of statistical life: A meta-analysis. *Indian Journal of Labour Economics*, *60*(4), 527–548. Retrieved March 06, 2018, from https://doi.org/10.1007/s41027-018-0102-y

Majumder, A., & Madheswaran, S. (2018). *Value of statistical life in India: A hedonic wage approach* (ISEC Working Paper No. 407). Retrieved November 03, 2018, from https://www.isec.ac.in/wp-content/uploads/2023/07/WP-407-Agamoni-Majumder-and-Madheswaran-Final.pdf

Miller, T. (2000). Variations between countries in values of statistical life. *Journal of Transport Economics and Policy*, *34*(2), 169–188. Retrieved August 05, 2016, from http://www.jstor.org/stable/20053838

Mrozek, J. R., & Taylor, L. O. (2002). What determines the value of life? A meta-analysis. *Journal of Policy Analysis and Management*, *21*(2), 253–270. Retrieved April 25, 2015, from http://www.jstor.org/stable/3325634

Nor, N. G. M., Yusoff, M. F. M., & Sohadi, R. U. R. (2001). The value of life and accident costing: A willingness to pay study amongst young motorcyclists in Malaysia. *Journal of the Eastern Asia Society for Transportation Studies*, *4*(5), 215–233. Retrieved July 09, 2016, from https://easts.info/on-line/journal/vol4no5/45020.pdf

Palanca-Tan, R. (2008). Value of statistical life estimates for children in Metro Manila, Inferred from Parents' Willingness to Pay for Dengue Vaccines, EEPSEA Research Report rr2008081, Economy and Environment Program for Southeast Asia (EEPSEA). Retrieved July 05, 2016, from https://ideas.repec.org/p/eep/report/rr2008081.html

Parada-Contzen, M., Riquelme-Won, A., & Vasquez-Lavin, F. (2012). The value of a statistical life in Chile. *Empirical Economics*, *45*(3), 1073–1087. Retrieved April 29, 2015, from https://link.springer.com/article/10.1007/s00181-012-0660-7

Parada-Contzen, M. V. (2019). The value of a statistical life for risk-averse and risk-seeking individuals. *Risk Analysis*, *39*, 2369–2390. Retrieved April 10, 2022, from https://doi.org/10.1111/risa.13329

Pollmann, D., Dohmen, T. J., & Palm, F. C. (2013). *Robust estimation of wage dispersion with censored data: An application to occupational earnings risk and risk attitudes* (Working Paper, IZA DP No. 6447). Retrieved July 15, 2018, from https://www.iza.org/publications/dp/6447/robust-estimation-of-wage-dispersion-with-censored-data-an-application-to-occupational-earnings-risk-and-risk-attitudes

Powell, D. M. (2009). *Three essays on the impacts of income taxes*. Massachusetts Institute of Technology. Department of Economics. Retrieved December 31, 2018, from http://hdl.handle.net/1721.1/49713

Rafiq, M., & Shah, M. K. (2010). The value of reduced risk of injury and deaths in Pakistan – Using actual and perceived risk estimates. *The Pakistan Development Review*, *49*(4), 823–837. Retrieved July 09, 2016, http://www.jstor.org/stable/41428692

Raudenbush, S. W. (1994). *Analyzing effect sizes: Random-effects models*. In H. Cooper, & L. V. Hedges (Eds.). New York: Russel Sage Foundation.

Rohlfs, C. (2012). The economic cost of conscription and an upper bound on the value of a statistical life: Hedonic estimates from two margins of response to the Vietnam draft. *Journal of Benefit-Cost Analysis*, *3*(3), 1–37. Retrieved June 19, 2015, from https://doi.org/10.1515/2152-2812.1107

Rohlfs, C., Sullivan, R., & Kniesner, T. J. (2012). New estimates of the value of a statistical life using air bag regulations as a quasi-experiment. *American Economic Journal: Economic Policy*, *7*(1), 331–354. Retrieved April 13, 2016, from https://www.aeaweb.org/articles?id=10.1257/pol.20110309

Roman, H. A., Hammitt, J. K., Walsh, T. L., & Stieb, D. M. (2012). Expert elicitation of the value per statistical life in an air pollution context. *Risk Analysis*, *32*(12), 2133–2151. Retrieved April 13, 2016, from https://doi.org/10.1111/j.1539-6924.2012.01826.x

Shanmugam, K. R. (2000). Valuations of life and injury risks-empirical evidence from India. *Environmental and Resource Economics*, *16*, 379–389. Retrieved June 19, 2015, from https://link.springer.com/content/pdf/10.1023/A:1008364502517.pdf

Shanmugam, K. R. (2001). Self-selection bias in the estimates of compensating wage differentials for job risks in India. *Journal of Risk and Uncertainty*, *22*(3), 263–275. Retrieved June 19, 2015, from https://doi.org/10.1023/A:1011135118675

Shanmugam, K. R. (2006). Rate of time preference and the quantity adjusted value of life in India. *Environment and Development Economics*, *11*(5), 569–583. Retrieved June 19, 2015, from https://www.cambridge.org/core/journals/environment-and-development-economics/article/abs/rate-of-time-preference-and-the-quantity-adjusted-value-of-life-in-india/A3BBB3BE8FB8EB5B1BB8B39D3B339854

Shanmugam, K. R. (2011). Discount rate for health benefits and the value of life in India. *Economics Research International*, *2011*, 1–5. Retrieved June 19, 2015, from https://doi.org/10.1155/2011/191425

Shanmugam, K. R., & Madheswaran, S. (2011). The value of statistical life. In A. K. Haque, M. N. Murty, & P. Shyamsundar (Eds.), *Environmental valuation in South Asia* (pp. 413–443). Cambridge University Press.

Simon, N., Cropper, M., Alberini, A., & Arora, S. (1999). *Valuing mortality reductions in India: A study of compensating wage differentials*. World Bank. Retrieved June 19, 2015, from https://documents1.worldbank.org/curated/en/582261468751139383/pdf/multi-page.pdf

Spengler, H., & Schaffner, S. (2007). *Using job changes to evaluate the bias of the value of a statistical life* (Ruhr Economic Paper No. 14, RWI – Leibniz-Institut für Wirtschaftsforschung, Ruhr-University Bochum, TU Dortmund University, University of Duisburg-Essen). Retrieved October 13, 2017.

Stanley, T. D., & Doucouliagos, H. (2012). *Meta-regression analysis in economics and business* (1st ed.). Routledge. Retrieved October 07, 2015, from T.D

Sunstein, C. R. (2004). *Are poor people worth less than rich people? Disaggregating the value of statistical lives* (John M. Olin Program in Law and Economics Working Paper No. 207). University of Chicago Law School. Retrieved October 08, 2015, from https://chicagounbound.uchicago.edu/cgi/viewcontent.cgi?article=1062&context=law_and_economics

Tekeşin, C., & Ara, S. (2014). Measuring the value of mortality risk reductions in Turkey. *International Journal of Environmental Research and Public Health*, *11*(7), 6890–6922. Retrieved June 19, 2015, from https://pubmed.ncbi.nlm.nih.gov/25000150/

Viscusi, W. (2003). *Racial differences in labour market values of a statistical life*. Economics and Business Discussion Paper Series, Harvard Law School (Discussion Paper No. 418). Retrieved October 23, 2018, from https://doi.org/10.2139/ssrn.404302

Viscusi, W. K. (2009). Valuing risks of death from terrorism and natural disasters. *Journal of Risk and Uncertainty*, *38*(3), 191–213. Retrieved June 12, 2017, from https://doi.org/10.1007/s11166-009-9068-y

Viscusi, W. K. (2011). Policy challenges of the heterogeneity of the value of statistical life. *Foundations and Trends in Microeconomics*, *6*(2), 99–172. Retrieved October 08, 2015, from https://scholarship.law.vanderbilt.edu/faculty-publications/95

Viscusi, W. K. (2015a). Pricing lives for corporate and governmental risk decisions. *Journal of Benefit Cost Analysis*, *6*(2), 227–246. Retrieved February 08, 2016, from https://www.cambridge.org/core/journals/journal-of-benefit-cost-analysis/article/pricing-lives-for-corporate-and-governmental-risk-decisions1/284B7CFD697F8C9DA3C87352BA84E012

Viscusi, W. K. (2015b). The role of publication selection bias in estimates of the value of a statistical life. *American Journal of Health Economics*, *1*(1), 27–52. Retrieved August 05, 2016, from https://doi.org/10.1162/ajhe_a_00002

Viscusi, W. K. (2017). Best estimate selection bias in the value of a statistical life. *Journal of Benefit Cost Analysis*, *9*(2), 205–246. Retrieved December 19, 2017, from https://doi.org/10.1017/bca.2017.21

Viscusi, W. K., & Hersch, J. (2008). The mortality cost to smokers. *Journal of Health Economics*, *27*(4), 943–958. Retrieved May 10, 2016, from https://doi.org/10.1016/j.jhealeco.2008.01.001

Viscusi, W., & Aldy, J. E. (2003). The value of a statistical life: A critical review of market estimates throughout the world. *Journal of Risk and Uncertainty*, *27*(1), 5–76. Retrieved October 23, 2015, from https://doi.org/10.1023/A:1025598106257

Viscusi, W. K., & Gentry, E. P. (2015). The value of a statistical life for transportation regulations: A test of the benefits transfer methodology. *J Risk Uncertain*, *51*, 53–77. https://doi.org/10.1007/s11166-015-9219-2.

Viscusi, W., & Hersch, J. (2001). Cigarette smokers as job risk takers. *Review of Economics and Statistics*, *83*(2), 269–280. Retrieved December 10, 2015, from http://www.jstor.org/stable/3211605

Viscusi, W. K., & Masterman, C. (2017a). Anchoring biases in international estimates of the value of a statistical life. *Journal of Risk and Uncertainty*, *54*(2), 103–128. Retrieved February 11, 2018, from https://scholarship.law.vanderbilt.edu/faculty-publications/1557

Viscusi, W. K., & Masterman, C. (2017b). Income elasticity and the global value of a statistical life. *Journal of Benefit Cost Analysis*, *8*(2), 226–250. Retrieved December 19, 2017, from https://doi.org/10.1017/bca.2017.12

Viscusi, W., Huber, J., & Bell, J. (2014). Assessing whether there is a cancer premium for the value of a statistical life. *Health Economics*, *23*(4), 384–396. Retrieved June 19, 2015, from https://doi.org/10.1002/hec.2919

Wang, H., & He, J. (2010). *The value of statistical life: A contingent investigation in China* (Policy Research Working Paper No. WPS 5421). World Bank. Retrieved December 31, 2018/July 05, 2016, from https://openknowledge.worldbank.org/entities/publication/8350466f-bf11-50a4-919b-1550cd489c2b

Wang, H., Cheng, Z., & Smyth, R. (2015). Are Chinese workers compensated for occupational risk? *Journal of Industrial Relations*, *58*(1), 111–130. Retrieved July 05, 2017, from https://doi.org/10.1177/0022185615598192

Yang, Z., Liu, P., & Xu, X. (2016). Estimation of social value of statistical life using willingness-to pay method in Nanjing, China. *Accident Analysis and Prevention*,

95(B), 308–316. Retrieved November 24, 2017, from https://doi.org/10.1016/j.aap.2016.04.026

Yusof, M. F. M., Nor, N. G. M., & Mohamad, N. A. (2011). Malaysian value of statistical life for fatal accident: A conjoint analysis approach. *Journal of Society for Transportation and Traffic Studies (JSTS)*, *2*(2), 30–40. Retrieved July 09, 2016, from https://www.semanticscholar.org/paper/Malaysian-Value-of-Fatal-and-Non-Fatal-Injury-due-Yusoff-Mohamad/64f1a310e78b78c0be70c151fc1944b636fe21cf

Appendices

Appendix 2A – Segmented labour market

Figure 2A.1 illustrates a segmented labour market with two different market offer curves and two levels of job risk. Workers 1 and 2 face market offer curve labelled "w(p)" while worker 3 faces a market offer curve labelled "z(p)". If both the market offer curves have same slope and the only difference between them arises because of their vertical intercept, then the wage–risk trade-offs are not affected. For a group of workers facing job risk level

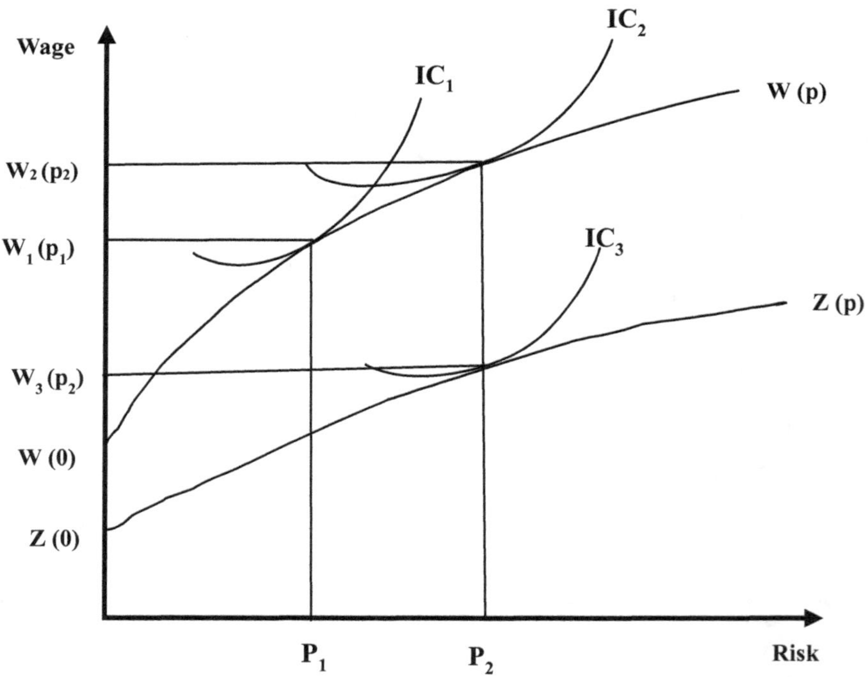

Figure 2A.1 Labour market segmentation.

Source: Majumder (2019).

$\mathbf{p}_2$, the average wage is "$\mathbf{w}_2(\mathbf{p}_2)$" and the compensating wage differential of the workers will be given by $[\mathbf{w}_2(\mathbf{p}_2)\text{-}\mathbf{w}(0)]$. Under the present scenario, both worker 2 and worker 3 should receive a wage premium of $[\mathbf{w}_2(\mathbf{p}_2)\text{-}\mathbf{w}(0)]$. However, this is not the case here. Worker 3, who is on a lower market offer curve "$\mathbf{z}(\mathbf{p})$", receives a compensating differential of $[\mathbf{w}_3(\mathbf{p}_2)\text{-}\mathbf{z}(0)]$ which is much lower than what worker 2 receives, being on a higher market offer curve "$\mathbf{w}(\mathbf{p})$". Thus, it can be inferred that two groups of workers can receive different wage premiums for facing identical job risk only if they are on different offer curves.

Appendix 2B – Summary of VSL studies between 2000 and 2024

Table 2B.1 **Summary of VSL studies based on U.S.A and other developed countries**

Sr. No	*Author, year, country*	*Title of the study*	*Type of study*	*Source of data*	*Findings*	*Value of statistical life (million)*
1.	Arabsheibani and Marin (2000) **UK**	Stability of Estimates of the Compensation for Danger	Hedonic Wage Study	Office for National Statistics and General Household Survey	• They attempted to replicate the study by Marin and Psacharopoulos (1982) using updated data (1985 onwards). • Studied the impact of including non-fatal risks and attempted to correct for endogeneity bias. • Found the non-fatal risk to have a negative impact on worker's wage. • Observed an increase in coefficient of fatal risk variable on endogenising the choice of risk.	£9.7 million

(*Continued*)

Table 2B.1 (Continued)

Sr. No	*Author, year, country*	*Title of the study*	*Type of study*	*Source of data*	*Findings*	*Value of statistical life (million)*
2.	Alberini et al. (2002) **USA & Canada**	The Willingness to Pay for Mortality Risk Reductions: A Comparison of the United States and Canada	Stated Preference Study	Contingent Valuation Survey	• This study empirically examines the influence of age and baseline health on WTP for fatality risk reduction. • They found the WTP is higher for immediate risk reduction compared to future risk reduction. • Found WTP increases with the size of risk reduction but varies little with respondent's age.	\$930,000 to \$4.8 (2000 US dollars)

(Continued)

Table 2B.1 (Continued)

Sr. No	*Author, year, country*	*Title of the study*	*Type of study*	*Source of data*	*Findings*	*Value of statistical life (million)*
3.	Chilton et al. (2002) **UK**	Public Perceptions of Risk and Preference-Based Values of Safety	Stated Preference Study	Contingent Valuation	• Estimates WTP for safety under three contexts – rail, domestic fires, and fires in public places – *relative to* the WTP for road safety. • Also examined respondents' perceptions of risk and attitudes to safety under different contexts. • Found that the impact of risk perceptions on trade-offs between averting death in different danger contexts is much less than what is recommended by value differentials that are currently implied in public policymaking.	Ratios: Rail/ Road =£1.003 Domestic fire/ Road = £0.890 Public place fire/ Road = £0.960 (2002 British Pound)
4.	Viscusi and Aldy (2003) **USA**	The Value of Statistical Life: A critical review of market estimates throughout the world	Meta-analysis	--	• Reviewed 100 VSL studies till 2002. Critically examined various econometric and other issues associated with estimation of VSL. • Conducted a meta-analysis and found income elasticity of VSL to be 5.0–6.0.	----

(*Continued*)

Table 2B.1 (Continued)

Sr. No	*Author, year, country*	*Title of the study*	*Type of study*	*Source of data*	*Findings*	*Value of statistical life (million)*
5.	Liu et al. (2003) **Taiwan**	Valuation of the risk of SARS in Taiwan	Stated Preference Study	Contingent Valuation Survey	• Attempted to study WTP to reduce the risk of infection and death from SARS. • Found that the WTP for risk reduction increased with the degree of risk reduction. • WTP for vaccine that protects from SARS was higher than WTP for other fatal risks.	$3–$12 (2003 US dollars)
6.	Aldy and Viscusi (2004) **USA**	Age variations in workers' Value of Statistical Life	Hedonic Wage Study	CFOI, CPS	• Used a life-cycle model to examine the relationship between individual's age and VSL. • They used age-specific job risk data by industry and occupation for the first time. • They found that VSL follows an inverted U-shaped relationship over an individual's life cycle. • They also found the VSLY to vary with individual's age.	$4.23 (general OLS Estimate) (1996$) At age of 60: $2.5–$3.0
7.	Chilton et al. (2004) **UK**	Valuation of Health Benefits Associated with Reductions in Air Pollution: Final Report	Stated Preference Study	Contingent Valuation Survey	• Attempted to estimate the WTP for reduction in health risk from air pollution. • Found WTP to rise with the number of months of additional life expectancy in normal health.	£1.1–£1.76 (2002 British Pounds)

(Continued)

Table 2B.1 (Continued)

Sr. No	Author, year, country	Title of the study	Type of study	Source of data	Findings	Value of statistical life (million)
					• WTP rises with per capita income. • WTP increased with the perceived probability that some family members would receive the proposed benefit from risk reduction.	
8.	Hammitt and Liu (2004) **Taiwan**	Effects of Disease Type and Latency on the Value of Mortality Risk	Stated Preference Study	Contingent Valuation Survey	• Examined the effect of type of disease and latency on WTP for reduction of environmental risks from chronic, degenerative disease. • WTP decreases with latency between exposure to pollutants and signs of any disease, at an annual rate of 1.5 per cent for a latency period of 20 years. • WTP for cancer risk reduction is found to be nearly one-third higher compared to WTP for reduction of a similar chronic, degenerative disease.	\$0.5–\$2.2

(Continued)

Table 2B.1 (Continued)

Sr. No	*Author, year, country*	*Title of the study*	*Type of study*	*Source of data*	*Findings*	*Value of statistical life (million)*
9.	Davis (2004) **USA**	The Effect of Health Risk on Housing Values: Evidence from a Cancer Cluster	Hedonic Price Study	Reported leukaemia cases between 1996 and 2002	• Studies the effect of an outbreak of paediatric leukaemia on housing Values in Nevada. • They found that the housing values declined by 15.6% during peak risk period for various risk measures and sizes of house.	(Value of Paediatric Leukaemia, VPL) $5.6 (2000 US dollar)
10.	Victor Brajer et al. (2004) **Iran**	From Diye to Value of Statistical Life: A Case Study for the Islamic Republic of Iran	Stated Preference Study	Contingent Valuation Survey	• Examined the WTP to avoid premature death and to assess the impact of cultural tradition Diye on preferences and WTP of individuals. • Found the Diye compensation amount to be similar to value obtained using Human Capital Approach (HCA). • VSL estimates were found to be 50 per cent higher than values obtained from HCA and Diye compensation.	$66,750 (2003 US dollars)

(Continued)

Table 2B.1 (Continued)

Sr. No	*Author, year, country*	*Title of the study*	*Type of study*	*Source of data*	*Findings*	*Value of statistical life (million)*
11.	Ashenfelter and Greenstone (2004) **USA**	Using Mandated Speed Limits to Measure the Value of Statistical Life	Hedonic Wage Study	Fatal Accident Reporting System	• Examines the impact of a US federal government law which raised the speed limit on rural interstate roads from 55 miles per hour to 65 miles per hour on fatalities on road. • They found that implementation of this law led to an increase in speed limit by 4% and road fatalities by 35%.	$1.03–$1.64 (1997 USD)
12.	Carlsson et al. (2004) **Sweden**	Is Transport Safety More Valuable in the Air?	Stated Preference Study	Contingent Valuation Survey	• Attempted to examine the WTP for fatality risk reduction based on modes of travel. • They found that an individual's WTP was significantly higher in the case of air travel than travelling by taxi. • Individual's WTP for fatality risk reduction vary significantly between modes of transportation; however, this doesn't necessarily suggest that different VSLs should be used.	------

(*Continued*)

Table 2B.1 (Continued)

Sr. No	*Author, year, country*	*Title of the study*	*Type of study*	*Source of data*	*Findings*	*Value of statistical life (million)*
13.	Kniesner and Kip Viscusi (2005) USA	Value of Statistical Life: Relative Position vs. Relative Age	Hedonic Wage Study	CFOI, CPS and PSID	• Attempted to examine the effect of relative position in wage distribution and relative age in life cycle consumption. • Found that including relative wage position in hedonic wage equation decreases the VSL. • Inclusion of consumption into the hedonic wage model increases VSL by nearly 20 per cent for middle-aged and old individuals.	\$4.7–\$4.8
14.	Alberini and Chiabai (2005) **Italy**	Urban environmental health and sensitive populations: How much are Italians willing to pay to reduce their risks?	Stated Preference Study	Contingent Valuation Survey	• Estimated the WTP for a fatality risk reduction from cardiovascular and respiratory causes. • They found that the WTP depends on respondent age and health. • The WTP is observed to increase with the size of risk reduction; however, it is not proportional to the amount of risk reduction.	€0.257–€5.8

(Continued)

Table 2B.1 (Continued)

Sr. No	*Author, year, country*	*Title of the study*	*Type of study*	*Source of data*	*Findings*	*Value of statistical life (million)*
					• WTP of elderly is less for a given risk reduction compared to younger individuals. Poor health is observed to raise WTP for risk reduction.	
15.	Kniesner et al. (2006) USA	Life-Cycle Consumption and the Age-Adjusted Value of Life	Hedonic Wage Study	CFOI, Consumption Expenditure Survey, PSID	• Empirically examined how the life-cycle consumption determines the shape of age-related VSL trajectory. • They provided consumption-adjusted estimates of VSL, which changes the age-related distribution of VSL. • They found that although VSLs of older individuals are lower than the peak VSL for middle-aged, they are still greater than the VSL of individuals aged 36 and below.	VSL without industry controls: $20.8 VSL with industry controls: $8.9

(*Continued*)

Table 2B.1 (Continued)

Sr. No	*Author, year, country*	*Title of the study*	*Type of study*	*Source of data*	*Findings*	*Value of statistical life (million)*
16.	Hinterman et al. (2006) **UK**	Estimating the Value of Safety with Labour Market Data: Are the Results Trustworthy?	Hedonic Wage Study	UK's Health and Safety Executive and British Household Panel Survey	• Found the coefficient of job risk to be negative or very large on correction of endogeneity issue using Garen's 2SLS procedure on a cross-section data. • Used panel data as well to correct for unobserved heterogeneity and endogeneity, but the risk coefficient were insignificant.	\$116–\$170 million (2000 US dollar)
17.	Itaoka et al. (2007) **Japan**	Age, Health, and the Willingness to Pay for Mortality Risk Reductions	Stated Preference Study	Contingent Valuation Survey	• Estimated the WTP for fatality risk reduction and studied the influence of age and health characteristics on the WTP. • They observed the WTP to increase with increase in age for their sample. • WTP of individuals with cancer was found to be lower compared to healthy individuals. However, WTP of individuals with heart disease was found to be high.	103–344 (yen)

(*Continued*)

Table 2B.1 (Continued)

Sr. No	*Author, year, country*	*Title of the study*	*Type of study*	*Source of data*	*Findings*	*Value of statistical life (million)*
18.	Hakes and Viscusi (2007) USA	Automobile Seatbelt Usage and the Value of Statistical Life	Stated Preference Study	Contingent Valuation Survey	• Estimated the WTP for fatality risk reduction due to an automobile accident. VSL estimates are based on seatbelt usage. • They found that the usage of seatbelts varies with attitudes towards risk, like smoking status and education. • They also found that individuals consistently balance expected benefits of safety against time and costs of discomfort from seatbelt use.	\$1.9–\$8.4
19.	Spengler and Schaffner (2007) **Germany**	Using Job Changes to Evaluate the Bias of the Value of Statistical Life	Hedonic Wage Study	Institut für Arbeitsmarkt und Berufsforschung and statutory accident insurance	• This study aimed at obtaining an unbiased estimate of VSL using cross-section as well as panel data sets. • They found that individual heterogeneity can lead to overestimation of VSL. • On the other hand, identifying wage–risk trade-offs using job-changer model (that shows the between job variation) and panel model may cause underestimation of VSL.	Pooled cross-section: € 6.1 Static first difference panel model: € 1.9 Job changer specification: € 3.5

(Continued)

Table 2B.1 (Continued)

Sr. No	*Author, year, country*	*Title of the study*	*Type of study*	*Source of data*	*Findings*	*Value of statistical life (million)*
20.	Marek Giergiczny (2008) **Poland**	Value of Statistical Life – the Case of Poland	Hedonic Wage Method and Stated Preference Method	Central Office of Work Safety and Polish Central Statistical Office, Contingent valuation Survey	• Used hedonic wage method as well as contingent valuation method to estimate the VSL for Poland. • They obtained the income elasticity of VSL to be 0.61. • The estimates of the contingent valuation survey failed an external scope test, which implies that the mean and median WTP didn't increase with the magnitude of risk reduction.	\$2.2 (US dollar)
21.	Viscusi and Hersch (2008) USA	The mortality cost to smokers	Hedonic Wage Study	CFOI and CPS Tobacco Use Supplement	• Attempted to estimate VSL of workers by their smoking status, age, and gender, and thereby estimate the value of their fatality risks. • Using a 3 per cent discount rate, they found the discounted expected mortality cost per pack to be \$222 for male smokers and \$94 for female smokers. • Using a 15 per cent or more discount rate, the cost falls to less than \$25 per pack.	\$7 (2006 US dollar)

(*Continued*)

Table 2B.1 (Continued)

Sr. No	*Author, year, country*	*Title of the study*	*Type of study*	*Source of data*	*Findings*	*Value of statistical life (million)*
22.	Carlsson et al. (2008) **Switzerland**	Value of statistical life and cause of accident: A choice experiment	Stated Preference Study	Choice experiment	• Attempted to estimate and compare the WTP for fatal risk reductions for traffic, drowning, and fire accidents. • They found VSL for fire and drowning accidents to be nearly one-third lower compared to traffic accidents. • The surveyed individuals were found to place a higher value on reducing a lower initial risk compared to a higher initial risk.	For fire: SEK 13.2, For drowning: SEK 12.6, For traffic accidents: SEK 20.0 (2007 Swedish Kronor)
23.	Aldy and Viscusi (2008) USA	Adjusting the value of statistical life for age and Cohort effects	Hedonic Wage Study	CFOI data for the period 1992–2000 and CPS	• This study uses an age-specific job risk and estimates VSL over the life cycle by pooling eight years of cross-sectional data. It also uses a minimum distance estimator to control for cohort effects based on year of birth. Finally, it examines whether there is variation in VSLY by age.	VSL from cross-section estimates: (18–24): \$3.7, (35–44): \$9.7, (55–62): \$3.5 Minimum distance estimator: \$7.8 at peak age of 46

(*Continued*)

Table 2B.1 (Continued)

Sr. No	Author, year, country	Title of the study	Type of study	Source of data	Findings	Value of statistical life (million)
					• They found that VSL increases and then decreases across population and over life cycle, but the trajectory differs according to cohort effects. • Inclusion of cohort effects yields a comparatively flat age-VSL function over life cycle. • VSLY is observed to follow an inverted U-shape relation with age.	
24.	Viscusi (2009) USA	Valuing risks of death from terrorism and natural disasters	Stated Preference Study	Contingent Valuation Survey	• This article's estimates of the value of reducing terrorism deaths and natural disaster deaths relative to traffic deaths. • They found that the value of reduction in death from terrorism is almost twice that of reductions in deaths from natural disasters. • Differences in utility values and not the differences in risk beliefs pertaining to exposure to risk seem to be mainly responsible for the higher valuation of reductions in deaths from terrorism risks.	--

(*Continued*)

Table 2B.1 (Continued)

Sr. No	*Author, year, country*	*Title of the study*	*Type of study*	*Source of data*	*Findings*	*Value of statistical life (million)*
25.	Hendryx and Ahern (2009) USA	Mortality in Appalachian Coal Mining Regions: The Value of Statistical Life Lost	Hedonic Wage Study	Centres for Disease Control and Prevention	• They examined the mortality rates in Appalachian coal mining areas during 1979–2005 and estimated the corresponding VSL. • They also evaluated the costs and benefits associated with the Appalachian coal mining economy. • They found that the cost of mining exceeds the benefit.	$18.563 billion to $84.544 billion (2005 US dollar)
26.	Powell (2009) USA	Using Income Tax Changes to Identify the Value of Statistical Life	Hedonic Wage Study	National Traumatic Occupational Fatality Surveillance System, CPS and NBER's Taxsim Program	• This paper estimates compensating differentials, keeping in view of the fact that these differentials depend on the income tax rate. • They found that changes in tax rate also cause differential wage changes on the basis of non-wage amenities. • They found that significant heterogeneity is present in the incidence of tax changes. • However, the VSL estimated in this paper is implausibly high, and omitted variable bias may have resulted in such high VSL.	$50–$75

(Continued)

Table 2B.1 (Continued)

Sr. No	*Author, year, country*	*Title of the study*	*Type of study*	*Source of data*	*Findings*	*Value of statistical life (million)*
27.	Evans and Schaur (2010) USA	A quantile estimation approach to identify income and age variation in the value of statistical life	Hedonic Wage Study	Health and Retirement Study	• Examined the variation of WTP for fatality risk reduction based on income and age differences. • They found that income heterogeneity causes more variation in VSL estimates compared to differences in age.	\$6.7 million (1998 US dollar)
28.	Hammitt and Haslinger (2010) USA	Valuing fatal risks to children and adults: Effects of disease, latency, and risk aversion	Stated Preference Study	Primary Survey	• This study examines the heterogeneity of WTP to reduce risks from fatal disease and trauma to adults and children. • They found that WTP to reduce fatal-disease risks is comparable to WTP for various cancer and non-cancer diseases. It is also comparable to WTP for reduction in motor-vehicle crashes. • WTP was uniformly larger for reducing risk to children compared to that of adults.	For adult: \$6–\$10 For children: and \$12–\$15

(*Continued*)

Table 2B.1 (Continued)

Sr. No	*Author, year, country*	*Title of the study*	*Type of study*	*Source of data*	*Findings*	*Value of statistical life (million)*
29.	Blomquist et al. **(2011)** USA	Willingness to pay for improving fatality risks and asthma symptoms: Values for children and adults of all ages	Stated Preference Study	Contingent Valuation Survey	• This study examined the effect of age on valuation of mortality and morbidity risks. • This study estimated the VSL for children and elderly people and the value of asthma control (VAC) for children as well as adults. • They found that WTP for asthma control was unrelated to individual's age. • VAC was found to be highest for young children and young adults, and it is lowest for older adults who are in their fifties and sixties.	Mean VSL: $3.8 Age 4:$14.1 Age 30:$3.7 Age 66:$6.7 Age 92:$1.5
30.	Kochi **(2011)** **Mexico,** USA	Endogeneity and estimates of the value of statistical life	Hedonic Wage Study	Survey of Income and Programme Participation	• This study presents a robustness analysis to correct endogeneity bias arising in cross-sectional hedonic wage studies. • He found that there exists considerable endogeneity bias in cross-sectional models.	

(*Continued*)

Table 2B.1 (Continued)

Sr. No	*Author, year, country*	*Title of the study*	*Type of study*	*Source of data*	*Findings*	*Value of statistical life (million)*
					• On controlling the unobserved heterogeneity, they found a 30–60 per cent decrease in VSL that is estimated using cross-section hedonic model. • They suggest that hedonic wage model should account for industry characteristics in order to avoid a possible upward bias in estimates of wage–risk trade-offs.	\$1.92–\$2.82
31.	Kniesner et al. (2012) USA	The Value of Statistical Life: Evidence from Panel Data	Hedonic Wage Study	PSID and CFOI for 1992–2002	• This study showed how the best available data and econometric methods influence estimated VSL and narrow the range of the estimates. • They controlled for various types of issues like measurement error, endogeneity, and worker heterogeneity to yield the VSL estimate.	\$7–\$12

(Continued)

Table 2B.1 (Continued)

Sr. No	*Author, year, country*	*Title of the study*	*Type of study*	*Source of data*	*Findings*	*Value of statistical life (million)*
					• They found that narrowing the range of cost-per-life-saved significantly reduces the indeterminacy range, and it has considerable practical results given the real distribution of policy performance.	
32.	Roman et al. (2012) **Canada**	Expert Elicitation of the Value per Statistical Life in an Air Pollution Context	Pilot Expert Judgement Study	Expert Elicitation Interviews	• This study introduces a novel method of elicitation of quantitative probabilistic judgements from subject matter experts on uncertainties in VSL estimates in the context of air pollution. • Results for each of the three selected experts were combined to develop example quantitative probabilistic uncertainty distributions for VSL that could be integrated into air quality models.	\$3–\$4

(*Continued*)

Table 2B.1 (Continued)

Sr. No	*Author, year, country*	*Title of the study*	*Type of study*	*Source of data*	*Findings*	*Value of statistical life (million)*
33.	Rohlfs et al. (2012) USA	New Estimates of the Value of Statistical Life Using Air Bag Regulations as a Quasi-Experiment	Hedonic Price Study	1974–2006 Fatality Analysis Reporting System	• Attempted to obtain the demand curve for airbags and the distribution of VSL across consumers. • This is the first study that provides VSL estimates based on external shocks to risks that are faced by consumers. • They found that a large portion of consumers assigned negative values to airbags, which may be because they distrust the technology. • VSL values for white, Asian, and other races are similar. • They found VSL to be slightly higher for consumers who are above the age of 60, as compared to consumers who are aged 30–59	\$7–\$13

(*Continued*)

Table 2B.1 (Continued)

Sr. No	*Author, year, country*	*Title of the study*	*Type of study*	*Source of data*	*Findings*	*Value of statistical life (million)*
34.	Rohlfs (**2012**) USA	The Economic Cost of Conscription and an Upper Bound on the Value of Statistical Life: Hedonic Estimates from Two Margins of Response to the Vietnam Draft	Hedonic Wage Study	Selective Service System and Statistical Abstract of the United States, 1961–1977	• Measured the cost of the Vietnam draft by using the decision to attend college and decision to enlist voluntarily for the war. • They estimated the cost of the draft to be approximately $115,000 for marginal military recruit. • The estimated cost for marginal college student was estimated to be only $30,000. • White men's WTP were much higher compared to that of Black men.	$7–$12 (2009 US dollar)
35.	Parada-Contzen et al. (**2012**) **Chile**	The value of statistical life in Chile	Hedonic Wage Study	Chilean Safety Association and Chilean National Socio-Economic Survey, 2006	• They estimated VSL and VSI for workers in Chile. • They corrected for the selectivity bias and endogeneity by using Garen's bias correction procedure. • On correction of endogeneity, VSL increased by almost a factor of three. • However, estimated values are lower than those of other developed countries.	Basic estimate: $4,625,958 Endogeneity-corrected estimate: $12,826,520 VSI: $30,840

(*Continued*)

Table 2B.1 (Continued)

Sr. No	*Author, year, country*	*Title of the study*	*Type of study*	*Source of data*	*Findings*	*Value of statistical life (million)*
36.	Kuhn and Ruf (2013) **Switzerland**	The Value of a Statistical Injury: New Evidence from the Swiss Labour Market	Hedonic Wage Study	Swiss Wage Structure Survey and Swiss Accident Insurance Fund	• Examines the presence of compensation for non-fatal risks and estimates the value of a statistical injury in Switzerland. • They found that using narrower samples, using accident risk at a lower level of aggregation, and using the wage component that is specific to the firm produces higher estimates of VSI. • Workers engaged in low-skilled jobs had statistically significant and positive compensation for non-fatal accident risk.	Value of Statistical Injury: 35,000 Swiss francs
37.	DeLeire et al. (2013) USA	Roy Model Sorting and Non-random Selection in the Valuation of a Statistical Life	Hedonic Wage Study	BLS, Department of Labour's Dictionary of Occupational Titles and CPS	• They corrected the downward bias in VSL estimates that arises from sorting of workers by idiosyncratic returns. • They use Roy Model, which is based on the idea that occupational sorting depends only on worker's wage.	For men: $18.755 million, For women: $29.299 million

(Continued)

Table 2B.1 (Continued)

Sr. No	*Author, year, country*	*Title of the study*	*Type of study*	*Source of data*	*Findings*	*Value of statistical life (million)*
					• The corrected estimate of VSL using Roy model is found to be nearly three to four times higher for men aged 18–60 than the value obtained using traditional methods.	
38.	Tekeşin and Ara (2014) **Turkey**	Measuring the Value of Mortality Risk Reductions in Turkey	Stated Preference Study	Choice Experiment	• Examined the WTP for fatality risk reduction due to four causes: lung cancer, other kinds of cancer, respiratory disease, and traffic accident. • They found lung cancer to have a premium of 213% relative to traffic accidents. • The peak VSL was estimated to be $0.8 million for age group 30–39. • They found that if Turkey complied with European Union air quality standards, then it would obtain welfare gains of about $373 million from reduction in premature mortality for the four study areas.	Region wise VSL: Afsin-Elbistan: $0.56 Kutahya-Tavsanli: $0.35, Ankara: $0.46 Pooled VSL: $0.49 (2012 US dollar)

(*Continued*)

Table 2B.1 (Continued)

Sr. No	*Author, year, country*	*Title of the study*	*Type of study*	*Source of data*	*Findings*	*Value of statistical life (million)*
39.	Viscusi et al. (2014) USA	Assessing whether there is a cancer premium for the Value of statistical life	Stated Preference Study	Stated Preference Survey	• This study examines the cancer risk premium for VSL using stated preference valuations of cancer risks for a nationally representative sample from the United States. • They estimated the VSL certainty premium to be \$1.5 million for eliminating a risk of cancer. • The estimated VSL in this study for an immediate risk of cancer is about 21 per cent higher compared to values for acute accidents in the United States. • This study also found that individuals who perceived their risk of exposure to be above the national average level have VSL that is 54% higher compared to the typical VSL.	\$10.85

(Continued)

Table 2B.1 (Continued)

Sr. No	*Author, year, country*	*Title of the study*	*Type of study*	*Source of data*	*Findings*	*Value of statistical life (million)*
40.	Viscusi (2015a) USA	Pricing lives for corporate and governmental risk decisions	Review of Studies	Previous studies on punitive damages in the United States	• This study examined how companies can use VSL to make risk decisions. In doing so, he presented the case study of ignition switch recall of General Motors in 2014. • Besides, this paper also puts forward cases of other auto recalls, which show that automobile companies have a bad legal experience with risk analysis. Mostly, companies use the court-outward method for wrongful death cases in doing the benefit-cost analysis of risks. • Companies should undertake systematic benefit-cost analysis of safety measures using VSL estimates rather than wrongful death cases. VSL can play a key role in awarding punitive damages and sanctioning policies in this respect.	$9.1

(*Continued*)

Table 2B.1 (Continued)

Sr. No	*Author, year, country*	*Title of the study*	*Type of study*	*Source of data*	*Findings*	*Value of statistical life (million)*
41.	Viscusi and Gentry (2015) USA	The value of statistical life for transportation regulations: A test of the benefits transfer methodology	Hedonic Wage Study	CFOI 2003–2008	• This study examines whether it is appropriate to use labour market-based VSL to value benefits of transport regulations. • They found that the average labour market-based VSI estimates fall on the lower end of the existing range of Department of Transportation's estimated VSI. • They found that the shift that BLS made from a job-based to an hour-based rate is better because it standardises risk on the basis of a uniform span of exposure. Besides, this method yields higher transport VSLs and lower non-transport VSLs compared to the job-based method. • They also found that transport VSL is comparable to non-transport VSL, after accounting for the injury rates.	$9.2

(Continued)

Table 2B.1 (Continued)

Sr. No	*Author, year, country*	*Title of the study*	*Type of study*	*Source of data*	*Findings*	*Value of statistical life (million)*
42.	Lee et al. (2015) **South Korea**	Value of statistical life estimation of carcinogenic chemicals for socio-economic analysis in Korea	Stated Preference Study	Contingent Valuation Survey	• This study estimates the WTP for fatality risk reduction from carcinogenic chemicals in Korea and thereby estimates the VSL of the sample. • They found that factors like location, age, household income, and quality of life significantly affect an individual's WTP for risk reduction. • The WTP was estimated to be 41205 Korean won per person.	796 (Korean Won)
43.	Viscusi (2015b) USA	The role of publication selection bias in estimates of the value of statistical life	Meta-analysis	17 labour market-based studies in the United States	• This article shows that publication selection bias was present in earlier US-based VSL studies, which used fatality risk data other than CFOI because CFOI data is less affected by measurement error and yields higher bias-corrected VSL estimates compared to earlier fatality risk measures.	$9.5 (2013 US dollar)

(*Continued*)

Table 2B.1 (Continued)

Sr. No	*Author, year, country*	*Title of the study*	*Type of study*	*Source of data*	*Findings*	*Value of statistical life (million)*
					• The sample of the meta-analysis comprises all published articles and working papers that estimated VSL based on CFOI data. • The results of this study indicate that publication bias has a statistically significant role in affecting the VSL estimates of studies. • The income elasticity estimated from this study ranges between 0.76 and 1.13.	
44.	Gentry and Viscusi (2016) USA	The fatality and morbidity components of the value of statistical life	Hedonic Wage Study	CFOI	• This study analyses and disentangles the mortality and morbidity components of VSL. • They found that after accounting for fatality risk and lost workday injury rate, workers receive an extra wage differential for morbidity risk related to fatality.	Value of morbidity risk: $1

(Continued)

Table 2B.1 (Continued)

Sr. No	*Author, year, country*	*Title of the study*	*Type of study*	*Source of data*	*Findings*	*Value of statistical life (million)*
					• The morbidity effect accounts for nearly 6–25 per cent of the total morbidity and fatality risk effect. • However, they find that the value of the fatality risk is a dominant component of VSL compared to the value of the morbidity risk.	
45.	Haddak (**2016**) **France**	Estimating the willingness to pay for road safety improvement	Stated-preference Study	Contingent Valuation Survey	• Examines the French households' WTP to reduce their risk of non-fatal injuries from road accidents. • The results of this study indicate that people have higher WTP for reducing the risk of heavy injuries compared to risk of minor and moderate injuries. • The results also indicate a strong influence of an individual's accidental experience on their WTP. • Young individuals aged 18–24 are WTP 24 euros more than people aged between 25 and 44 years. People aged 45–64 and 65–74 were WTP 6 euros less than the young people.	---

(*Continued*)

Table 2B.1 (Continued)

Sr. No	*Author, year, country*	*Title of the study*	*Type of study*	*Source of data*	*Findings*	*Value of statistical life (million)*
46.	Lee and Taylor (2017)	Randomised Safety Inspections and Risk Exposure on the Job: Quasi-experimental Estimates of the Value of Statistical Life	Quasi-experimental Design	10-year panel data from OSHA and the US Census Bureau	• This study uses randomised safety inspections at workplace to ascertain CWD for risky working conditions and thereby estimate VSL. • They found that inspections are effective in decreasing plant-level fatality risks by nearly 50 per cent, and these reductions last for the entire study period. • It was observed that after inspection, the wages of workers are decreased by an average of 2–3 per cent. • They also found that fringe compensation benefit payments comprise of nearly 35 per cent of the wage differentials, and incorporating them increases the VSL estimates.	\$6–\$10 (2016 US dollar)
47.	Lavettiy (2017) USA	The Estimation of Compensating Wage Differentials: Lessons from the Deadliest Catch	Stated Preference Study	Survey undertaken between 2003 and 2009	• Estimated VSL for commercial fishing deckhands working in Alaskan Bering Sea and Aleutian Islands fisheries.	Marginal VSL: \$4.13–\$5.04

(*Continued*)

Table 2B.1 (Continued)

Sr. No	*Author, year, country*	*Title of the study*	*Type of study*	*Source of data*	*Findings*	*Value of statistical life (million)*
					• Used a set of longitudinal survey data for estimation of the CWD. • He found that marginal aversion to fatal risk decreases as the level of risk rises.	
48.	Viscusi and Masterman **(2017b)** USA	Income Elasticity and the Global Value of Statistical Life	Benefit Transfer Method	68 VSL Studies	• This article suggests that transferring a base VSL from the US labour market estimates is the best way to calculate VSL for countries which have insufficient or unreliable data. The VSL should be adjusted for the differences in incomes of the two countries. • They used the benefit transfer method to calculate VSL for 189 countries. • Using a fixed effects specification, they estimated the income elasticity of VSL within the United States to be between 0.5 and 0.7, while it is slightly higher than 1.0 in case of non-US countries. • Using Quantile regression they found that income elasticity of VSL declines as VSL level increases.	Base VSL: \$9.6 Mean VSL: \$13.5, Mean of US studies: \$13 Mean of non-US-based studies: \$15.6

(*Continued*)

Table 2B.1 (Continued)

Sr. No	*Author, year, country*	*Title of the study*	*Type of study*	*Source of data*	*Findings*	*Value of statistical life (million)*
49.	Viscusi and Masterman (2017a) USA	Anchoring Biases in International Estimates of the Value of Statistical Life	Meta-analysis	68 VSL studies that are classified on the basis of five different governmental and non-governmental sources of job-related fatality data that they used	• This article presents the first comparison of the publication selection biases in the United States and international estimates. • They found that publication selection biases significantly affect the VSL estimates of international studies. • The publication selection bias varies across VSL distribution and it is more prominent for larger VSL estimates. • VSL estimates from other countries are expected to be lower than the US studies because of income differences between the countries. This form of bias effect is consistent with international studies that rely on the US estimates as an anchor for reasonable VSL estimates.	$9.6

(*Continued*)

Table 2B.1 (Continued)

Sr. No	*Author, year, country*	*Title of the study*	*Type of study*	*Source of data*	*Findings*	*Value of statistical life (million)*
					• This study suggests that it is better to use the baseline VSL estimate of $9.6 million that has been adjusted for bias for generating international VSL estimates rather than depending on direct estimates for other countries. • To estimate the VSL, they have used the usual range of income elasticity, which is between 0.6 and 1.0.	
50.	Viscusi (2018) USA	Best Estimate Selection Bias in the Value of a Statistical Life	Meta-analysis	1025 VSL Estimates from 68 Studies	• This article examines the magnitude and direction of publication selection bias based on meta-analyses of studies comprising of "best set" of VSL estimates (in which researchers select a single best estimate from certain articles) and an "all-set" dataset (which contains all VSL estimates reported in the studies).	Full sample bias-adjusted estimate: $8.1, For US CFOI sample: $11.4

(*Continued*)

Table 2B.1 (Continued)

Sr. No	*Author, year, country*	*Title of the study*	*Type of study*	*Source of data*	*Findings*	*Value of statistical life (million)*
					• This study found that all the specifications indicate that publication selection bias has a significant impact on VSL estimates from both the types of datasets. • Another important finding is that the best estimate selection bias may cause some major additional selection effects other than publication bias. • The income elasticity estimated from this study ranges between 0.53 and 0.85.	
51.	Parada-Contzen (2019) Chile	The Value of Statistical Life for Risk-Averse and Risk-Seeking Individuals	Hedonic Wage Study	Chilean Survey of Social Protection (EPS), Chilean Safety Association (ACHS), Primary Survey-177 Observations	• This study examines the effect of risk aversion on the wage–risk trade-off of individuals. • Smoking behaviour and hypothetical gambles were used as proxies for risk aversion. Additional proxies were alcohol-drinking behaviour, stock ownership, and retirement investments.	Full sample: $24 (USD), for Smokers: $3.59, for non-smokers: $2.85, for the risk-averse in lotteries: $2.55, for non-risk averse in lotteries: $6.47

(*Continued*)

Table 2B.1 (Continued)

Sr. No	*Author, year, country*	*Title of the study*	*Type of study*	*Source of data*	*Findings*	*Value of statistical life (million)*
					• The study found that risk premium decreases as financial risk aversion increases, while it increases as smoking aversion increases. • The risk premium for risk-averse people appears only among non-drinkers, and patterns for stock ownership and retirement savings match direct risk-aversion measures.	
52.	Greenstone and Nigam **(2020)** USA	Valuing mortality risk in the time of COVID-19			•	Value of preventing 100,000 COVID-19 deaths are US$1 trillion
53.	Ananthapavan et al. **(2021)** **Australia**	Systematic Review to Update 'Value of Statistical Life' Estimates for Australia	Meta-analysis-Systematic Review	18 VSL studies published between 2007–2019	• Australian evidence on VSL is scarce; there is still uncertainty about which VSL or VSLY value best fits the Australian context.	Median VSL: AUD $7.3

(*Continued*)

Table 2B.1 (Continued)

Sr. No	*Author, year, country*	*Title of the study*	*Type of study*	*Source of data*	*Findings*	*Value of statistical life (million)*
					• Study suggests to use, for sensitivity analyses, AUD $7.3m (international median, elasticity 0.5) as the high VSL and AUD $4.3m (Australian guidance, 2017) as the low VSL • We recommend that consideration be given to increasing the base case • Suggested increasing the base VSL value used in public policy decision-making in Australia from AUD $4.3 million to AUD $7.0 million.	
54.	de Wit et al. (2024) **Netherlands**	The value of statistical life in reducing fire risk: A choice experiment among Dutch citizens	Stated-Preference Study: Choice Experiment	Primary survey – 504 Dutch adults	• The study examined the trade-off between house-fire death risk reductions and tax increases and estimated the VOSL for fire risk in the Netherlands. • People are willing to pay more to prevent death irrespective of the amount of tax.	EURO 15–22

Source: Author's own compilation.

Table 2B.2 **Summary of VSL studies from developing countries including India**

Sr. No	*Author, year, country*	*Title of the study*	*Type of study*	*Source of data*	*Findings*	*Value of statistical life (million)*
1.	Simon et al. (1999) **India**	Valuing Mortality Reductions in India, A Study of Compensating Wage Differentials	Hedonic Wage Study	Indian Labour Yearbook and Occupational Wage Survey (OWS)	• This study estimated VSL for Indian workers and compared it with the VSL obtained from Benefit Transfer Approach (BTM). • This is the first VSL study in India that is completely based on secondary data which attempted to estimate VSL for the whole country. • They found the job-related risks to have a positive relation with worker's wage. • The estimated VSL was found to be between 20 and 48 times the value obtained using human capital approach • The VSL to foregone earnings ratio was found to be quite larger for India compared to the United States. Thus, they found that transferring VSL estimates from the United States to India using BTM undervalues Indian VSL	\$6.4–\$15 (1999 US dollar)

(*Continued*)

Table 2B.2 (Continued)

Sr. No	*Author, year, country*	*Title of the study*	*Type of study*	*Source of data*	*Findings*	*Value of statistical life (million)*
2.	Shanmugam (2000) **India**	Valuations of Life and Injury Risks – Empirical Evidence from India	Hedonic Wage Study	Report of Chief Inspector of Factories	• This study estimated VSL and VSI for industrial workers of Chennai city in India • The estimates of this study are based on a primary survey in Chennai during 1987–1990. • Results indicated that positive CWDs are paid to workers in the sample. • The estimated VSL is much lower compared to developed country estimates.	INR 13.78 (Indian Rupees)
3.	Shanmugam (2001) **India**	Self-Selection Bias in the Estimates of Compensating Differentials for Job Risks in India	Hedonic Wage Study	Report of Chief Inspector of Factories	• This study attempts to correct the VSL estimate of the earlier study for the self-selection bias. • This study used modified selectivity bias correction method for correction of the self-selection bias. • The results of this study indicated that selectivity bias exists, and correction of the bias raised the VSL estimate substantially.	INR 56.07 (Indian Rupees)

(Continued)

Table 2B.2 (Continued)

Sr. No	*Author, year, country*	*Title of the study*	*Type of study*	*Source of data*	*Findings*	*Value of statistical life (million)*
4.	Nor et al. (2001) **Malaysia**	The value of life and accident costing: a willingness to pay study amongst young motorcyclists in Malaysia	Stated Preference Study	Contingent Valuation Survey	• This study examined the WTP for fatality risk reduction among motorcycle riders, especially young riders between the ages of 15 and 20. • The initial results indicated that young riders had higher WTP for a certain level of fatality risk reduction compared to seniors; however, the subsequent regression analysis indicated that these results are not robust.	1.2 (RM)
5.	Ghani and Yusoff (2003) **Malaysia**	Value of life of Malaysian motorists: Estimates from a nationwide survey	Stated Preference Study	Contingent Valuation Survey	• This paper presents the WTP for fatal risk reduction from traffic fatalities based on a nationwide survey similar to the national survey done by Jones-Lee et al. (1985, 1993) in Great Britain. • The survey was based on respondents' WTP to reduce a pre-specified risk of his/her own death. • The respondents' WTP didn't vary with the degree of fatality risk reduction.	1.2–3.1 (Malaysian Ringgit)

(*Continued*)

Table 2B.2 (Continued)

Sr. No	*Author, year, country*	*Title of the study*	*Type of study*	*Source of data*	*Findings*	*Value of statistical life (million)*
6.	Mahmud (2005) **Bangladesh**	Measuring trust and the value of statistical lives: Evidence from Bangladesh	Stated preference and choice experiment	Contingent Valuation Survey	• This study uses contingent valuation survey to examine the impact of training respondents on probabilities and fatal risk reduction on their WTP. • This study also estimated the VSL using CVM as well as choice experiment. • They found that the WTP of the trained as well as the untrained respondents was affected by the degree of risk reduction. • The VSL of the trained sample was found to be higher than the untrained sample of respondents. • Training was helpful in decreasing the downward bias since the WTP was comparatively higher for the trained respondents.	$1,783–$2,922

(*Continued*)

Table 2B.2 (Continued)

Sr. No	*Author, year, country*	*Title of the study*	*Type of study*	*Source of data*	*Findings*	*Value of statistical life (million)*
7.	Shanmugam (2006) **India**	Rate of time preference and the quantity adjusted value of life in India	Hedonic Wage Study	Report of Chief Inspector of Factories	• This study attempts to estimate implicit discount rate that workers use in discounting their future life years using the data from his earlier study in 2000. • This study uses the discounted expected life years approach to calculate the discount rate. • The discount rate estimated from this study is 7.6 per cent and 7.9 per cent using two different specifications. • The estimated discount rate in this study was comparable to the market interest rate on debt to private creditors during 1990 which was around 8 per cent.	Value per year of life: INR 0.97–INR 1.06 (Indian Rupees)
8.	Hammitt and Zhou (2006) **China**	The economic value of air-pollution-related health risks in China: a contingent valuation study	Stated preference and choice experiment	Contingent Valuation Survey	• This study estimated the value of three health outcomes associated with air pollution: cold, chronic bronchitis, and death. • This study was conducted in Beijing, Anqing, and rural areas near Anqing during 1999.	US$4,000 and US$17,000

(*Continued*)

Table 2B.2 (Continued)

Sr. No	*Author, year, country*	*Title of the study*	*Type of study*	*Source of data*	*Findings*	*Value of statistical life (million)*
					• They found a negative and significant relationship between age and VSL for all the regions except Beijing for which they found insignificant results. • The average median WTP to avoid an event of cold range between \$3 and \$6, while the WTP to avoid chronic bronchitis ranges between \$500 and \$1,000.	
9.	Madheswaran (2007) (Mumbai & Chennai) INDIA	Measuring the value of statistical life: estimating compensating wage differentials among workers in India	Hedonic Wage Study	Report of Chief Inspector of Factories	• This study estimates VSL based on primary survey of industrial workers in the cities of Chennai and Mumbai, India. • This study showed that the blue-collar workers in the sample are compensated for fatal and injury risks associated with job. • An interesting result from this study is that workers from backward social class earns significant wage premium in blue-collar jobs compared to other workers.	VSL Chennai: INR 15.4, Mumbai: INR 14.8 VSI Chennai: INR 6470 Mumbai: INR 9000 (Indian Rupees)

(Continued)

Table 2B.2 (Continued)

Sr. No	*Author, year, country*	*Title of the study*	*Type of study*	*Source of data*	*Findings*	*Value of statistical life (million)*
10.	Bhattacharya et al. (2007) **Delhi, India**	The value of mortality risk reductions in Delhi, India	Stated Preference Study	Contingent Valuation Survey	• This study estimated the WTP for fatality risk reduction from road accidents in Delhi. • Respondents were presented with three scenarios under most of the road fatalities take place: pedestrians, two-wheeler users, and while travelling. • They found that respondent's WTP rises with their income, size of risk reduction and exposure to risk of road traffic, which was measured by the time taken for travel and whether respondents drive motorcycles or not. • The WTP amount for high-risk individuals obtained in this study was found to be nearly 1.75 times the discounted flow of personal earnings.	VSL for low income group:123,000 PPP$, For middle income group: 149,000 PPP$ For high income group: 179,000 PPP$ For high exposure individuals: 150,000 PPP$

(Continued)

Table 2B.2 (Continued)

Sr. No	*Author, year, country*	*Title of the study*	*Type of study*	*Source of data*	*Findings*	*Value of statistical life (million)*
11.	Palanca-Tan (2008) **Manila, Philippines**	Value of statistical life estimates for children in metro Manila, inferred from parents' willingness to pay for Dengue vaccines	Stated Preference Study	Contingent Valuation Survey	• This study examined parent's WTP for dengue vaccines for their children in Metro Manila. • The result of this study indicates that the demand for vaccines increased significantly with the household income. • The WTP, on the other hand, increased significantly with lower prices of the vaccines.	\$0.70–\$0.80
12.	Rafiq and Shah (2010) **Pakistan**	The Value of Reduced Risk of Injury and Deaths in Pakistan – Using Actual and Perceived Risk Estimates	Hedonic Wage Study	Industrial fatal accidents records of the Punjab Employees Social Security Institute (2006–2007)	• This is the first study in Pakistan that attempts to evidence CWD for blue-collar workers of manufacturing sector of Lahore. • They found that workers are compensated for job risk in formal private sector in Pakistan. • Workers earn higher income for facing higher fatality risks on the job.	\$122,047 (10.4 million PKR)–\$435,294 (37 million PKR) value per year of life

(*Continued*)

Table 2B.2 (Continued)

Sr. No	*Author, year, country*	*Title of the study*	*Type of study*	*Source of data*	*Findings*	*Value of statistical life (million)*
13.	Cameron et al. (2010) **Cambodia**	The Value of Statistical Life and Cost-Benefit Evaluations of Landmine Clearance in Cambodia	Stated Preference Study	Contingent Valuation Survey	• This study estimated the WTP for fatality risk reduction from landmine-related accidents in Cambodia so that the VSL obtained from this study can be used for cost-benefit analysis (CBA) of landmine clearance. • They found that the value obtained from foregone earnings method is much lesser than what this study obtained using WTP method. • The results indicate that comparatively wealthy individuals and individuals who know landmine victims have a higher VSL. • Individuals who have to visit forests to collect firewood and have higher fatality risk due to landmines also have higher VSL. • Lower VSLs were found for people residing in affected villages.	$0.4

(*Continued*)

Table 2B.2 (Continued)

Sr. No	*Author, year, country*	*Title of the study*	*Type of study*	*Source of data*	*Findings*	*Value of statistical life (million)*
					• The CBA of landmine clearance using VSL estimated in this study suggests that targeted clearance for all land use types is economic. They found the net benefits of clearing irrigation systems to be more than six times the cost.	
14.	Benkhalifa (2010) **Tunisia**	The value of mortality risk reductions in the Tunisian building and manufacturing industries	Hedonic Wage Study	Caisse nationale de la sécurité sociale	• This study intends to measure the value of fatality risk reduction for workers engaged in construction and manufacturing industries of Tunisia. • They found positive and significant fatal risk premium, implying a higher value of mortality risk in the building and the manufacturing industries. • Workers in the building industry are paid a higher wage compared to other industries.	448663.32 Dinnars (Manufacturing) 689280.5 (Building)

(*Continued*)

Table 2B.2 (Continued)

Sr. No	*Author, year, country*	*Title of the study*	*Type of study*	*Source of data*	*Findings*	*Value of statistical life (million)*
15.	Wang and He (2010) **China**	The value of statistical life: a contingent investigation in China	Stated Preference Study	Contingent Valuation Survey Conduction during 2000	• This study estimated the WTP for cancer risk prevention in three provinces of China during 2000. • They found that the average WTP of elderly people (over 55 years) was significantly lower compared to younger people. • The marginal value of reducing the anticipated incidence of cancer mortality by one in the population was found to be 60 times average annual household income, while the elasticity of WTP was comparatively low for their study. • The income elasticity of WTP was estimated to be 0.42.	Mean VSL: 795,000 Yuan Marginal VSL: 73,000 Yuan
16.	Shanmugam (2011) **India**	Discount Rate for Health Benefits and the Value of Life in India	Hedonic Wage Study	Report of Chief Inspector of Factories	• This study attempts to estimate the discount rate for health benefits and VSL using the data from his earlier study in 2000.	INR 20 (Indian Rupees)

(Continued)

Table 2B.2 (Continued)

Sr. No	*Author, year, country*	*Title of the study*	*Type of study*	*Source of data*	*Findings*	*Value of statistical life (million)*
					• The life cycle model has been utilised to estimate the discount rate. • The real discount rate is estimated to range between 2.4 and 5.1 per cent.	
17.	Shanmugam and Madheswaran (2011) **India**	The Value of Statistical Life	Hedonic Wage Study	Report of Chief Inspector of Factories	• This study used the data from Shanmugam (2000) and estimated the VSL, adjusting for selectivity bias, wealth effect, and other issues related to VSL. • The results of this study indicated that workers are paid a positive wage premium for fatal and non-fatal job risks. • Compensation benefits have a significant influence on worker's wage and workers are not short-sighted when deciding job risk choices.	VSL: INR 10.28 Selectivity bias corrected VSL: INR 67.73 VSI:4876 Discount rate: 7.6 per cent

(*Continued*)

Table 2B.2 (Continued)

Sr. No	*Author, year, country*	*Title of the study*	*Type of study*	*Source of data*	*Findings*	*Value of statistical life (million)*
18.	Yusof et al. (2011) **Malaysia**	Malaysian value of statistical life for fatal injury. In road accident: A conjoint analysis approach	Stated Preference Study	Choice Experiment	• This study examines the WTP for fatality risk reduction due to road accidents in all 13 states of Malaysia, including Federal Territory Kuala Lumpur. • They found that the respondents having higher income show higher WTP and therefore have higher VSL compared to others having lower income. • The results show that respondents owning vehicles have higher VSL compared to others. • Respondents who faced with an event of accident are willing to pay more for fatality risk reduction compared to others.	RM 1.15–RM 1.45

(*Continued*)

Table 2B.2 (Continued)

Sr. No	*Author, year, country*	*Title of the study*	*Type of study*	*Source of data*	*Findings*	*Value of statistical life (million)*
19.	Hoffmann et al. (2012) **Mongolia**	The willingness to pay for mortality risk reductions in Mongolia	Stated Preference Study	Contingent Valuation Survey Conducted during 2010	• Estimated the WTP of residents of Ulaanbaatar, Mongolia, for reductions in mortality risk of the size and type typically provided by air pollution policy. • This study attempted to build a stronger empirical basis for the transfer of environmental health valuation estimates among developed and developing countries by administering the same survey instrument used in studies of seven other developed and developing countries. • Results indicate that people of Ulaanbaatar place a high value on fatality risk reduction compared to their income	$493,000 (PPP US dollar)

(*Continued*)

Table 2B.2 (Continued)

Sr. No	*Author, year, country*	*Title of the study*	*Type of study*	*Source of data*	*Findings*	*Value of statistical life (million)*
20.	Benkhalifa et al. (2013) **Africa**	Estimated hedonic wage function and value of life in an African country	Hedonic Wage Study	Tunisian *Caisse nationale de la sécurité sociale* 2002	• This is the first CWD study based on job risks of workers engaged in private sector in Tunisia, Africa. • Results of this study indicate that Tunisian workers are provided CWD for job risks. • The union workers and workers engaged in permanent jobs and in manufacturing sector were found to have higher VSL than other workers.	$643,800 (2000 US dollar)
21.	Hua Wang (2014) **China**	Estimating the Economic Value of Statistical Life in China: A Study of the Willingness to Pay for Cancer Prevention	Stated Preference Study	Contingent Valuation Survey Conducted during the year 2000	• This study examined the WTP for a hypothetical cancer vaccine which is likely to be effective for one year. • They found that the WTP varies significantly with respondents' attitude towards cancer vaccines on the basis of their age, gender, and geographical location. The females were found to have higher average values of risk reduction than males.	481–814 thousand Yuan (2000 prices)

(*Continued*)

Table 2B.2 (Continued)

Sr. No	*Author, year, country*	*Title of the study*	*Type of study*	*Source of data*	*Findings*	*Value of statistical life (million)*
					• The results indicated that the morbidity-based average values of cancer risk reduction are around 0.481 million Yuan for a group of respondents who had normal demand for cancer vaccine.	
22.	Wang et al. (2015) **China**	Are Chinese Workers Compensated for Occupational Risk?	Hedonic Wage Study	2012 China Labour Force Dynamics Survey and Pearl River Delta Survey in 2008	• This study estimates the CWD for job risk in urban labour market of China. • They used dataset on all workers in the country as well as the data on migrant workers from the Pearl River Delta. • This study accounted for the issues of endogeneity of job risk and unobserved worker heterogeneity. • Results indicate that workers earn significantly negative wage premium in risky job. An average migrant worker engaged in risky jobs earns about 3.38 per cent lower hourly wages compared to workers engaged in safe jobs.	---

(Continued)

Table 2B.2 (Continued)

Sr. No	*Author, year, country*	*Title of the study*	*Type of study*	*Source of data*	*Findings*	*Value of statistical life (million)*
					• Workers engaged in risky jobs especially those who involve exposure to dust, earn significantly negative CWD. • Only local urban workers were found to earn a significantly positive CWD for exposure to chemicals.	
23.	Ainy et al. (2016) **Iran**	Cost Estimation of Road Traffic Injuries among Iranian Motorcyclists Using the Willingness to Pay Method	Stated Preference Study	Contingent Valuation Survey	• This study examines the WTP for fatality risk reduction from traffic accidents among motorcyclists in Iran. • Respondents in this study comprised of individuals ageing between 18 and 65 years having high school or above levels of education. • The average WTP among motorcyclists was estimated to be 888,110 IRR. • They found that the WTP depends on the earlier experience of an accident, distance of daily commute, and helmet usage. • The cost of traffic injuries obtained from this study is quite high compared to the global average.	VSL: $104,874,178 VSI: $230,127,985 (PPP US dollar)

(*Continued*)

Table 2B.2 (Continued)

Sr. No	*Author, year, country*	*Title of the study*	*Type of study*	*Source of data*	*Findings*	*Value of statistical life (million)*
24.	Yang et al. (2016) **China**	Estimation of social value of statistical life using willingness to pay method in Nanjing, China	Stated Preference Study	Primary survey	• This study estimated the subjective VSL and social VSL in the city of Nanjing in China. • They examined the WTP for traffic risk reduction. • The results indicate that the mixed logit model is better than the fixed coefficient binary logit model. • They found that the WTP is significantly affected by factors like individual's income, education, gender, age, driving age (for motorists) and individual's occupation. • Other factors that affected the WTP were the reduction in mortality rate and alteration in travel cost. • They estimated the social VSL on the basis of the tax system that showed the contribution of various income groups towards social funds.	Social VSL: 7,184,406 RMB Mean VSL for motorists: 3,729,493 RMB Mean VSL for motorists: 3,281,283 RMB

(Continued)

Table 2B.2 (Continued)

Sr. No	*Author, year, country*	*Title of the study*	*Type of study*	*Source of data*	*Findings*	*Value of statistical life (million)*
25.	Leon and Miguel (**2017**) **Africa**	Risky transportation Choices and the Value of Statistical Life	Revealed Preference Study	Transportation choice survey, accident reports in newspapers and accident data between 2005 and 2012 from UN's Engineering Department.	• This paper estimated the trade-offs individuals are willing to make between mortality risk and cost as they travel to and from the international airport in Sierra Leone to Freetown and have to cross an estuary that is roughly 16 km. • Travellers have to choose from among multiple transport options – namely, ferry, helicopter, hovercraft, and water taxi, with each alternative having different accident risks, trip durations and travelling costs. • Results of this study indicated that African traveller's WTP for reduction in mortality risk was lower than non-African travellers' WTP.	African travellers: $577,000 For non-African travellers: $924,000

(*Continued*)

Table 2B.2 (Continued)

Sr. No	*Author, year, country*	*Title of the study*	*Type of study*	*Source of data*	*Findings*	*Value of statistical life (million)*
26.	Huang et al. (2017) **China**	Willingness to pay to reduce health risks related to air quality: evidence from a choice experiment survey in Beijing.	Stated Preference Study	Choice Experiment	• Conducted a choice experiment survey in Beijing to estimate the WTP for reduction in death risk or the risk of becoming ill due to air pollution. • They also examined the effect of payment regimes (i.e. new tax contribution or a tax reallocation) on WTP and the relationship between age and VSL. • They found no evidence of a relationship between individual's age and VSL. • They found that the payment regimes affect individual's choices and results in different VSL and VSI for different payment groups.	VSL: RMB 5.24 million (US$774,000) and VSI: RMB 1.13 million (US$167,000)

Source: Author's own compilation

Appendix 2C – Empirical specification of mixed effects regression model

The specification for the mixed effects regression is given below:

$$VSL_j = \beta_0 + \sum_{k=1}^{p} \beta_k X_{jk} + u_j + e_j \tag{2.3}$$

VSL_j is re-estimated VSL for '*m*' studies in the sample. β_0 is the constant term. X_{jk} is the vector of explanatory variables from study 'j'.β_1 ,β_2 . . . .β_p capture the fixed effects of study characteristics on VSL. As shown in equation (2.3), the model includes a composite error term consisting of a random effect u_j and an estimation error e_j which are assumed to be independently distributed with zero means and variances σ_u^2 and σ_{VSLj}^2 respectively. The random error component u_j captures the unobserved factors that influence the $\mathrm{VSL_j}$ conditional on the study characteristics X_{jk} is given by the following expression.

$$\sigma_{\mathrm{VSLj*}}^2 = Var(u_i + e_j) = \sigma_u^2 + \sigma_{\mathrm{VSLj}}^2 \tag{2.4}$$

According to Raudenbush (1994), Weighted Least Squares (WLS) technique is suitable for estimating equation (2.3) since mixed-effects regression model is based on the assumption of heteroscedasticity. Thus, WLS is employed to estimate the mixed-effects regression model, with the optimal weights given by the following expression. (2.5)

$$w_j = \frac{1}{\sigma_{VSLj}^2 *} = \frac{1}{\left(\sigma_u^2\right) + \left(\sigma_{VSLj}^2\right)} \tag{2.5}$$

If the estimation error e_j is assumed to be the sole source of variation in VSL estimates, the variance of the random error term σ_u^2 in equation (2.5) becomes zero, and the optimal weight simplifies to $w_j = \frac{1}{\sigma_{VSLj}^2}$. Under this assumption, a fixed-effects model is sufficient to explain the observed variation in VSL estimates. However, a mixed-effects regression model accounts for unobserved and uncontrollable factors that also contribute to differences in VSL estimates across studies. Therefore, the variance of the random error term σ_u^2 must be incorporated into the weighting scheme. In this case, the values of σ_u^2 and σ_{VSLj}^2 must be estimated separately. While the value of σ_{VSLj}^2 can be directly obtained from the data reported in individual studies included in the meta-analysis, the value of σ_u^2 must be estimated independently, as it is not provided in the original studies. An alternative approach to using equation (2.5) for weighting is to apply the inverse of the sample size of each study as weights in the meta-analysis. In this study, the inverse of the sample size of the VSL studies is used as the weighting scheme for estimating equation (2.3) using WLS (Majumder & Madheswaran, 2017).

Table 2C.1 Description of the studies included in the meta-analysis

Sr. No.	Year of publication	Authors	Country	Sample size	Average income (1)	Risk coefficient (φj)	Death risk (2)	Compensation	Endogeneity of risk	White workers sample	Union sample	Age	Age ^2	VSLj	Standard Error (VSLj)
1	1990	Meng and Smith	Canada	777	34292.049	0.04023	1.2	0	0	0	0	0	0	13,79,569	2554757.63
2	1991	Berger and Gabriel	USA	22,837	47992.537	0.0018	0.97	0	0	0	0	0	0	86,38,657	1515553.79
3	1991	Gegax et al.	USA	228	46118.927	0.0168	8.6075	0	0	0	1	0	0	30,99,192	1564458.30
4	1991	Kniesner and Leeth – 1	Japan	20	32861.89	4.422	0.32	0	0	0	0	0	0	1,45,31,528	6707897.00
5	1991	Kniesner and Leeth – 2	Australia	44	28648.537	1.729	1.4	1	0	0	0	0	0	49,53,332	1753538.64
6	1991	Kniesner and Leeth – 3	USA	8,868	38382.915	0.1365	4.36	1	0	0	0	1	1	5,23,927	310246.31
7	1991	Leigh	USA	1502	38612.012	0.0021	1.34	0	0	0	0	0	0	81,08,523	2467596.64
8	1992	Cousineau et al.	Canada	32,713	33636.512	0.00162	0.764	0	0	0	0	0	0	54,49,115	526993.71
9	1992	Martinello and Meng	Canada	4,352	32805.183	0.1087	2.5	0	0	0	0	1	0	35,65,923	1077318.24
10	1994	Siebert and Wei	UK	1,353	17723.305	0.9075	0.332	0	1	0	1	0	0	1,60,83,899	7993985.67
11	1995	Lanoie et al.	Canada	63	52777.5	0.052	2.73	0	0	0	1	1	1	2,74,44,300	8684905.06
12	1995	Leigh	USA	1,528	33516.293	0.00376	1.1016	0	0	0	1	0	0	1,26,02,126	1237929.87
13	1997	Liu et al.	Taiwan	18,987	11055.659	0.0123	2.252	0	0	0	0	0	0	13,59,846	120928.95
14	1997	Miller et al.	Australia	18,850	30211.39	0.675	0.68	0	0	0	0	0	0	2,03,92,688	1553136.97
15	1999	Kim and Fishback	South Korea	321	18731.561	0.094	4.85	0	0	0	0	0	0	17,60,767	368361.24
16	1999	Simon et al.	India	1454	1968	0.324	0.0149	0	0	0	0	0	0	6,16,81,251	50177208.46
17	1999	Meng and Smith	Canada	1,503	25793.89	0.1035	1.8	1	0	0	0	0	0	26,69,668	691623.74
18	2000	Arabsheibani and Marin	UK	3,608	33089.854	1.0542	0.5	0	0	0	0	0	0	3,48,83,324	5233807.01
19	2001	Gunderson and Hyatt	Canada	2,014	33694.354	0.082	1.67	0	1	0	0	0	0	2,76,29,370	3924626.42
20	2001	Shanmugam	India	522	3445.5366	0.0529	1.04407	0	1	0	0	1	1	1,82,26,889	8147916.20
21	2003	Leeth and Ruser	USA	45001	28194.878	0.116	0.9757	1	0	0	0	0	0	32,70,606	704871.95
22	2003	Viscusi	USA	83,625	34533.622	0.0053	0.362	1	0	1	0	1	1	1,83,02,820	1726681.10
23	2004	Viscusi	USA	99,033	34070.89	0.0017	0.402	1	0	0	0	1	1	57,92,051	681417.80
24	2004	S. Madheswaran 1	India	550	5977.5317	0.0098	1.135	0	0	0	1	0	0	58,57,981	1337438.60
25	2004	S. Madheswaran 2	India	535	6313.2868	0.0089	1.255	0	0	0	1	0	0	56,18,825	530227.92
26	2005	Kniesner, Viscusi, Woock & Ziliak	USA	2108	46411.043	0.0013	0.59	0	0	1	1	1	0	60,33,436	1856441.74

(Continued)

Table 2C.1 (Continued)

Sr. No.	*Year of publication*	*Authors*	*Country*	*Sample size*	*Average income (1)*	*Risk coefficient (φj)*	*Death risk (2)*	*Compensation*	*Endogeneity of risk*	*White workers sample*	*Union sample*	*Age*	*Age ^2*	*VSLj*	*Standard Error (VSLj)*
27	2006	Rafiq and Mir Kalan Shah	Pakistan	1000	3942.1896	0.141	1.17	1	0	0	1	1	0	55,58,487	4139299.06
28	2006	Hintermann, Alberini and Markandya	UK	2599	24605.923	0.0625	0.186	0	1	1	1	0	0	15,37,87,019	31449288.20
29	2007	Hannes Spengler and Sandra Schaffner	Germany	88115	22879.313	0.007	0.82	1	0	0	1	0	0	1,60,15,519	34318969.96
30	2007	W. Kip Viscusi and Joni Hersch 1	USA	66844	26091.241	0.0026	0.2989	0	0	0	1	0	0	67,83,723	3130948.87
31	2007	W. Kip Viscusi and Joni Hersch 2	USA	212067	31196.458	0.0022	0.3844	0	0	0	1	0	0	68,63,221	3119645.80
32	2008	Giergiczny	Poland	116514	10289.517	0.0574	1.8	0	0	0	1	0	0	59,06,183	288106.49
33	2010	Abdelaziz Benkhalifa	Tunisia	4103	84.634147	0.119	7.79	0	1	0	1	1	0	10,071	2268.20
34	2011	S. Madheswaran	India	522	9203.2951	0.0111	1.044	1	1	0	1	0	0	1,02,15,658	1406921.58

Note: (1) In USD 2005 and (2) Number of deaths per ten thousand workers (Majumder & Madheswaran 2016, 2017).

3 Occupational health and safety in India

3.1 Introduction

A safe and healthy workplace is not only a basic right but also vital for achieving sustainable growth, productive jobs, and decent work for everyone. However, workers across the world continue to face occupational hazards from known as well as unknown factors. In 2019, around 2.93 million workers died globally due to work-related factors, a 12 per cent rise compared to 2000. About 2.6 million of these deaths occurred due to occupational diseases, and 330,000 deaths were attributed to work-related accidents. While over 395 million workers worldwide endured a non-fatal injury. Asia and the Pacific region account for nearly 63 per cent of global work-related fatalities, as this region comprises the highest working population in the world. Agriculture, forestry and fishing, mining, construction, and manufacturing have been persistently at the top of the list of most hazardous sectors and represent 60 per cent of all fatal occupational injuries (International Labour Organization (ILO), 2023a). Across the world, the toll highlights ongoing struggles to protect workers from occupational risks.

Rapid and large-scale industrialisation has not only helped the developing nations to grow faster but also led to the mushrooming of unregulated industries with low safety and health standards. Therefore, the number of work-related accidents and diseases has been mounting in many developing countries. In emerging economies like India, while there has been progress through revisions of some existing legislations or implementation of some new legislations related to worker's welfare, the large size of the workforce and prevalence of precarious employment make safeguarding workers' health and safety a continuing challenge.

Work-related accidents cause immense hardship for workers and lead to loss of work. The economic burden of poor occupational safety and health practices has been estimated to be 4 per cent of global gross domestic product every year (ILO, 2024). For the developed countries, the key issue is work-related diseases, while for the developing countries it is work-related deaths. The ILO report indicates that many developing countries have poor reporting systems and coverage of OSH. During 2001, the number of

DOI: 10.4324/9781003628262-3

work-related deaths in India was estimated to be 40,000 by the ILO, while India reported this number to be 222. Thus, only a fraction of the actual number of work-related deaths and diseases are covered in most developing countries (International Labour Organization, 2005).

The ILO recently launched the "*Global Strategy on Occupational Safety and Health 2024–2030*" to strengthen worldwide efforts for safer workplaces. The strategy aims to put workers' well-being at the centre, supporting the ILO's mission of social justice and decent work for all. The strategy calls on ILO Members to focus on three main areas: (1) Improved national OSH frameworks: strengthening national OSH systems through better governance, data, and upskilling; (2) Stronger coordination and investment through partnerships: improving coordination, partnerships, and investment at both national and global levels; and (3) Enhanced workplace OSH management systems: advancing workplace OSH management by applying ILO-OSH 2001 principles, promoting gender-responsive guidance, and addressing specific risks across sectors and occupations. The 2024–2030 plan of action builds on the 2003 strategy, updated to reflect today's world of work. ILO plans to work towards these key areas through promotion of international labour standards, knowledge sharing, awareness, and advocacy, focusing on research and collection of OSH data, technical and policy analysis support to its members for ratification and implementation of international labour standards (ILS), and specific codes of practice and guidelines (International Labour Organization, 2023b).

International Labour Standards are in the form of conventions and recommendations on the rights of workers and the responsibilities of the competent authorities, employers, and employees (Alli, 2008). All the member states of the ILO are obliged to ratify these conventions. India is a member state of the ILO, but it has not ratified 54 technical conventions pertaining to OSH (Ratifications for India n.d., ILO). Two of these fundamental conventions on OHS that are yet to be ratified by India are: Occupational Safety and Health Convention, 1981 (C155) and Promotional Framework for Occupational Safety and Health Convention, 2006 (C187) (Up-to-date Conventions and Protocols not ratified by India n.d., ILO).

Workers spend a major portion of their day at the workplace. Hence, a safe and healthy workplace is essential for boosting workers' productivity. However, most often workers work in an unsafe work environment and face numerous health hazards. Occupational hazards include the risk of accidents and of contracting occupational diseases. A worker can get exposed to various occupational hazards such as physical hazards (like heat and cold stress, light, noise, vibration, and radiation); chemical hazards (like liquids, dust, gases, solvents, pesticides, et cetera); biological hazards (like fluid, bacteria, viruses, protozoa, et cetera); mechanical hazards (like machines or moving machine parts, slips, and falls); psychological hazards (like work-related stress, workplace violence, et cetera); and ergonomic hazards (like lifting, uncomfortable posture, and improper adjustments at workstations and tools) (Occupational Hazard, 2014).

Unsafe work conditions and hazardous jobs are the main reasons behind the occurrence of industrial accidents. Such incidents impose huge economic loss on employers and employees besides causing loss of life and limb of employees. The major loss for employers arises from damage to machinery, equipment, raw materials, interruption in production activities in the factory, and payment of huge compensation to the dead and injured employees. For employees, the cost of such accidents includes loss in earnings, medical expenses due to injury, et cetera. The family of the injured person also bears various sufferings and hardships if the person becomes disabled due to the accident. These accidents not only affect individual workers but also society at large.

India has thousands of registered as well as unorganised sector factories classified as hazardous, located in major industrial states such as Gujarat, Maharashtra, Tamil Nadu, Karnataka, and Odisha. These factories contribute substantially to the national economy but possess high occupational and environmental safety risks. Nearly 1861 industrial units classified as major accident hazard (MAH) are located across 301 districts and 25 states and 3 Union Territories in India (DGFASLI, 2024). Some of the major industrial disasters in India include the Bombay Docks Explosion (1944), Bhopal Gas Tragedy (1984), Jaipur Oil Depot Fire (2009), Korba Chimney Collapse (2009), Mayapuri Radiological Incident (2010), Tarapur Chemical Explosion (2016), boiler explosion at NTPC power plant (2017), Vizag Gas Leak (2020), Dahej Chemical Plant Fire (2020), and Thane boilers explosion (2024). More recently, there has been an increase in the frequency and intensity of industrial accidents in India. All these incidents underscore the need for more research in occupational safety and health. During 2010–2014, the incidence of fatal industrial accidents and injuries was highest in Gujarat among the industrial states of India (Annual Report, National Crime Records Bureau, 2010–2014). Hence, this book presents a labour market analysis and VSL study from Gujarat.

This chapter begins with a brief overview of the Indian economy and the performance of major sectors (section 3.2). Section 3.3 discusses the occupational safety and health scenario in India. This section begins with an overview of the Indian labour market, followed by a discussion on legislations related to labour safety and welfare in India. The following section (i.e. Section 3.4) begins with a brief overview of Gujarat's economy which serves as the study area for this research and then discusses the scenario of occupational safety and health in Gujarat. This section also presents a few labour welfare programmes and legislations specific to Gujarat. Since the background of occupational safety and health is already set by the earlier sections, Section 3.5 includes a discussion on the available sources of secondary data on job-related deaths and injuries in India. This is followed by an analysis of the data from India and, specifically, Gujarat, where the labour market study was undertaken. This data is presented for the time 2010–2015, which collaborates with the period during which the study was undertaken. In Section 3.6, the job risks for different industries of the study region, that is, Ahmedabad district of Gujarat state are estimated. These job risks will be used in the following chapter to estimate the VSL and VSI of the workers in the study. Section 3.7 concludes the chapter.

3.2 Brief overview of the Indian economy

India is among the world's fastest-growing economies and aims to sustain this growth, with the goal of achieving high middle-income status by 2047, the 100th year of its independence (World Bank, 2024). In the past, the industrial sector has been the major driving force of the Indian economy. However, the growth of this sector has slowed down recently owing to policy reforms like demonetisation, implementation of the Goods and Services Tax (GST), and the global COVID-19 pandemic by the Indian Government. The Quick Estimates of Indices of Industrial Production (IIP) indicate that growth in the Mining, Manufacturing, and Electricity sectors during July 2025 was (–) 7.2 per cent, 5.4 per cent, and 0.6 per cent, respectively (Press Information Bureau, 2025). Table 3.1 shows the contribution of various sectors of the Indian economy towards annual real Gross Value Added (GVA) at constant prices of 2011–2012.

Before the COVID-19 pandemic, the contribution of the service sectors (see columns 3, 4, and 5, Table 3.1) to the GVA was growing, while the contribution of the agriculture sector (see column 1, Table 3.1) and the industry sector (see column 2, Table 3.1) was shrinking (Economic Survey, 2024–2025). The post-pandemic scenario indicates recovery in all the sectors of the Indian economy. Despite challenges of supply chain disruptions, low demand for exports, and aggressive US trade policies, India's manufacturing sector continued to register fast growth in 2024–2025. Given a brief introduction on the performance of the Indian economy, the next section presents the condition of OSH in India.

3.3 Regulatory and institutional framework of occupational safety in India

In the past few decades, there has been an enormous expansion of industries in India, especially after the economic liberalisation of 1991. Since then, the Indian labour market has been evolving to cope up with the competitive environment of world trade. Over the past few decades, the Indian labour market has undergone significant changes, including shifts in job patterns and employment relationships, rising levels of self-employment, increased subcontracting and outsourcing, growth in home-based work, and a larger number of workers employed away from their primary establishments. The Indian labour market is also characterised by a high prevalence of informal employment. Almost 90 per cent of the workers are engaged in informal work, which includes a considerable proportion of informal workers in the formal sector. Besides, about half of the total workers are self-employed,

Table 3.1 Contribution of sectors towards annual real GVA at constant prices (at 2011–2012 prices)

Sectors						
	(1)	*(2)*	*(3)*	*(4)*	*(5)*	*(6)*
Years	*Agriculture, forestry & fishing, mining and quarrying*	*Manufacturing, construction, electricity, gas and water supply*	*Trade, hotels, transport & communication*	*Financial real estate and professional services*	*Public administration, defence and other services*	*GVA at basic prices*
2014–2015	1.2	6.7	9.4	11.0	8.3	7.2
2015–2016	2.1	9.5	10.2	10.7	6.1	8.0
2016–2017	7.3	7.5	7.7	8.6	9.3	8.0
2017–2018	4.5	7.1	10.3	1.8	8.3	6.2
2019–2020	1.6	5.9	7.2	7.0	7.5	5.8
2021–2022 (1st RE)	4.8	–1.3	6.0	6.8	6.6	3.9

Source: Economic Survey, Ministry of Finance, Government of India (2024–2025).

Note: RE: Revised Estimates

which is one of the highest in the world. Another key characteristic is the segmentation of the labour market based on worker's gender, location, occupation, social groups, and geographical regions. India has one of the lowest female labour force participation rates in the world, and workers face significant gender inequalities (Institute for Human Development & International Labour Organization, 2024).

These changes have led to various problems pertaining to the management of occupational safety and health risks at workplaces. The transfer and adoption of new technologies have created new hazards. Besides, many of the conventional hazards still exist at the workplace. Exposure to physical, chemical, and biological substances at the workplace with undiscovered risks, an increase in the number of hazardous industries, and high levels of work-related stress are some of the major factors leading to serious health and environmental risks (National Policy on Safety, Health and Environment at Workplace, 2009). There is an urgent need for effective policymaking to address the emerging OSH issues and cover areas that are yet untouched by regulatory lenses. Besides, many of the existing legislations need to be amended on the basis of the changes in the labour market. Given the scenario of OSH in India, the next section sheds some light on the existing legislations and programmes related to labour welfare in India.

3.3.1 Legislations and programmes on labour welfare in India

India has always been a source of cheap labour for the world. Since the colonial era, under British Rule, Indian labourers toiled hard under deteriorating work conditions and minimal pay to produce goods for the West as well as for its own people. The labour welfare movement began in India during the early 19th and 20th centuries with the aim of improving the working conditions of Indian labour and providing them with various benefits like health insurance, compensation for injury, regular payment of wages, et cetera. Thereafter, the first Factories Act (1881) was enacted in India. The formation of the ILO in 1919 was yet another benchmark in the labour welfare movement in India. In 1920, the All-India Trade Union Congress was formed, which further aided the Indian labour welfare movement. Thus, labour movements in India have led to the enactment of several laws protecting the rights and interests of the workers. Some of these legislations are discussed below.

The Factories Act (1948) was the first labour legislation enacted in independent India. Two broad objectives of this act are to ensure safety measures at the workplace and to promote the health and welfare of the factory workers besides checking the unregulated growth of factories. The key provisions of this act include facilities and conveniences that are to be maintained on the factory premises (especially for large factories), ensuring safety, sanitation, and hygiene of workers; guidelines on working hours, overtime wages, employment, and night shifts of women workers; maintaining records of workers, their leaves, wages for overtime and leave, employment of children, notice of accidents, diseases, et cetera; and obligations related to hazardous processes. Special emphasis has been given to the health and safety of the workers through provisions of proper toilets, bathing facilities, and safe drinking water for factory workers; provisions for first-aid boxes; safety appliances for workers; additional safety measures for handling hazardous substances; guidelines to report accidents, diseases, and dangerous occurrences in the factory to the Factory Inspector within 48 hours, et cetera.

The Workmen's Compensation Act (1923) is one of the earliest legislations that made provisions for compensation for disabilities and the death of workers. This legislation intends to provide assistance to the workmen or to their dependents in case of work-related accidents. It outlines all the guidelines regarding the conditions under which compensation is given to the workers, liability of employees in case of injury and death of workers, and a list of rates at which compensation benefit is provided to workers for various types of injuries, disabilities, and fatalities. This Act is amended from time to time by the government. In 2010, this Act was renamed as the Employee's Compensation Act.

Another important piece of legislation pertaining to labour welfare is the Employees' State Insurance (ESI) Act, which was first enacted in 1948. This Act has provisions for sickness benefits, work injuries, maternity benefits, medical facilities, et cetera for the workers. Employees covered under the ESI programme are eligible to obtain medical facilities for themselves as well as for their dependents. Besides, the dependents are entitled to family pension in the event of the death of an insured worker due to work-related injury or occupational disease.

The Mines Act (1952) is a major legislation pertaining to the safety and welfare of mine workers. This Act made provisions for drinking water, sanitary facilities, medical facilities, first-aid boxes and first-aid rooms, et cetera at mines. It also laid guidelines on work hours, night shifts, extra work hours, overtime, extra wages for overtime, employment of women, et cetera (Mines Act, 1952).

The Dock Workers (Safety, Health and Welfare) Act, which was enacted in 1986, intends to ensure the safety, health, and welfare of dock workers. It made provisions for safe working conditions of workers, prevention of fire and explosion, handling of dangerous substances, and providing protective equipment or protective clothing, sanitary and washing, medical supervision and investigation of work-related accidents, dangerous occurrences and diseases, et cetera (Dock Workers Act, 1986).

The Environment Protection Act of 1986 laid down guidelines for planning and execution of a nationwide programme for prevention, control and abatement of environmental pollutants from various sources. This legislation has set up the standards for emission of various pollutants and guidelines for prevention of any accidents which may cause environmental pollution and handling of hazardous substances (Environment Protection Act, 1986).

Unorganized Workers' Social Security Act (2008) intend to provide social security and ensures the welfare of the unorganised sector workers. Unorganised sector workers have been kept out of the purview of the labour welfare legislation for a long time. However, this act empowered the central and state governments to develop appropriate welfare programmes related to skill development, health benefits, disability benefits, maternity benefits, provident funds, compensation benefits, old age pensions, et cetera for unorganised sector workers. Besides, a National Social Security Board for Unorganised Workers has been formed to advise the government on developing various programmes, monitoring them, and reviewing the registration of unorganised sector workers.

Another major legislation in this context is The National Policy on Safety, Health and Environment at Workplace, which was issued by the Ministry of Labour and Employment, Government of India, in 2009 with the goal of building and developing the safety, health, and environment at the workplace. The objectives of the National Policy are continuous reduction in the incidence of work-related fatal injuries, non-fatal injuries and diseases, building a more comprehensive database on OSH, creating community awareness regarding safety, health, and environment at workplace and creating "green jobs" (jobs that preserve or protect the environment) to improve safety at workplace. However, to achieve these objectives, a well-coordinated national effort is necessary.

The Occupational Safety, Health and Working Conditions (OSHWC) Code, 2020, consolidates 13 central labour laws into a single framework to streamline workplace safety and welfare in India. The 2020 Bill replaces nine laws related to social security. It is applicable to establishments with ten or more workers, as well as mines and docks, and it introduces uniform definitions, unified registration through the Shram Suvidha portal, and comprehensive employer duties covering health, safety, and welfare facilities. It also regulates working hours, overtime, and contract labour. A notable effort has been made to consider the well-being of the informal sector, gig, and platform workers, including migrant workers. The 2019 bill has the provision for notifying schemes for social security funds, while the 2020 bill has provision for these workers to be registered. Conditions for employing contract workers engaged in precarious works have also been mentioned under this new bill (Directorate General Factory Advice Service & Labour Institutes, 2020). Though not fully in force yet, the Code marks a major step towards modernising labour laws and ensuring standardised workplace safety across industries.

The OSH-related legislations are compiled concisely in Table 3.2. Most of these legislations and programmes that have been discussed under this section aim at improving occupational health and safety in the workplace. The key question that arises here is: Does this legislation ensure safety at workplace? It is the responsibility of the factory inspectors to ascertain whether

Table 3.2 Few environmental, health, and safety legislations and labour laws in India

Year	*Labour laws*	*A few highlights*
1923	The Workmen's Compensation Act	Compensation rates for various types of injuries, disabilities, fatality, et cetera.
1948	Factories Act	Regulate work conditions, employment, wages, overtime work, health, hygiene, sanitation, and safety provisions for factory workers.
1948	The Employees' State Insurance Act	Insurance for all factory workers, benefit rates for work injuries and fatalities, et cetera.
1952	The Employees' Provident Fund and Miscellaneous Provisions Act	Guidelines for factory employees and workers for joining and contributing to funds, interest rates, fund withdrawal, et cetera.
1952	The Mines Act	Guidelines for mine owners and agents, and provisions for mine workers' health, safety, working and living conditions.
1963	The Personal Injuries (Compensation Insurance) Act	Impose liability on employers for payment of compensation to injured workers and provide insurance for employers against such liabilities.
1976	The Iron Ore Mines, Manganese Ore Mines and Chrome Ore Mines Labour Welfare Fund Act	Finances welfare promotion activities of workers employed in the iron ore mines, manganese ore mines, and chrome ore mines.
1976	The Equal Remuneration Act	Made provisions for payment of equal remuneration to men and women workers and prevention of discrimination in workplace.
1983	The Dangerous Machines Act	Regulating production, supply, distribution, and use of product of any industry producing dangerous machinery; securing welfare of workers operating such machineries; and compensation for injury and death while operating such machineries.
1986	Dock Workers (Safety, Health and Welfare) Act	Made provisions for safety, health, and welfare of dock workers.
1986	The Environment Protection Act	Guidelines for control and prevention of environmental pollution caused by industrial production activities.
1989	The Manufacture, Storage & Import of Hazardous Chemicals Rules	Rules and guidelines for manufacturing, import and storage of hazardous chemicals, inspection of factories for such substances, safety audits of factories, major accident control, et cetera.

(*Continued*)

Table 3.2 (Continued)

Year	*Labour laws*	*A few highlights*
1996	The Building & Other Construction Workers (Regulations of Employment and Conditions of Service) Act	It intends to regulate employment and work conditions of building and other construction workers besides ensuring their safety, health, and welfare.
2000	The Municipal Solid Waste (Management and Handling) Rules	Guidelines and responsibilities of State Government, Union territories, Central Pollution Control Boards and municipality for management and handling of municipal solid waste.
2008	The Unorganised Workers' Social Security Act	Responsibilities of state and central government for social security and other benefits for unorganised sector workers.
2020	Occupational Safety, Health and Working Conditions Code (OSHWCC),	Simplified and consolidated regulations on workplace safety and welfare, protecting the rights of all workers, including gig and migrant workers, and making working hours, safety measures, and leave policies the same across all sectors.

Source: Author's compilation from different government legislations.

the rules and regulations under various OSH-related legislations are followed and maintained in the factory or not. They are also responsible for enquiring into and reporting work-related accidents and injuries to concerned authorities. However, the number of factory inspectors appointed by the government has always been lower than what is required. In 2016, out of the 874 sanctioned posts for factory inspectors, only 663 were filled up. There is an urgent need to appoint more factory inspectors to ensure OSH at the workplace. This will also facilitate the collection of reliable and precise data pertaining to industrial accidents. Another major concern is with the workers who work at various factories on contractual basis (be it in the organised or unorganised sector) and have to bear the burden of work-related health and safety hazards. These workers are not covered by major OSH legislations in India. Even though ten years have passed since Unorganized Workers' Social Security Act (2008) was enacted, no special programme has been formulated to ensure OSH at the workplace for the unorganised workers.

3.3.2 *Role of DGFASLI in ensuring OSH*

This section briefly highlights the role of the Directorate General Factory Advice Service & Labour Institutes (DGFASLI) in ensuring OSH at workplace. It is one of the prime government bodies that assist the Ministry of Labour and Employment in formulation of policy related to safety, health, and welfare of workers in factories and docks. DGFASLI also offers diploma courses in industrial safety, which is an essential prerequisite for selection of Safety Officers by the government. It provides in-service training of Factory Inspectors from time to time. It conducts research in areas of industrial safety, work-related health hazards, industrial hygiene, industrial psychology, and industrial physiology.

A key task of DGFASLI is to compile the statistics on industrial accidents. The Factory Advice Services (FAS) division under DGFASLI has a statistical cell that gathers and compiles statistics on factory accidents and other information pertaining to administration of Factories Act. This information is utilised in preparation and execution of national-level policies on OSH and for preparing replies to Parliament questions (About DGFASLI, n.d.). The information pertaining to work-related accidents is collected by factory inspectors at the factory level. This information is then sent to the respective state office of Directorate of Industrial Safety and Health (DISH). The DISH office of each state compiles this information and sends it to DGFASLI annually.

An important thing to note is that The Factories Act, 1948, assigns obligation to the factories to report the number of deaths and injuries occurring due to industrial accidents to the Factory Inspectors. This is a major loophole in the Factories Act because this provides an opportunity to the factories to shun to report industrial accidents. Even though the Factories Act has been amended several times since independence, this important issue has never received any attention. Therefore, this leads to numerous unreported industrial accidents in India. The statistics that DGFASLI has on industrial injuries are provided by factories that submit returns. There is no way of estimating the number of injuries in the factories that do not submit returns. Besides, the information on the number of work-related accidents occurring in the unorganised sector of the country is not available. This is another major shortcoming of the secondary data on work-related accidents in India. Therefore, the Ministry of Labour and Employment should make some effort to find out a way to obtain this information from the unorganised sector as well.

3.4 An overview of Gujarat's economy and occupational safety landscape

Gujarat is known to be the engine of growth for the Indian economy mainly because of its strong economic fundamentals. The average growth in the real Gross State Domestic Product for Gujarat has been 8.5 per cent during 2012–2013 to 2021–2022, which is above India's average growth rate of 5.6 per cent. In 2021–2022, the largest sectors that contribute to this State's GSVA are Industry (49.3 per cent) and Services (34.7 per cent). Between 2013–2014 and 2022–2023, manufacturing recorded the highest growth of 8.8 per cent per annum, followed by service and agriculture sectors. In 2022–2023, about 23.8 per cent of the state's total workforce were engaged in manufacturing (NITI Aayog, 2025).

The industrial sector of this state is highly developed. This state has the highest geographical area under Special Economic Zone development in India. The contribution of Gujarat towards total industrial output of the country is 18.14 per cent, which is the highest among all the Indian states during 2019–2020 (Directorate of Economics and Statistics, 2019–2020). Table 3.3 shows the contribution of major sectors of the economy towards the Gross State Value Added (GSVA) during 2016–2017 at constant prices. The contribution of the primary, secondary, and tertiary sectors is 18.7 per cent, 45.5 per cent, and 35.8 per cent, respectively, to the total GSVA during 2016–2017 at constant prices.

As observed from Table 3.3, the contribution of the industrial sector has been the highest among the three major sectors of the Gujarat economy. Within the industrial sector, the contribution of the manufacturing sector has consistently been the highest during the given period. Given that Gujarat is a major industrial hub in India and a significant share of its state income comes from the industrial sector, OSH at workplace is very crucial for this industrialised state.

Gujarat has a vast industrial base with numerous industries. However, the major categories of industries in Gujarat are dairy, textiles, engineering, cement and ceramics, gems and jewellery, chemicals, petrochemicals, drugs, and pharmaceuticals. The share of seven major industry groups (by NIC Code, 2008) in Net Value Added during 2014–2015 and 2019–2020 is given in Figure 3.1. There are seven major groups of industry that contribute 83.82 per cent to the net value added by the factory sector in 2014–2015 and 72.8 per cent in 2019–2020. Manufacturing textiles has been the key industrial group that comprised 11.58 per cent of the factories in the State and employed nearly 18.99 per cent of people in 2014–2015 and 17.62 per cent

Table 3.3 Percentage contribution of major sectors to Gross State Value Added of Gujarat at constant prices (at 2011–2012 prices)

Sr. No.	*Sectors*	*Contribution towards GSVA (in percentage)*				
		2012–2013	*2013–2014*	*2014–2015*	*2015–2016*	*2016–2017*
1.	**Primary**	19.0	20.9	19.3	19.4	18.7
1.1.	Agriculture (Crops and live stocks)	13.6	16.5	14.8	13.0	12.4
2.	**Secondary**	**43.5**	**42**	**44.3**	**45.0**	**45.5**
2.1.	Manufacturing	31.9	30.5	33.4	34.7	35.5
3.	**Tertiary**	37.5	37.0	36.5	35.6	35.8

Source: State Domestic Product Gujarat State, Directorate of Economics and Statistics (2016–2017).

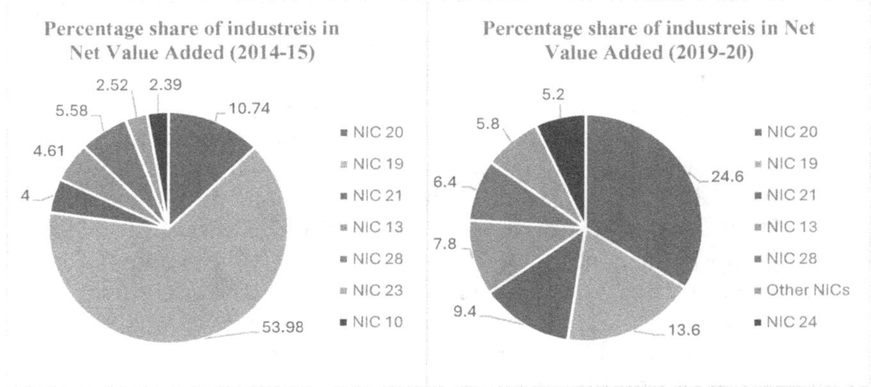

Figure 3.1 Percentage share of major manufacturing industry groups of Gujarat in Net Value Added in 2014–2015 and 2019–2020.

Source: Author's creation based on Socio Economic Review 2017–2018 and 2022–2023 of Gujarat State.

As per NIC code 2008: NIC 10: Manufacture of food products, NIC 13: Manufacture of Textiles, NIC 19: Manufacture of Coke, Refined Petroleum Products & Nuclear Fuel, NIC 20: Manufacture of Chemical & Chemical Products, NIC 21: Manufacture of Pharmaceuticals, NIC 23: Manufacture of other non-metallic mineral products, NIC 24: Manufacture of basic Metals, NIC 28: Manufacture of machinery and equipment n.e.c.

of employment in factories in 2019–2020. On the other hand, manufacturing of coke and refined petroleum products is the key industrial group in terms of fixed capital in both time periods.

3.4.1 *Occupational safety and health in Gujarat*

This section sheds some light on the OSH scenario in Gujarat. It also discusses a few existing labour legislation and welfare programmes of this state.

The Directorate of Industrial Safety and Health (DISH), Labour and Employment Department, Government of Gujarat, oversees the matters of OSH at workplace in Gujarat. The key task of the department is to ensure effective implementation of various labour laws and to protect the health and safety of workers. The aim of this department is to prevent work-related accidents, eliminate their pain and suffering, and ensure overall labour welfare (About Department, Mission, DISH, 2019).

The activities of Labour and Employment Department of Gujarat are also focused on the following areas:

- Awareness creation on OSH amongst workers and factory management through various seminars and programmes.
- To organise Safety Conference annually in order to stay aware of the latest trends in OSH at workplace.

- Provide Shram Awards to workers in order to encourage and appreciate their contribution to the industry.
- To facilitate the execution of welfare programmes for Construction workers.
- Conduct Health & Hygiene Survey in various industrial sectors.

There are other government institutions in Gujarat contributing to safety and health at workplace. The Occupational Health & Research Centre and Industrial Hygiene Laboratory of Gujarat examine occupational diseases. These two government bodies also conduct Industrial Hygiene surveys in various manufacturing processes to detect and prevent occupational diseases.

3.4.2 Labour laws and welfare programmes in Gujarat

The government of Gujarat has issued many programmes and enacted various legislations related to labour welfare and safety. Some of these labour laws and welfare programmes are presented in this section. A major legislation that was enacted in 1963 by the Gujarat legislature was The Gujarat Factories Rules. Under this legislation, guidelines are provided for construction and expansion of factories, registration of factories, renewal, and transfer of licence for factories. This Act directs all the factories in the state to prepare a policy related to the Health & Safety of workers at work and revise it on a regular basis. It provides guidelines for employment and payment of workers, instruction on maintenance of cleanliness and hygiene at factories, and health and safety of workers at workplace. This legislation also made provisions for medical examination of workers employed in 'hazardous processes' by qualified medical practitioners referred to as Factory Medical Officer (Gujarat Factories Rules, 1963).

The Gujarat Payment of Unemployment Allowance to Workmen (In Factories) Act, 1981, is another noteworthy legislation enacted by the Gujarat legislature. This Act makes provision for payment of unemployment allowance to factory workers who are rendered jobless because of the employer who is unable to provide them with job due to power shortage and other related reasons. In such a scenario, workers are paid unemployment allowance at the rate of 50 per cent of their basic wages and daily dearness allowance during the period.

Another legislation is the Gujarat Physically Handicapped Persons (Employment in Factories) Act (1982), which ensures that physically handicapped people are employed. This Act directs all the existing and new factories with 200 or more employees to reserve a certain number of job positions for people who are registered as physically handicapped.

A major OSH legislation enacted by the Gujarat government is the Manufacture, Storage and Import of Hazardous Chemicals Rules (1989), which is based on the powers conferred by Sections 6, 8, and 25 of the Environment (Protection) Act during 1986. It provides guidelines for the storage and handling of hazardous chemicals at workplace. Under this Act, factories need to identify hazardous chemicals (as per the criteria provided under the Act) and take necessary measures to reduce their consequences to workers and environment. The workers handling such hazardous chemicals at workplace must be given full information, training, and equipment to ensure their safety. The concerned authority must undertake inspection at least once in a year of industrial activity, which involves the use of hazardous chemicals. Another legislation that has been founded on the powers conferred by Sections 6, 8, and 25 of the Environment (Protection) Act (1986) was enacted in 1996. It is called the Chemical Accidents (Emergency Planning, Preparedness, and Response) Rules, 1996. This legislation provides guidelines to the Central, State, and District level governments to set up Crisis Groups and Crisis Alert Systems for management of chemicals according to the provisions of rule. Since Gujarat has a large number of chemical factories, these two legislations pertaining to chemicals and hazardous substances are very important for maintaining OSH at workplace.

Besides various legislations, the government of Gujarat started the Shramik Suraksha Accident Group Insurance programme in 1996 to provide insurance to unorganised sector workers. This programme covers workers employed in unorganised sector from accidental death at workplace. The premium is paid to insurance companies by the State Government on behalf of workers. The programme was revised in 2005, and new provisions have been made for compensation in case of partial disability due to accidents, permanent disability, and accidental death.

3.5 Analysis of characteristics and OSH data of registered factories in India

This section presents the secondary information pertaining to registered factories of India and Gujarat. The purpose of this and the succeeding sections is to provide background information related to the present study.

The Annual Survey of Industries (ASI) is the main source of industrial statistics in India. This survey covers all factories registered under the Factories Act, 1948. Some of the important indicators generated based on ASI are the number of factories, employment in factories, wages paid to workers, invested capital, capital formation, input, output, depreciation, and value added on an annual basis.

DGFASLI, Indian Labour Bureau, and National Crime Investigation Bureau (NCIB) maintain statistics on industrial accidents in India. The office of DISH in various states and UTs also maintains an annual record of the number of deaths and injuries due to factory accidents. However, such information is hardly available in the public domain. Even if some data are available, those are either inadequate or unamenable to further analysis. Therefore, researchers have to work with these limitations. Thus, inadequacy of job risk-related information is key concern in most developing countries, including India.

3.5.1 Registered factories, factory employment, and wages in India

At present, India is the most populous country in the world, and its experiencing demographic dividend as about 7–8 million young workers are added annually to the Indian labour force. Ernst and Young (2023) predicts that India will become the third-largest economy in the world by 2027, with a sustained growth of 5–6 per cent for the next 15 years. The GDP of the country will be US$7 trillion by 2030 (Department of Economic Affairs, India, 2023). Despite high economic growth, Indian labour market conditions did not witness any drastic structural transformation in employment conditions. The share of construction and service sector employment increased from 23 per cent in 2000 to 32 per cent in 2019, while the manufacturing sector employment remained stagnant, in a range of 12–14 per cent (MOSPI, 2021). Given this information, Table 3.4 presents the number of registered factories, employment in registered factories, and payment of wages to factory workers in India during the period 2000–2001 to 2018–2019.

The average growth in factory wages in India during 2001–2016 is 11.9 per cent. In 2010–2011, ASI changed its methodology to include non-operational units with past or potential production, causing a sudden jump in the reported number of factories; hence, total factory counts before and after are not comparable, though operational factories remain comparable. On the other hand, the average growth in number of registered factories is 3.6 per cent, and factory employment during this period is 4.2 per cent. While the growth in the number of registered factories and factory employment goes hand in hand, the growth in wages has been more during the given time period. In 2000–2001, employment in factories was 6.1 million, which rose to 9.9 million in 2010–2011 and to 12.7 million in 2018–2019.

All three parameters (i.e. growth in registered factories, factory employment, and wage payment) follow similar pattern over the given time period. During 2001–2002, the growth rates were low mainly because of deceleration in growth of industrial sector. Besides, industries were affected by low prices of commodities and output globally. The 9/11 terror attack in the United States aggravated the situation further (Economic Survey, 2001–02). However, the Indian economy made a significant improvement during 2002–2003 as the industrial sector started performing well and grew at 6.4 per cent. Therefore, the growth of all three parameters is positive during 2002–2003. The growth rate of India was quite high at 9.7 per cent (GDP at factor cost, constant prices 1999–2000) during 2006–2007 and 9.0 per cent during 2007–2008. However, in 2008–2009, it recorded a growth of 6.7 per cent, which was lower compared to the previous years. The growth of all three parameters during 2006–2007 is high owing to high economic growth. However, the rate of growth in registered factories, factory employment, and payment of wages fell during 2007–2008 despite a high growth rate of the Indian economy. In 2008–2009, a deceleration was observed in the manufacturing industry mainly because of fall in exports, fall in domestic demand, and rise in input prices. During the same time period, the global financial crisis took place. Figure 3.2

Table 3.4 Number of registered factories, factory employment, and payment of wages to factory workers in India during 2000–2019

	Number of registered factories	*Growth in the number of registered factories* (in %)*	*Number of factory workers*	*Growth in the number of factory workers* (in %)*	*Wages paid to workers (Rupees in lakh)*	*Growth in wages* (in %)*
2000–01	131268		6135238		2934792	
2001–02	128549	−2.1	5957848	−2.9	2900951	−1.2
2002–03	127957	−0.5	6161493	3.4	2968905	2.3
2003–04	129074	0.9	6086908	−1.2	3047777	2.7
2004–05	136353	5.6	6599298	8.4	3363505	10.4
2005–06	140160	2.8	7136097	8.1	3766366	12.0
2006–07	144710	3.2	7880536	10.4	4429135	17.6
2007–08	146385	1.2	8198110	4.0	5103023	15.2
2008–09	155321	6.1	8776745	7.1	5977184	17.1
2009–10	158877	2.3	9157802	4.3	6894071	15.3
2010–11	211660	33.2	9901970	8.1	8564552	24.2
2011–12	217554	2.8	10438365	5.4	9985579	16.6
2012–13	222120	2.1	10051626	−3.7	11089620	11.1
2013–14	224576	1.1	10444404	3.9	12649644	14.1
2014–15	230435	2.6	10755288	3.0	14048488	11.1
2015–16	233116	1.2	11148079	3.7	15609839	11.1
2016–17	234865	0.7	11662947	4.6	17353716	11.1
2017–18	237684	1.2	12224422	4.8	19280066	11.1
2018–19	242395	1.9	12798588	4.6	21576035	11.9

Source: Annual Survey of Industries (2000–01 to 2018–19), Ministry of Statistics and Programme Implementation (MOSPI), Central Statistical Office (CSO).

* Calculated by author.

indicates that all three parameters increased during 2008–2009, which is contrary to expectations. On the other hand, the year 2010–2011 was exceptional because of a sudden surge in the growth of all the parameters, especially the growth in registered factories. However, the growth rate in factories declined sharply during 2012–2013 because of the slowdown in economic growth. During this time period, a decline in the growth rate of the manufacturing sector was also observed. On the other hand, the decline in factory employment and wages was sharper during 2013–2014, after which it started increasing.

3.5.2 *Registered factories, factory employment, and wages in Gujarat*

Table 3.5 presents the number of registered factories, employment in registered factories, and wages paid to factory workers in Gujarat from 2000–2001 to 2018-19. The employment in Gujarat during the given time more than doubled from 0.55 million in 2000–2001 to 1.48 million in 2018-19. The pattern of growth in the number of factories and wages for workers goes hand in hand (see Figure 3.3). However, certain years show negative growth rate in

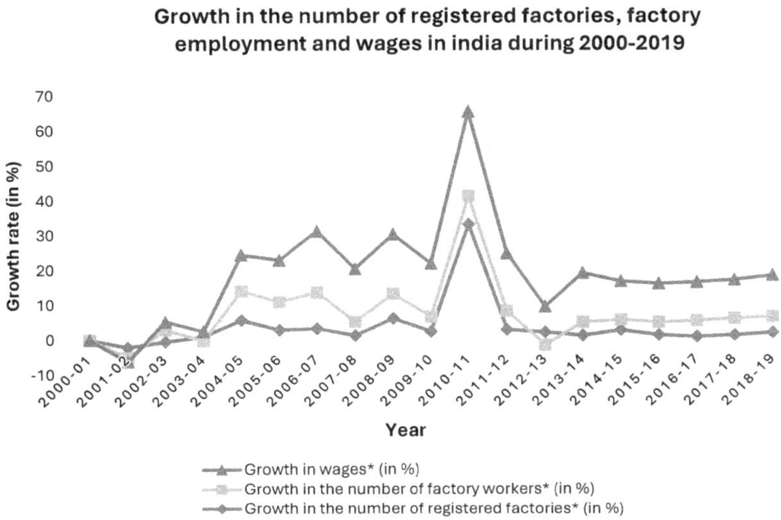

Figure 3.2 Growth in the number of registered factories, factory employment, and wages in India during 2000–2019.

Source: Author's creation based on Annual Survey of Industries (2000–01 to 2018–19), MOSPI, CSO.

Table 3.5 Number of registered factories, factory employment, and payment of wages to factory workers in Gujarat during 2000–2019

Year	*Number of registered factories*	*Growth in the number of registered factories* (in %)*	*Number of factory workers*	*Growth in the number of factory workers* (in %)*	*Wages paid to workers (Rupees in lakh)*	*Growth in wages* (in %)*
2000–01	14090		553704		261108	--
2001–02	13950	-1.0	521528	-5.8	252562	-3.3
2002–03	13180	-5.5	528217	1.3	257003	1.8
2003–04	12795	-2.9	538080	1.9	278787	8.5
2004–05	13603	6.3	606847	12.8	324874	16.5
2005–06	14055	3.3	669324	10.3	367361	13.1
2006–07	14327	1.9	749597	12.0	444958	21.1
2007–08	15107	5.4	797443	6.4	528857	18.9
2008–09	14863	-1.6	871459	9.3	593380	12.2
2009–10	15576	4.8	890600	2.2	679673	14.5
2010–11	21282	36.6	992050	11.4	855537	25.9
2011–12	22220	4.4	1059789	6.8	1032731	20.7
2012–13	22587	1.7	1046462	-1.3	1131969	9.6
2013–14	22876	1.3	1049725	0.3	1209240	6.8
2014–15	23433	2.4	1103204	5.1	1426146	17.9
2015–16	24426	4.2	1192093	8.1	1726995	21.1
2016–17	25966	6.3	1246650	4.6	1056017	8.7
2017–18	26,586	2.3	1403204	12.6	2239676	19.3
2018–19	26842	1	1489381	6.1	2559875	14.3

Source: Annual Survey of Industries, Ministry of Statistics and Program Implementation (2000–01 to 2018–19), Ministry of Statistics and Programme Implementation (MOSPI), Central Statistical Office (CSO). * Calculated by author.

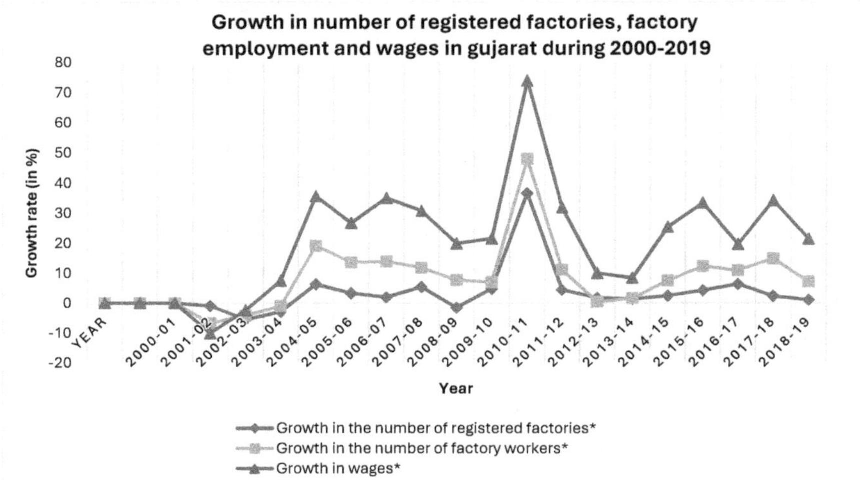

Figure 3.3 Growth in number of registered factories, factory employment, and wages in Gujarat during 2000–2019.

Source: Author's creation based on Annual Survey of Industries (2000–01 to 2018–19), MOSPI, CSO.

the number of factories and employment of workers. During 2001, Gujarat faced a massive earthquake, which hit the economy of the state adversely. This is the major reason for a sudden decline in the number of factories and factory employment during the post-disaster years. The impact of this major natural calamity lasted till 2003–2004, after which the economic condition of the state improved, and positive growth was observed in the number of factories. Specifically, the growth in employment and wages paid to workers surged up suddenly from 2003–2004 to 2004–2005. A decline in the number of registered factories and factory employment is observed during 2008–2009 for Gujarat due to global financial crisis that adversely affected the Indian economy. The decline in wages paid to workers was much less during 2007–2008. The year 2010–2011 was exceptional because of a sudden surge in all three parameters. The key reason behind this may be the fiscal and monetary stimulus post-financial crisis, which led to stronger economic growth in 2009–2010 and 2010–2011. All three parameters declined during 2012–2013 onwards because of the slowdown in economic growth, leading to a decline in the growth of manufacturing sector that averaged at 0.2 per cent per annum in 2012–2013 and 2013–2014. During, another slump in the growth of all three parameters was observed.

Given the discussion on the registered factory and factory employment in the state of Gujarat, the next table provides information on the number of registered factories and factory employment in various districts of Gujarat. There are 33 districts in the state of Gujarat. The office of DISH, Government of Gujarat, has grouped the districts into four major regions: Surat region, Vadodara region, Ahmedabad region, and Rajkot region. The district-wise information on the number of registered factories and factory employment is reported according to these four major regions. Table 3.6 presents the district-wise information on the number of registered factories and employment in those factories during the year 2015. The total number of registered factories comprises the working as well as closed factories that are registered in the districts of Gujarat.

As observed from Table 3.6, Ahmedabad district has the highest number of total registered factories and highest number of working factories. Dang district has the lowest number of registered factories. On the other hand, Surat district has the highest number of workers employed in factories, and Dang district has the lowest factory employment. Region-wise, again Ahmedabad region has highest number of total registered factories, while Vadodara region has the lowest number of registered factories. Surat region has highest number of workers employed in factories, and Vadodara region has the lowest factory employment.

This study focuses on the manufacturing sector since the contribution of this sector to the NVA of Gujarat is huge. From the last table, it is observed that Ahmedabad district has the highest number of registered factories and working factories in Gujarat. Therefore, Ahmedabad district is selected as the region of this study. In this respect, Table 3.7 presents the number of registered factories and the average employment by gender in the manufacturing industries of Ahmedabad district during 2015.

Manufacture of chemicals and chemical products has the largest number of working factories, while manufacture of leather and leather products had the lowest number of working factories in Ahmedabad during 2015. From the employment point of view, manufacture of textiles has the highest number of total workers and male workers. Female workers are higher in number in manufacture of pharmaceuticals, medicinal chemicals and botanical products, and manufacture of other non-metallic mineral products.

Given the scenario of registered factories and factory employment and wages in India, Gujarat, and its districts, the next section presents the information on work-related injuries.

3.5.3 Work-related fatal and non-fatal injuries in India

The incidence of various kinds of accidents and health risks has risen over past decade in India. The statistics on Accidental Deaths & Suicides in India published by the National Crime Investigation Bureau (NCIB), Ministry of Home Affairs, Government of India, indicate that the number of deaths in India due to factory or machine accidents has declined by 12.8 per cent during 2015 compared to the previous year. As observed from Table 3.8, the number of such deaths was recorded to be 797 during 2014; it has marginally reduced to 695 during 2015.

There are some fluctuations observed in the number of fatal and non-fatal injuries due to factory or machine accidents in India over the time 2000–2015 (see Figure 3.4). The number of fatal injuries is much higher than the number

Table 3.6 Number of registered factories and factory employment in the districts of Gujarat during 2015

Sr. No.	*Name of the district*	*Registered factories*			*Employment in factories*
		Working factories	*Closed factories*	*Total number of factories*	
1.	Surat	3131	480	3611	294305
2.	Tapi	76	1	77	3280
3.	Navsari	582	203	785	48441
4.	Valsad	2601	138	2739	141939
5.	Dang	4	0	4	94
6.	Bharuch	1756	950	2706	190912
7.	Narmada	10	8	18	1189
Total of Surat Region (A)		**8160**	**1780**	**9940**	**680160**
8.	Vadodara	3007	797	3804	112703
9.	Chota Udepur	178	43	221	3619
10.	Panchmahal	441	359	800	25095
11.	Dahod	85	33	118	4242
12.	Anand	763	352	1115	22327
13.	Kheda	519	298	817	24589
14.	Mahisagar	52	8	60	1020
Total of Vadodara Region (B)		**5045**	**1890**	**6935**	**193595**
15.	Mehsana	995	275	1270	50037
16.	Banaskantha	165	49	214	5867
17.	Patan	179	71	250	6079
18.	Gandhinagar	1437	312	1749	54897
19.	Arvalli	52	8	60	1433
20.	Sabarkantha	242	84	326	8440
21.	Ahmedabad	7507	2673	10180	265182
Total of Ahmedabad Region (C)		**10577**	**3472**	**14049**	**391935**
22.	Rajkot	1608	1017	2625	50142
23.	Morbi	1435	63	1498	67261
24.	Surendranagar	497	194	691	14138
25.	Kutch	489	126	615	74926
26.	Jamnagar	548	319	867	20024
27.	Devbhumid-varka	75	41	116	10407
28.	Bhavnagar (Alang)	189	91	280	35855
	Bhavnagar	528	0	528	17855
29.	Botad	83	0	83	1512
30.	Junagadh	319	124	443	6152
31.	Amreli	180	26	206	6566
32.	Girsomnath	161	20	181	12046
33.	Porbandar	106	25	131	5062
Total of Rajkot Region (D)		**6218**	**2046**	**8264**	**321946**
Total (A+B+C+D)		**30000**	**9188**	**39188**	**1587636**

Source: Directorate of Industrial Safety and Health, Ahmedabad.

Table 3.7 Number of working factories and average employment by gender in the manufacturing sector of Ahmedabad district, Gujarat (2015)

Two digit NIC Code (2008)	*Description of the industry*	*No. of working factories*	*Average No. of workers employed*		
			Male workers	*Female workers*	*Total workers*
10	Manufacture of food products	397	13078	410	13488
11	Manufacture of beverages	97	919	4	923
12	Manufacture of tobacco products	14	1267	2	1269
13	Manufacture of textiles	628	41277	743	42020
14	Manufacture of wearing apparel	192	7142	592	7734
15	Manufacture of leather and related products	13	254	0	254
16	Manufacture of wood and products of wood and cork, except furniture; manufacture of articles of straw and plaiting materials	254	2786	11	2797
17	Manufacture of paper and paper products	156	3543	19	3562
18	Printing and reproduction of recorded media	158	3555	28	3583
19	Manufacture of coke and refined petroleum products	29	1175	11	1186
20	Manufacture of chemicals and chemical products	1236	28002	664	28666
21	Manufacture of pharmaceuticals, medicinal chemical and botanical products	193	22229	1868	24097
22	Manufacture of rubber and plastics products	345	10245	224	10469
23	Manufacture of other non-metallic mineral products	274	8032	1039	9071
24	Manufacture of basic metals	797	22741	184	22925
25	Manufacture of fabricated metal products, except machinery and equipment	905	28188	106	28294
26	Manufacture of computer, electronic and optical products	40	1095	6	1101
27	Manufacture of electrical equipment	187	6572	77	6649
28	Manufacture of machinery and equipment	897	27882	198	28080
29	Manufacture of motor vehicles, trailers and semi-trailers	109	4939	85	5024
30	Manufacture of other transport equipment	15	266	0	266

(*Continued*)

Table 3.7 (Continued)

Two digit NIC Code (2008)	*Description of the industry*	*No. of working factories*	*Average No. of workers employed*		
			Male workers	*Female workers*	*Total workers*
31	Manufacture of furniture	50	1037	3	1040
32	Other manufacturing	49	1287	124	1411
33	Repair and installation of machinery and equipment	47	1437	15	1452

Source: Directorate of Industrial Safety and Health, Ahmedabad.

Table 3.8 Number of fatal injuries in India due to factory or machine accidents during 2000–2015

Year	*Number of fatal injuries*			*Number of non-fatal injuries*		
	Male	*Female*	*Total*	*Male*	*Female*	*Total*
2000	528	97	625	228	29	257
2001	560	81	641	166	12	178
2002	561	113	674	271	39	310
2003	625	87	712	219	15	234
2004	610	105	715	15	254	239
2005	578	98	671	305	17	322
2006	742	127	869	434	19	453
2007	731	105	836	425	29	454
2008	764	94	858	422	39	461
2009	906	138	1044	489	63	552
2010	916	127	1043	568	61	629
2011	966	125	1091	605	49	654
2012	920	87	1007	576	49	625
2013	848	107	955	562	56	618
2014	700	97	797	508	46	554
2015	613	82	695	551	43	594

Source: Accidental Deaths & Suicides in India, National Crime Records Bureau (NCRB), Ministry of Home Affairs (2001–2015), Government of India.

of non-fatal injuries arising due to factory or machine accidents. This pattern is just the opposite of what is being observed at global level. As already mentioned in the introduction section, the number of non-fatal injuries worldwide is much higher than the number of fatal injuries due to factory accidents. For a country like India, where a large proportion of population is engaged in industrial sector (both organised and unorganised), the number of non-fatal injuries is expected to be quite high. However, the statistics indicate otherwise. This clearly indicates that there is a major loophole with reporting and collection of secondary data on industrial fatalities and injuries in India.

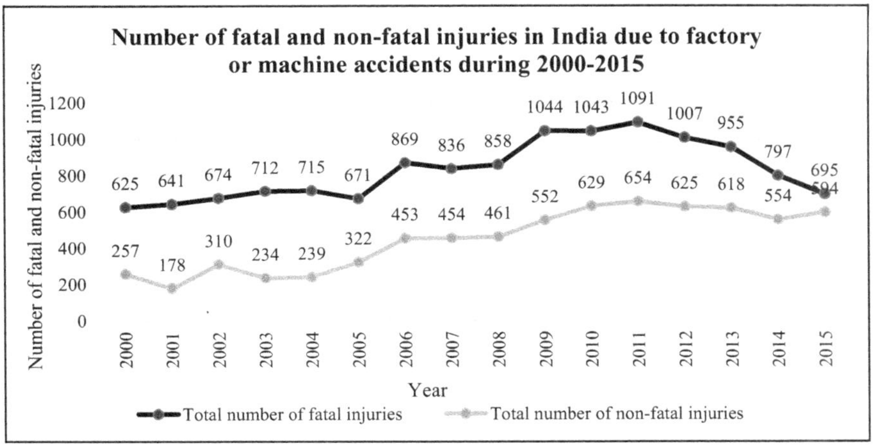

Figure 3.4 Number of fatal injuries in India due to factory or machine accidents during 2000–2015.

Source: Author's creation based on Accidental Deaths & Suicides in India, National Crime Records Bureau (NCRB), Ministry of Home Affairs, Government of India.

As observed from Table 3.8, the number of fatal injuries was highest during 2011 and lowest during 2015. On the other hand, the number of non-fatal injuries recorded is highest during 2011 and lowest during 2001. However, both types of injuries were quite high from 2009 to 2013, after which they started falling. The number of fatal and non-fatal injuries is much higher among male workers compared to female factory workers.

The information on the number of fatal injuries due to factory or machine accidents in India is available by age groups. There are five age groups: below 14 years, 15–29 years, 30–44 years, 45–59 years, and above 60 years. Even though employment of labour below 14 years of age is prohibited in India, Table 3.9 shows that there are a considerable number of deaths in this age group. The highest work-related fatal injuries are observed to occur in the age groups 15–29 years, 30–44 years, and 45–59 years. The number of deaths of workers above 60 years of age is lower compared to the other age groups.

It is expected that, with the growth in factories and employment, workers would demand higher levels of safety at workplace, thereby decreasing the number of industrial accidents. The simple analysis undertaken in the earlier sections of this chapter indicates a declining trend in the number of accidents with increase in number of factories during 2014 and 2015.

Figure 3.5 shows the trend in work-related fatal injuries for a few Indian states during 2010–2014. The numbers presented here pertain to a five-year average (i.e. during 2010–2014) of the total number of deaths due to industrial accidents in each state. As observed, the average number of fatal injuries

Table 3.9 Number of fatal injuries by age groups in India due to factory or machine accidents during 2000–2015

Year	*Number of fatal injuries by age group*					
	Below 14	*15–29*	*30–44*	*45–59*	*Above 60*	*Total number of fatal injuries*
2000	23	256	249	81	16	625
2001	18	235	271	103	14	641
2002	18	246	294	103	13	674
2003	12	261	314	112	13	712
2004	25	261	287	123	19	715
2005	5	278	272	99	17	671
2006	24	369	333	122	21	869
2007	14	314	354	131	23	836
2008	14	337	352	132	23	858
2009	40	363	439	174	28	1044
2010	20	388	442	172	21	1043
2011	28	409	418	192	44	1091
2012	35	343	414	197	18	1007
2013	19	319	421	171	25	955
2014	9	312	312	136	28	797
2015	7	291	258	126	13	695

Source: Accidental Deaths & Suicides in India, National Crime Records Bureau (NCRB), Ministry of Home Affairs, Government of India.

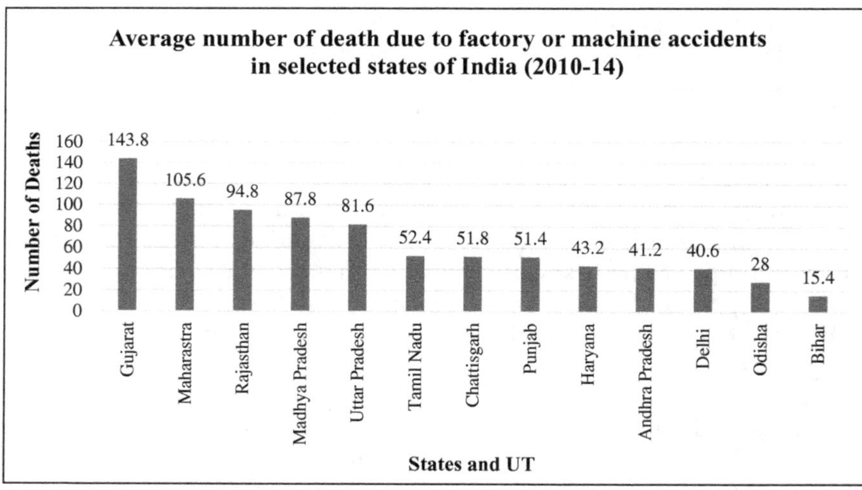

Figure 3.5 Average number of factory or machine accidents in selected states of India during 2010–2014.

Source: Author's creation based on Accidental Deaths & Suicides in India, National Crime Records Bureau (NCRB), Ministry of Home Affairs, Government of India.

is highest in the state of Gujarat, followed by Maharashtra, Rajasthan, and Madhya Pradesh. Uttar Pradesh, Karnataka, and West Bengal are the other states where an upward trend in fatal industrial occurrences is visible. In the past, Maharashtra and Tamil Nadu recorded the highest number of fatal injuries due to factory or machine accidents in India. However, the data indicate that such accidents are highest in the state of Gujarat. Gujarat is a highly industrialised state, and it has many industrial clusters which consist of large variety of industries, like textiles, pharmaceuticals, chemicals, steel, food products, et cetera. Most of these industries engage workers in risky jobs.

3.5.4 Work-related fatal and non-fatal injuries in Gujarat

This section presents a discussion on the scenario of work-related fatal and non-fatal injuries in Gujarat. The information pertaining to this has been obtained from the DISH office at Ahmedabad, Gujarat. Table 3.10 shows the total number of fatal and non-fatal injuries in manufacturing industries of Gujarat during 2001–2014. Since industry-wise information was unavailable, yearly information on the total number of injuries is presented in Table 3.10.

During the period 2001–2014, considerable fluctuations were observed in the number of fatal injuries in manufacturing industries of Gujarat. As observed from Figure 3.6, the number of fatal injuries was lowest during 2006 and highest during 2011. It was comparatively stable during 2012 and 2013, after which it increased again during 2014. On the other hand, the non-fatal injuries exhibit less fluctuations during the given time (see Figure 3.7). It

Table 3.10 Number of fatal and non-fatal injuries in manufacturing industries of Gujarat during 2001–2014

Year	*Number of fatal injuries*	*Number of non-fatal injuries*
2001	175	7756
2002	218	7814
2003	209	7664
2004	205	7300
2005	185	5574
2006	161	4842
2007	189	3151
2008	176	2875
2009	173	2984
2010	221	2430
2011	249	3014
2012	216	2781
2013	218	2285
2014	240	1751

Source: Directorate of Industrial Safety and Health, Ahmedabad.

Figure 3.6 Number of fatal injuries in manufacturing industries of Gujarat during 2001–2014.

Source: Majumder (2019).

Figure 3.7 Number of non-fatal injuries in manufacturing industries of Gujarat during 2001–2014.

Source: Majumder (2019).

is observed to be highest during 2001 and lowest during 2014. Overall, a declining trend is observed in the number of non-fatal injuries over the years.

Table 3.11 presents the data on the number of non-fatal injuries in various manufacturing industries of Gujarat. This information is available at two-digit level of NIC code of 1998 (which is given by Ministry of Statistical Program Implementation, Government of India), and it is obtained from the website of Directorate of Industrial Safety and Health, Ahmedabad. As observed from this table, during 2016, the total number of non-fatal injuries in the manufacturing industries of Gujarat was 1097. Manufacture of textiles

Table 3.11 Number of fatal and non-fatal injuries in the manufacturing industries of Gujarat during 2016

Two digit NIC Code (1998)	*Description of the industry*	*Number of non-fatal injuries*	*Number of fatal injuries*
15	Manufacture of Food Products and Beverages	24	10
16	Manufacture of Tobacco Products	0	0
17	Manufacture of Textile	402	47
20	Manufacture of Wood and Products Wood and Cork	5	4
21	Manufacture of Paper and Paper Products	12	16
22	Publishing, Printing and Proof recorded Media	3	1
23	Manufacture of Cock Refined Petro Products and N. Fuel	50	7
24	Manufacture of Chemical and Chemical Products	236	57
25	Manufacture of Rubber and Plastics Products	18	9
26	Manufacture of Other Non-metallic Mineral Products	20	13
27	Manufacture of Basic Metals	112	31
28	Manufacture of Fabricated Metal Products	106	11
29	Manufacture of Machinery and Equipment n.e.c	61	11
31	Manufacture of Electrical Machinery and Apparatus	35	6
34	Manufacture of Motor Vehicles Trainers and Semi	4	1
35	Manufacture of Transport Equipment	9	0
Total		1097	224

Source: Directorate of Industrial Safety and Health, Ahmedabad.

has the highest number of non-fatal injuries, while for the manufacture of tobacco products, it is nil. On the other hand, fatal injuries are highest in manufacture of chemicals and chemical products and nil in manufacture of tobacco products. Manufacture of textiles shows a high number of fatal injuries as well as non-fatal injuries among all industries.

On comparing the number of fatal and non-fatal injuries in India as opposed to Gujarat, we find a clear mismatch in the number of non-fatal injuries that have been reported during the given time. It is expected that the number of injuries reported at the national level will be much higher than the number reported by an individual state (since the total number of injuries at national level is obtained by summing up the information obtained from all the states in the country). However, the secondary data contradicts this expectation. Similarly, the number of injuries recorded by the DISH office of Ahmedabad at the state level is found to be much higher compared to the figures that have been reported at the national level by the National Crime Records Bureau (NCRB). In this context, the data provided by the office of DISH is much more realistic. Therefore, the ILO's observation on under-reporting of the number of fatal and non-fatal accidents in India can be justified from this simple mismatch of information at the state and national level.

The analysis of the secondary data on accidental occurrences in industries from different states in India indicates that Gujarat has the highest number of deaths from industrial accidents over the last few years. In this study, Gujarat is selected as the study location. Ahmedabad district of Gujarat is selected for field study since it has the highest number of registered factories in the state. Based on the background provided in previous sections, the next section provides a further analysis of secondary information on Ahmedabad district of Gujarat.

3.6 Estimating job risks in Gujarat's manufacturing industries

The number of fatal and non-fatal injuries varies considerably over years. These numbers can be particularly high if there is a major catastrophe in any year, causing several deaths. Thus, information on job risks is generally collected for a span of time (such as five years, ten years, or more) to weed out the effect of such sudden fluctuations. In this study, five years of data have been used to weed out the effect of sudden fluctuations in the data.

The information on employment of blue-collar male workers and work-related fatal and non-fatal injuries in manufacturing industries of Ahmedabad has been obtained from the office of DISH, Ahmedabad. Out of the 23 manufacturing industries, complete information was available for only 13 types of manufacturing industries for a period of five years (2010–2014). The male workers engaged in blue-collar jobs are selected as the sample units in this study because they are more susceptible to job injuries than other types of workers. All this information aids in estimation of job risk variables used in this study. Different studies select different scales for estimating job risks. For this study, the scale of fatal risk is one lakh, and the scale of injury risk is 1,000. This implies that the probability of work-related fatal risk is 0.00001 and the probability of work-related injury risk is 0.001.[1] Thus, for each of the 13 selected industries, the average probability of job-related fatal risks per one lakh workers and that of injury risk per 1,000 workers over the years 2010–2014 have been computed. The estimated job risks for the 13 types of manufacturing industries are presented in Table 3.12.

From among the 13 industries listed in Table 3.12, the workers in manufacturing paper and paper products (NIC 21) have the highest probability of fatal risk. This implies that on average, 44 out of one lakh workers die in manufacture of paper and paper products. On the other

Table 3.12 Average probability of fatal risk per one lakh workers and average probability of injury risk per one thousand workers in selected manufacturing industries of Ahmedabad district, Gujarat

Sr. No.	*NIC (2004)*	*Industry*	*Average probability of fatal risk (per one lakh workers)*	*Average probability of injury risk (per 1000 workers)*
1	15	Mfg. of Food Products and Beverages	7.49	0.74
2	17	Mfg. of Textile	9.17	2.29
3	20	Mfg. of Wood and Products Wood and Cork	22.96	0.37
4	21	Mfg. of Paper and Paper Products	43.78	0.95
5	23	Mfg. of Cock Refined Petro Products and Nuclear Fuel	19.62	9.47
6	24	Mfg. of Chemicals and Chemical Products	15.49	2.69
7	25	Mfg. of Rubber and Plastics Products	10.25	0.91
8	26	Mfg. of Other Non-Metallic Mineral Products	18.31	0.47
9	27	Mfg. of Basic Metals	16.57	0.82
10	28	Mfg. of Fabricated Metal Products	12.91	0.48
11	29	Mfg. of Machinery and Equipment	34.46	1.4
12	31	Mfg. of Electrical Machinery and Apparatus	17.01	1.48
13	35	Mfg. of Transport Equipment	22.38	3.55
Total			**19.26**	**1.97**

Source: Computed based on information from Directorate of Industrial Safety and Health, Ahmedabad.

hand, workers in manufacturing of food and food products (NIC 15) face lowest risk of death among all industries. The job-related injury risk is lowest for the workers in manufacturing wood and wood products (NIC 20), while those in manufacturing of coke and refined petroleum products (NIC 23) have the highest risks of injury. The mean fatal and injury risks for all 13 industries taken together are 19.26 per one lakh workers and 1.97 per one thousand workers, respectively. These job-related fatal and injury risks are essential for estimation of VSL and VSI that is undertaken in the next few chapters.

3.7 Conclusion

This chapter provides an overview of OSH in India and compiles the existing legislations related to labour safety and welfare. Major issues are identified as the enforcement of existing OSH legislation in the country. Being a member of the ILO, India has not yet ratified many important ILO conventions related to OSH. Unless these conventions are ratified, India cannot ensure safety of individuals at workplace and reduce the number of work-related accidents.

Another key issue pertains to the availability of job risk data in India. Most data are unavailable to the public, and obtaining them is extremely difficult. In developed countries like the United States, information on work-related accidents is available based on an individual's gender, age, race, cohort, occupation, industry, et cetera. This type of information is necessary to facilitate in-depth research on health and mortality risk reduction in a country. For example, availability of job risk data by an individual's age would enable researchers to examine the benefit of a health risk reduction policy for individuals belonging to different age groups. However, in India, the secondary data on job risk is available only by industry at the two-digit NIC code. This is a major shortcoming of secondary data on job risks in India, which prevents researchers from undertaking extensive research on health and mortality risk reduction. Besides, under-reporting of accidents is very common in developing countries, including India. The analysis of the available secondary data in this chapter indicates that industrial accidents are on the rise. Considering the underreporting of such incidents exists, the true magnitude of work-related fatalities, diseases, and injuries would be even higher. Hence, the government should emphasise building a framework for reporting occupational mishaps to ensure a safer workplace and well-being of workers. Creating an adequate database on job risks for India will enable evidence-based research, which in turn would aid policy decisions related to OSH.

Building on this discussion and analysis of data, the next chapter presents a study from the highly industrialised Indian state of Gujarat, where work-related accidents are very common. Using the labour market data from Gujarat, the VSL and VSI are estimated.

Note

1 The following formula has been used to calculate the probability of fatal risk per one lakh workers for a particular year:

Probability of fatal risk per one lakh workers

$$= \frac{\textit{Total number of fatal injuries for a NIC}}{\textit{Total number of blue collar workers for a NIC}} \times (100{,}000)$$

Similarly, the probability of injury risk per one thousand workers for a particular year has been calculated by the following formula:

Probability of injury risk per one thousand workers

$$= \frac{\textit{Total number of non fatal injuries for a NIC}}{\textit{Total number of blue collar workers for a NIC}} \times (1{,}000)$$

Reference list

Alli, B. O. (2008). Occupational Hazards and risks: The problems and the ILO response. In *Fundamental principles of occupational health and safety* (2nd ed., pp. 3–22). Geneva: International Labour Office.

The Building & Other Construction Workers (Regulations of Employment and Conditions of Service) Act. (1996). Retrieved December 12, 2018, from https://labour.gov.in/sites/default/files/BOCW.pdf

The Dangerous Machines Act. (1983). Retrieved September 29, 2018, from http://legislative.gov.in/sites/default/files/A1983-35.pdf

Department of Economic Affairs (DEA). (2023). *Economic survey 2022–23*. Government of India. Retrieved May 23, 2025, from https://www.indiabudget.gov.in/budget2023-24/economicsurvey/doc/echapter.pdf Accessed 23/05/2025

Directorate General Factory Advice Service & Labour Institutes. (2020). *Occupational safety, health and working conditions code, 2020 – Gazette notification*. Ministry of Labour & Employment, Government of India. Retrieved December 23, 2025, from https://dgfasli.gov.in/public/Admin/Cms/AllPdf/OSH_Gazette.pdf

Directorate General Factory Advice Service & Labour Institutes. (2024, July–September). *INDOSHNEWS: Occupational safety, health and the environment at the workplace* (Vol. 10, No. 3). Ministry of Labour & Employment, Government of India. Retrieved May 23, 2025, from http://www.dgfasli.gov.in

Directorate General, Factory Advice Service & Labour Institutes. (n.d.). *About DGFASLI*. DGFASLI. Retrieved May 11, 2018, from http://www.dgfasli.nic.in/about1.htm

Directorate of Economics and Statistics. (2016–17). *State domestic product Gujarat state*. Government of Gujarat. Retrieved August 19, 2018, from https://gujecostat.gujarat.gov.in/uploads/publicationsecmanagment/sdppublication1606202305_07_23_10_44_36.pdf

Directorate of Economics and Statistics. (2019–20). *Socio-economic review, Gujarat state*. Government of Gujarat. Retrieved August 19, 2018, from https://invest-india-revamp-static-files.s3.ap-south-1.amazonaws.com/s3fs-public/2020-03/Gujarat%20Socio%20Economic%20review.pdf

Directorate of Industrial Safety & Health, Government of Gujarat. (1963). *The Gujarat factories rules, 1963*. Retrieved August 06, 2018, from https://dish.gujarat.gov.in/Images/dish/pdf/01The_Gujarat_Factories_Rules_1963.pdf

Dock Workers (Safety, Health and Welfare) Act. (1986). Retrieved September 12, 2018/April 01, 2017, from http://dgfasli.nic.in/html/dockact/act1986.htm

Economic Survey 2001–02. (2002). *Macroeconomic overview for 2001–2002*. Ministry of Finance. Retrieved April 01, 2017, from https://www.indiabudget.gov.in/budget_archive/es2001-02/welcome.html

The Employees' Provident Fund and Miscellaneous Provisions Act. (1952). Retrieved September 19, 2018, from https://www.epfindia.gov.in/site_docs/PDFs/Downloads_PDFs/EPFAct1952.pdf

The Employees State Insurance Act. (1948). *Benefits*. Retrieved September 20, 2018, from https://www.esic.nic.in/attachments/actfile/a4be21587177569bb213b8254b83148e.pdf

The Environment Protection Act. (1986). *General powers of the central government*. Retrieved September 20, 2018, from http://envfor.nic.in/legis/env/env1.html

The Equal Remuneration Act. (1976). Retrieved September 26, 2018, from https://labour.gov.in/sites/default/files/equal_remuneration_act_1976_0.pdf

Ernst & Young. (2023). *India – Towards becoming the third largest economy in the world*. Retrieved December 23, 2025, from https://www.ey.com/en_in/insights/tax/economy-watch/india-towards-becoming-the-third-largest-economy-in-the-world

Factories Act. (1948). Retrieved September 21, 2018, from https://labour.gov.in/sites/default/files/TheFactoriesAct1948.pdf

ILO News. (2005, September 18). *Global workplace deaths vastly under-reported, says ILO*. International Labour Organization. Retrieved September 03, 2018, from http://www.ilo.org/global/about-the-ilo/newsroom/news/WCMS_005176/lang--en/index.htm

Institute for Human Development, & International Labour Organization. (2024). *India employment report 2024: Youth employment, education and skills* (3rd ed.). International Labour Organization. Retrieved April 07, 2025, from https://www.ilo.org/publications/india-employment-report-2024-youth-employment-education-and-skills

International Labour Organization. (2023a). *A call for safer and healthier working environments* [Report]. International Labour Organization. Retrieved February 10, 2025, from https://www.ilo.org/publications/call-safer-and-healthier-working-environments

International Labour Organization. (2023b). *Global strategy on occupational safety and health*. Retrieved February 10, 2025, from https://www.ilo.org/resource/policy/global-strategy-occupational-safety-and-health

International Labour Organization. (2024). *ILO helpdesk: Business, occupational safety and health*. International Labour Organization. Retrieved February 10, 2025, from https://www.ilo.org/resource/other/ilo-helpdesk-business-occupational-safety-and-health

International Labour Organization. (n.d.). *Safety and health at work*. International Labour Organization. Retrieved February 10, 2025, from http://www.ilo.org/global/topics/safety-and-health-at-work/lang--en/index.htm

International Labour Organization. (n.d.). *Up-to-date conventions and protocols not ratified by India*. International Labour Organization. Retrieved September 23, 2018, from https://www.ilo.org/dyn/normlex/en/f?p=1000:11210:0

The Iron Ore Mines, Manganese Ore Mines and Chrome Ore Mines Labour Welfare Act. (1976). Retrieved August 25, 2018, from http://legislative.gov.in/sites/default/files/A1976-55.pdf

Labour and Employment Department. (2019). *About department, mission*. Director Industrial Safety and Health. Retrieved July 01, 2024, from https://dish.gujarat.gov.in/about-mission.htm

Majumder, A. (2019). *Valuation of statistical life: A study on compensating wage differential* (Doctoral dissertation, University of Mysore).

The Manufacture, Storage & Import of Hazardous Chemicals Rules. (1989). Retrieved September 18, 2018, from http://www.moef.nic.in/legis/hsm/hsm2.html

The Mines Act. (1952). *Provisions as to health and safety*. Retrieved September 21, 2018, from http://www.dgms.gov.in/writereaddata/UploadFile/Mines%20Act,%201952.pdf

Ministry of Finance, Government of India. (2025). *Economic survey 2024–25*. Department of Economic Affairs. Retrieved December 23, 2025, from https://www.indiabudget.gov.in/economicsurvey/?utm_source

Ministry of Home Affairs. (2001–2015). *Accidental suicides and deaths in India*. National Crime Records Bureau. Retrieved September 23, 2018, from http://ncrb.gov.in/StatPublications/ADSI/PrevPublications.htm

Ministry of Labour and Employment. (2009). *National policy on safety, health and environment at workplace*. Government of India. Retrieved January 04, 2019, from https://labour.gov.in/policies/safety-health-and-environment-work-place

Ministry of Statistics and Program Implementation. (2000–01 to 2018–19). *Annual survey of industries*. Central Statistical Office. Retrieved June 03, 2025, from https://microdata.gov.in/NADA/index.php/catalog/ASI/?page=1&sort_order=desc&ps=15&repo=ASI

Ministry of Statistics and Program Implementation (MOSPI). (2021). *Annual survey of industries (ASI) 2020–21*. Retrieved June 03, 2025, from https://microdata.gov.in/NADA/index.php/catalog/ASI/?page=1&sort_order=desc&ps=15&repo=ASI

The Municipal Solid Waste (Management and Handling) Rules. (2000). Retrieved August 01, 2018, from http://www.moef.nic.in/legis/hsm/mswmhr.html

NITI Aayog. (2025). *Macro and fiscal landscape of the State of Gujarat*. Government of India. Retrieved May 23, 2025, from https://www.niti.gov.in/sites/default/files/2025-03/Macro-and-Fiscal-Landscape-of-the-State-of-Gujarat-1.pdf

Occupational Hazard. (2014). *Retrieved from Ministry of Environment, Forest and Climate Change, Government of India*. ICMR. Retrieved September 03, 2016, from http://www.niohenvis.nic.in/occupational_hazard.html

The Personal Injuries (Compensation Insurance) Act. (1963). Retrieved August 05, 2018, from http://www.legislative.gov.in/sites/default/files/A1963-37.pdf

Press Information Bureau. (2025, August 28). *Quick estimate of index of industrial production and use-based index for the month of July 2025 (base 2011–12 = 100)*. Government of India. Retrieved December 23, 2025, from https://www.pib.gov.in/pressreleasepage.aspx?PRID=2161516&utm_source=chatgpt.com&reg=3&lang=2

The Unorganized Workers' Social Security Act. (2008). Retrieved August 06, 2018, from https://www.ilo.org/dyn/travail/docs/686/Unorganised%20Workers%20Social%20Security%20Act%202008.pdf

Workmen's Compensation Act. (1923). Retrieved August 08, 2018, from https://labour.gov.in/sites/default/files/TheWorkmenAct1923(1).pdf

The World Bank. (2024). *India overview: Development news, research, data*. Retrieved December 23, 2025, from https://www.worldbank.org/en/country/india/overview

4 Measuring value of statistical life and injury from Gujarat

4.1 Introduction

This chapter sets out the detailed theoretical and empirical framework of the study and introduces the core challenges in estimation of VSL. To begin with, the literature is examined to identify the gaps that motivate further investigation. The literature on VSL estimation in India is sparse, with the majority of studies employing the compensating wage differential method. Simon et al. (1999) provided the first VSL estimates for India, drawing exclusively on secondary data sources. They undertook an analysis which indicated that the benefit transfer method (BTM) yields an underestimated VSL for India. Shanmugam (2000) is a pioneer study on VSL in India that is based on a primary survey of blue-collar workers in manufacturing industries of Chennai during 1990. The subsequent studies by Shanmugam (2001, 2006, 2011) and Shanmugam and Madheswaran (2011) are all based on the same dataset. Madheswaran (2007) is another noteworthy study. This study has utilised primary data on factory workers from two Indian cities, Chennai and Mumbai, that were collected in 2001. The only stated preference-based study in India has been undertaken by Bhattacharya et al. (2007), which examined the WTP for fatality risk reduction from traffic accidents in Delhi.

In view of the limited VSL literature for India, it is apparent that existing studies are based on old datasets. Over time, the Indian labour market has experienced substantial changes in the nature of work, the handling of hazardous materials, and workers' exposure to chemical and other occupational risks. These developments suggest that patterns of job-related risk and workplace accidents require renewed examination. There is therefore a strong need for a new study in India to examine workers' preferences towards job risk, determine whether compensating wage differentials exist for hazardous jobs, and estimate the value of statistical life and injury.

The chapter begins with the theory of CWD. This theory explains how the wage differentials for job risks observed in a hedonic labour market aid in estimating the implicit trade-off between money and small risks of death and injury. The next section presents the empirical framework of the study based on the Hedonic Wage Approach, which is used for the estimation of VSL and

DOI: 10.4324/9781003628262-4

VSI. Following section introduces the common Issues such as choice of appropriate functional form, unobserved heterogeneity and selectivity bias are which are quite common in hedonic wage studies. Hence, these issues are addressed using approaches like flexible functional form analysis and incorporating the wealth effect and selectivity bias in the estimation of the hedonic wage model. This is followed by a discussion on the data and variables used in this study. The basic and selectivity bias-corrected estimates of VSL and VSI are then presented. Following this, the issue of wealth effect is examined using logistic regression, and VSL is generated using the alternative BTM approach for comparison with the results of this study. The chapter ends with a discussion on the implications of the results of this study on health and safety policies in India.

4.2 Theory of compensating wage differential and hedonic wage approach

Adam Smith's theory of Compensating Wage Differential (CWD) suggests that jobs with a higher likelihood of death and injury will require a wage premium, all else equal. Thus, workers need to be paid higher wages to offset any job risks. CWD is the amount that an employer pays to convince workers to take up risky jobs. Alternatively, it is the amount that workers would forego from their wages so that employers can use that amount to make their workplace safer. Thus, the market forces of demand and supply match the risk-loving workers with firms offering risky jobs, and the risk-averse workers are matched with firms offering safe jobs (Borjas, 2013, p. 204). Thaler and Rosen (1976) developed a hedonic wage framework to explain that wage differentials arise to compensate workers for the unpleasant job characteristics, such as riskiness of a job. Thaler and Rosen (1976) empirically verified the hedonic wage framework. They describe the transaction in the labour market as tied sales of product characteristics. In the labour market, workers exchange their labour while also accepting non-monetary job attributes. Similarly, firms demand labour while offering non-monetary job characteristics, such as job risk, to workers. Within the hedonic framework, wages therefore implicitly reflect the level of risk associated with a job (Majumder & Madheswaran, 2018).

4.2.1 Examining CWD for risky jobs from a hedonic labour market

The idea that different jobs have different attributes drives a hedonic labour market. Based on this hedonistic nature of the job, two workers may have different job risk preferences despite having similar skills. Job risk is an intricate concept which necessitates a distinction between the probability of death and injury on one hand and the degree of severity of the injury on the other (Thaler & Rosen, 1976).

To examine how CWD arises in a hedonic wage labour market, a simple example can be used. Let there be a situation in which workers have the option of choosing between two jobs: the first job is completely safe, such that the probability of injury risk is nil, while the second job is highly risky, such that the probability of injury risk is one. Assuming that all the workers are aware of the levels of job risk and given the market wage associated with each type of job, the workers' utility function can be written as follows:

$$\textbf{Utility of worker} = \mathbf{f}\left(\mathbf{w}, \textbf{on the job injury or fatality risk}\right) \quad \textbf{(4.1)}$$

Equation (4.1) shows that workers are not only concerned with the wage that they receive in a job but also the level of injury or fatality risk associated with the job. If workers prefer higher wages, the additional utility that the worker derives from one rupee increase in his income will be positive, given the job risk level. Considering job risk to be a "bad", additional utility derived from one unit increase in job risk level will be negative, given his initial wages. The relationship between the worker's choice of job risk level and wage level can be represented using indifference curve. A positively sloped indifference curve is appropriate in this case because workers will be convinced to take up risky jobs only if they are paid higher wages, given that their utility level remains constant (Borjas, 2013).

While the workers must choose the level of job risk and corresponding wages, the firms are faced with the choice of either providing safe work conditions or risky work conditions to the workers. Since providing safe work conditions is expensive, this decision affects a firm's balance sheet. To make the workplace safer, a firm must divert its resources from production of output, and therefore, the profits of the firm are affected. The only way in which a firm can keep its profit level constant and provide safe work environment for its workers is by paying lower wages to them. On the other hand, a risky firm which earns higher profits must pay higher wages to the workers to persuade them to work in a risky work environment. Thus, a firm would provide safe work conditions if the additional cost incurred by the firm in paying higher wages to the workers exceeds the productivity gain per worker. On the contrary, if the productivity gain per worker is higher than the additional cost on labour, the firm will prefer maximising its profit and providing unsafe work conditions (Borjas, 2013). The relationship between job risk levels and corresponding wage offers by a firm can be shown using iso-profit curve or market offer curve. This curve is concave from below, with all points along the curve yielding a constant level of profit. Since the law of diminishing returns arises in production of safety at workplace, the iso-profit curve of firms is concave in shape. Figure 4.1 shows that workers face a market opportunity locus represented by "**w (p)**" that is the outer envelope of the individual firm's market offer curve.

The indifference curves faced by workers and the iso-profit curves faced by the firms in a hedonic labour market are illustrated in Figure 4.1. For simplicity, it is assumed here that there are two workers (worker 1 and worker 2) and two firms (firm 1 and firm 2) in the hedonic labour market. A worker intends to maximise his expected utility given the set of wage–risk offers along indifference curves. The slope of the indifference curves reflects

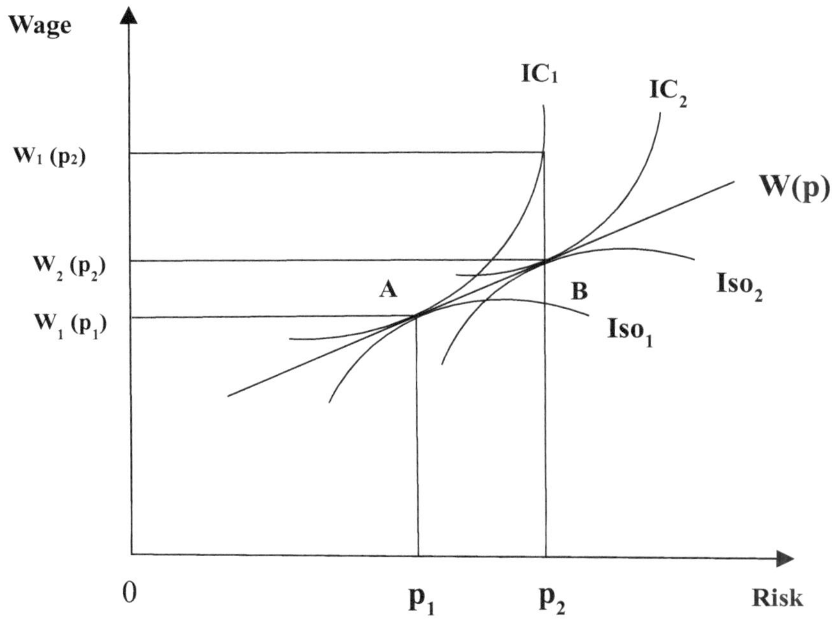

Figure 4.1 Equilibrium condition in hedonic labour market.
Source: Majumder & Madheswaran (2018).

workers' preferences towards job risk. As illustrated in Figure 4.1, the indifference curve of worker 1 is steeper than that of worker 2. This implies that worker 1 dislikes job risk while worker 2 is fine with taking up job risks. On the other hand, firm 1 provides a safe work environment while firm 2 provides a risky work environment.

In a hedonic labour market, the CWD model matches the risk-averse workers with safe firms and risk-taking workers with unsafe firms (Borjas, 2013). As a result, the risk-averse worker 1 maximises utility at point A, whereas the risk-loving worker 2 maximises utility at point B. A worker's optimal wage–risk combination is determined at the point of tangency between the worker's indifference curve and the firm's iso-profit curve (Majumder & Madheswaran, 2018). The observed relationship between wages and job attributes is summarised by a hedonic wage function or market opportunity locus, "**w (p)**", which comprises all the points at which workers' indifference curves are tangent to market offers. The market opportunity locus yields the average rates of wage–risk trade-off across workers. While a random sorting of workers and firms takes place in a usual labour market equilibrium, the equilibrium in a hedonic labour market is different in the sense that the workers self-select across a range of firms (Borjas, 2013).

The subsequent paragraphs describe the derivation of the wage–risk trade-off from labour market equilibrium. The standard model used to estimate VSL specifies that a worker is initially endowed with an income of "w" that depends on only two probable states in his life. These two states are good health state (u) and ill health state due to injury (v). Thus, the utility derived by the worker from his income or wealth under the good health state is "u (w)" and utility under ill health is "v (w)". The probability of occurrence of each state is (1-p) and p, respectively. Since rational individuals will always prefer good health to ill health, the utility derived under good health will be greater than utility derived under ill health, that is, $\mathbf{u}(\mathbf{w}) > \mathbf{v}(\mathbf{w})$. The marginal utility derived from his income is higher in good health than in ill health, therefore, $\mathbf{u}'(\mathbf{w}) > \mathbf{u}''(\mathbf{w}) > 0$. Since an insurance plan doesn't cover all types of pain and misery (Dionne, 1982), the worker is risk averse in both states. Therefore, his marginal utility from income is strictly decreasing under both states, that is, $\mathbf{v}''(\mathbf{w}), \mathbf{v}''(\mathbf{w}) < 0$. Given this information, the state-dependent Von-Neumann-Morgenstern expected utility function of the individual is:

$$\mathbf{Z} = (\mathbf{1} - \mathbf{p}) \times \mathbf{u}\ (\mathbf{w}) + \mathbf{p} \times \mathbf{v}\ (\mathbf{w})$$

In this model, a worker must pay an amount "x" from his income "w" to reduce the probability of his premature death from "p" to "$\mathbf{p}_1$" keeping the expected utility constant. Thus, the value of "x" that satisfies the following equality needs to be estimated.

$$\mathbf{Z} = (\mathbf{1} - \mathbf{p}) \times \mathbf{u}\ (\mathbf{w}) + \mathbf{p} \times \mathbf{v}\ (\mathbf{w}) = (\mathbf{1} - \mathbf{p}_1) \times \mathbf{u}\ (\mathbf{w} - \mathbf{x}) + \mathbf{p}_1 \times \mathbf{v}\ (\mathbf{w} - \mathbf{x})$$

To find the workers' WTP for risk reduction (i.e. the optimal trade-off between risk and income), the above equation is differentiated with respect to the income (w) and risk (p) keeping the expected utility constant.

$$WTP = \frac{dw}{dp} = \frac{u(w) - v(w)}{(1 - p)u'(w) + pv'(w)} > 0$$

The WTP shows the marginal rate of substitution between a worker's income and the level of job risk. It also represents the slope of the hedonic wage function, which is positive, implying that workers should receive higher remuneration with a rise in the job risk level. From a worker's point of view, this amount reflects his marginal willingness to accept risk as well as his marginal willingness to pay for more safety. From an employee's point of view, it resembles a firm's marginal cost of providing more safety as well as a reduction in its marginal cost for an increase in risk (Majumder & Madheswaran, 2018).

4.2.2 *Econometric specification for hedonic wage model*

This section shows the econometric specification that represents the hedonic wage function, along with a discussion on a few estimation issues.

The hedonic wage function is obtained by modifying the earning function given by Jacob Mincer (1974). It shows that wage is a function of worker's personal characteristics (age, education, and experience) and non-monetary job attributes (level of difficulty involved in doing a job, and the level of risk associated with it). The hedonic wage equation is given by equation (4.2).

$$LnW_i = \alpha + \beta_1 p_i + \beta_2 q_i + \sum {}_k \gamma_k X_{ki} + \epsilon_i \quad (4.2)$$

Here, $\mathbf{W_i}$ is after-tax hourly wage of workers, $\mathbf{X_{ki}}$ is a vector of worker's personal characteristics and job characteristics, $\mathbf{p_i}$ is the fatal risk, and $\mathbf{q_i}$ is the job-related injury risk, $\in_i$ is the random error term. From equation (4.2), the wage–risk trade-off is obtained, and utilised for basic VSL and VSI estimation. However, the basic hedonic equation suffers from issues like endogeneity of job risk on wage and heterogeneity among workers. Only a few studies have been corrected for these problems. In the Indian context, only Shanmugam (2001) has accounted for these problems.

4.2.3 *Derivation of VSL using wage–risk trade-off*

Differentiating equation (4.2) with respect to fatal risk **'p'** yields the wage–risk trade-off for fatal risk. Therefore,

$$\frac{dw}{dp} \times \frac{1}{w} = \beta_1$$

$$\text{Or, } \frac{dw}{dp} = (\beta_1 \times w) \quad (4.3)$$

Similarly, to obtain the wage–risk trade-off for injury risk, equation (4.2) is differentiated with respect to injury risk **'q'**.

$$\frac{dw}{dp} \times \frac{1}{w} = \beta_2$$

$$\text{Or } \frac{dw}{dp} = (\beta_2 \times w) \quad (4.4)$$

These trade-offs yield VSL and VSI estimates for the sample. Firstly, the estimated trade-offs are annualised by multiplying them with the annual work hours, which is 2160[1] for this study. The annualised trade-off indicates the wage premium received by workers for facing job risks. The annual wage–risk trade-off for fatal risk is multiplied by one lakh, which is the scale of fatal risk, yielding the VSL estimate for this study. Therefore,

$$VSL = (\textit{Annual wage-risk trade-off for fatal risk}) \times 1{,}00{,}000$$

$$VL = (\widehat{\beta}_1 \times \overline{w} \times 2160) \times 1,00,000$$

Similarly, multiplying the annualised trade-off for injury risk by 1,000 yields the estimate of VSI.

$$VSL = (\textit{annual wage-risk trade-off for non fatal risk}) \times 1,000$$

$$VSL = (\widehat{\beta}_2 \times \overline{w} \times 2160) \times 1,000$$

Here, the estimated trade-off for fatal risk is $\widehat{\beta_1}$, estimated trade-off for injury risk is $\widehat{\beta_2}$ and after tax mean hourly wage is $\overline{w}$.

4.3 Issues with estimation of hedonic wage equation

This section discusses the three major issues with estimation of hedonic wage equation and provides ways to resolve them.

4.3.1 *Determining the functional form for hedonic wage equation*

Considerable debate exists in the VSL literature regarding the appropriate functional form for estimating the hedonic wage equation. While a semi-logarithmic specification is commonly used, the choice of functional form requires careful examination, as it depends on multiple factors and is not prescribed by economic theory. To address this issue, the study uses normal probability plots and the Box-Cox transformation to identify the most suitable functional form for the hedonic wage equation.

4.3.2 *Wealth effect*

A well known issue in VSL estimation is the impact of worker's wealth on choice of job risk. As mentioned in Chapter 2, a positive relationship exists between an individual's income level and his VSL. It is observed that individuals who are employed in the finest jobs are paid more compared to those engaged in riskier jobs. For example, an accountant is paid more than an individual operating machines in the factory. This observation raised an obvious question amongst researchers: does the wage increase with the riskiness of job? Since job safety is a normal good, an increase in a worker's wealth will lead to an increase in his demand for safety. Thus, a rich individual will tend to select safer job (Majumder & Madheswaran, 2018). Therefore, an inquiry has been made to examine the wealth effect in this study.

4.3.3 *Endogeneity and the issue of selectivity bias*

Another issue arises from selectivity bias. Selectivity bias is introduced through unobserved worker differences and the endogenous relationship between job risk and wages. A worker's attitude towards job risk is an important determinant of VSL. A risk-averse worker will put a high value on safety and will have a higher VSL. In contrast, a risk-loving worker who assigns a lower value to safety will have smaller VSL. Thus, the workers self-select themselves into different jobs having different risk levels creating the issue of selectivity bias. This study attempts to address this issue and correct the selectivity bias to provide more accurate VSL estimate. There are many other unobserved characteristics of workers that may affect their earnings in hazardous jobs. For example, workers who are observed to be cool-headed are more efficient in doing risky jobs. In the previous section, it was discussed that wealthier individuals tend to select safer jobs since safety is a normal good. Similarly, individuals with higher human capital (say, higher levels of education) will have an income effect, which will lead them to select safer jobs. Such disturbances are considered as unobserved heterogeneity among workers, which result in workers with higher earnings to select safe jobs. This implies that the disturbances which affect worker's wage are correlated with the unobserved disturbances that affect their choice of job risk. Thus, the choice of job risk is endogenous to worker's earnings, and it leads to selectivity bias (Garen, 1988). In such a situation, estimation of hedonic wage equation using ordinary least squares technique will yield biased results. Heckman's selectivity bias correction techniques are commonly used to resolve the issue of selectivity bias. However, this method is not applicable in this study since the endogenous choice variable is continuous. The simultaneous equation technique is more appropriate in this scenario. Therefore, Garen's modified selectivity bias correction technique has been used in this study. However, the structure of the disturbance in this model is different from other simultaneous equation models because unobservable factors affect the marginal return to job risks. This technique modifies the hedonic wage equation such that the structure of the disturbance term is altered.

$$\boldsymbol{Log}\ w_i = \alpha + \beta_1 p_i + \beta_2 q_i + \sum_k X_{ki}\gamma_k + \epsilon \qquad \ldots (4.5)$$

Here "ϵ" comprises three disturbances: ϵ_1, φ_1 and φ_2, such that; $\epsilon = \epsilon_1 + \varphi_1 \boldsymbol{p_i} + \varphi_2 \boldsymbol{q_i}$. "$\epsilon_1$" captures the effect of unobserved factors which influence worker's wage irrespective of the job risk **pi** and **qi**. Additional disturbance terms φ_1 and φ_2, represent the unobserved factors whose effect on worker's wage depends on the job risks **pi** and **qi.** It is assumed that the disturbances are correlated with each other, and they are normally distributed with a zero mean and a positive variance. The optimal choice of job risks **pi** and **qi** is dependent on the marginal loss in expected utility and marginal gain in expected earnings for taking up riskier jobs. Thus, the higher the values of φ_1 or φ_2, higher will be the marginal gain in earnings for taking up risky jobs.

Since safety is a normal good, counterweighing income and substitution effect arise for a choice of job risk. The disturbance term "$\in_1$" raises the earnings of a worker and therefore produces an income effect which induces a worker to select safer job. Similarly, factors such as having dependent children, which influences the worker's degree of risk aversion (denoted as Z), his asset and non-wage income (denoted as **Y**) produce an income effect. The first-order approximation of the job risks can be written as follows.

$$p_i = \pi_0 + X_{ki}\pi_1 + \pi_2 Z + \pi_3 Y + \eta \quad (4.6)$$

$$q_i = \delta_0 + X_{ki}\delta_1 + \delta_2 Z + \delta_3 Y + \mu \quad (4.7)$$

In equations (4.6) and (4.7), the error terms η and μ represent unobserved heterogeneity that may depend on the disturbances of the wage equation (i.e. ϵ_1, φ_1 and φ_2). The factors included in (X_{ki}) the factors affecting a worker's degree of risk aversion (Z) and non-wage income (Y) are expected to reduce the job risk levels ($\mathbf{p_i}$ and $\mathbf{q_i}$) and increase the earnings of the worker.

The final econometric model comprises equations (4.5), (4.6), and (4.7), and it resembles a standard triangular system of equations. The disturbances of equation (4.5) are correlated with disturbances of equations (4.6) and (4.7), and the unobservable factors embedded in φ_1 and φ_2 play a key role in determining the choice of job risk by the workers. Since the disturbance terms are correlated, $E(\varphi_1 p_i + \varphi_2 q_i + \epsilon_1) \neq 0$ and a crucial assumption of OLS is violated, yielding biased results. Reliable estimates can be obtained if values of $\boldsymbol{\eta}$ and $\boldsymbol{\mu}$ are replaced with their unbiased estimates, that is, $\hat{\eta}$ *and* $\hat{\mu}$. Besides, interaction of the predicted residuals $\hat{\eta}$ and $\hat{\mu}$ with the job risk variables (**p** and **q**) would reveal the underlying effect of unobserved worker heterogeneity. Thus, the bias-corrected hedonic wage equation is given by (4.8), which can be estimated using OLS to yield consistent results.

$$LnW_i = R\beta + Z_1\hat{\eta} + Z_2\hat{\mu} + Z_3\hat{\eta}p + Z_4\hat{\mu}p + Z_5\hat{\eta}q + Z_6\hat{\mu}q + \theta \quad (4.8)$$

Here, $R = (\alpha + \beta_1 p_i + \beta_2 q_i + \sum_k X_{ki}\gamma_k)$

This modified equation corrects not only the standard simultaneity bias but also the bias arising from unobserved factors affecting marginal return to job risks.

The next few sections of this chapter solve the above-discussed issues one by one to produce the basic and selectivity bias-corrected estimates of VSL and VSI.

4.4 Source and description of data

This study uses primary as well as secondary information to estimate the value of statistical life and Injury. The key focus of the previous chapter was on the sources of secondary information on job risks and the estimation of the objective job risk measures for this study. It also presented an analysis of the secondary data on the labour market, which laid the foundation for developing the sampling procedure of the study. The section discusses the sampling procedure.

The empirical implementation of the hedonic wage model, which was discussed at the beginning of this chapter, requires detailed information on workers' earnings, job risk, worker's personal and job characteristics. Since secondary information is available only on job risk measures, the only way to obtain individual-level information on workers is to conduct a cross-sectional micro-level primary survey. The required data were obtained from a survey undertaken in the Ahmedabad district of Gujarat during the period October 2016 to February 2017 (see the Appendix for the survey questionnaire).

This study adopted a multi-stage random sampling design, given the large and relatively homogeneous population under consideration. In the first stage, the Ahmedabad district of Gujarat was chosen as the study area due to having highest concentration of registered factories in the state. In the second stage, sample selection was based on the nature of employment. The analysis focused exclusively on male blue-collar workers employed in manufacturing industries. This choice was guided by data obtained from the Directorate of Industrial Safety and Health (DISH), which indicated that reported cases of occupational injuries and fatalities during the period 2010–2014 involved only male workers. Workers employed in other sectors covered under the Factories Act, such as services, railways, and coal mining, were therefore excluded from the sample. In the third stage, the selected workers were stratified into 13 industrial groups using the National Industrial Classification (NIC) 2004 codes. This industrial classification was used to link workers in the sample to objective measures of job risk, namely the average probability of fatal injuries per 100,000 workers and injury risks per 1,000 workers. The objective job risk measures are available only at the industry level and do not account for occupational differences within industries. Thus, workers within the same industry are assumed to face identical levels of risk. However, this simplifying assumption may lead to a mismatch between measured and actual workplace risk exposure. Such measurement issues are common in labour-market-based VSL studies in developing countries, where detailed secondary data on occupational risks by industry and job type are often unavailable. The problem is particularly pronounced for white-collar workers, who typically experience safer working environments (Garen, 1988). Although the lack of detailed risk data prevents the complete elimination of measurement error, this study seeks to mitigate its impact by restricting the sample to blue-collar workers, who are more likely to face comparable and observable workplace risks (Majumder and Madheswaran, 2018, 2020, 2022).

Approximately 1 per cent of workers from each stratum were selected in the sample, resulting in an initial sample size of 438. Comprehensive information on all registered factories in Ahmedabad, including factory names and addresses, workforce size, and industry classification based on two-digit National Industrial Classification (NIC) codes published in 2004 was obtained from a factory registry compiled by the (DISH). The DISH office classifies registered factories in Ahmedabad into four industrial regions (Divisions 1, 2, 3, and 4). Using this registry, factories were randomly drawn from each of these four regions. From each selected factory, around five to six workers were randomly surveyed. Primary data were collected through face-to-face interviews using a pre-tested questionnaire (see Appendix for the survey questionnaire). Following data cleaning, questionnaires containing incomplete or insufficient information were excluded. As a result, the final analytical sample consisted of 430 workers (Majumder & Madheswaran, 2018, 2020, 2022).

4.4.1 Descriptive statistics of variables

The descriptions of variables, along with their mean and standard deviation, are enlisted under Table 4.1. The objective job risk measures are calculated from secondary data, while the information on the other variables is obtained from the primary survey.

The dependent variable in the analysis is workers' after-tax hourly wage. Hourly wages were computed using the monthly and daily earnings reported by workers during the primary survey and were subsequently verified against wage records maintained by the factories. The average hourly wage among workers in the sample was INR 42.96.

This study employs two objective measures of job-related risk, namely FATAL and INJURY, which represent the average probability of fatal accidents per 100,000 workers and injuries per 1,000 workers, respectively. As reported in Table 4.1, the data indicate that, on average, there are 19 fatalities per 100,000 workers and two injuries per 1,000 workers annually. A subjective job risk measure (i.e. ENVDANGER) is developed using the information obtained from the primary survey. This variable equals one when a worker reports exposure to environmentally hazardous or unhealthy working conditions and zero otherwise. In the sample, around 61 per cent of workers indicated that their jobs involved such work conditions. The variable is included as a subjective proxy for job risk to compare workers' perceptions with objective measures of job risk. However, the estimation of VSL and VSI relies exclusively on the objective risk indicators, FATAL and INJURY, and does not use the subjective measure ENVDANGER. The subjective job risk measure yields a value of danger which indicates the wage premium that a worker receives if he perceives his job to be risky.

The personal characteristics of workers comprise of their level of job experience and education, the number of dependents at home, their caste and origin, income of other family members, and ownership of house, land, and vehicle. The mean years of experience of the workers in the sample are 18 years. There are four dummy variables indicating education level of workers in the sample. The sample is largely composed of workers with higher secondary education, whereas graduates account for only 6 per cent of the sample. Only 16 per cent of the workers in the sample belong to

Table 4.1 Descriptive statistics of variables used in the study

Variable	*Description*	*Mean & standard deviation*
Dependent variable		
HOURLY WAGE	After tax hourly wage of workers	42.96 (12.72)
Independent variables		
• Risk Variables		
FATAL	Average probability of fatal risk per one lakh workers	19.26 (10.30)
INJURY	Average probability of injury risk per one thousand workers	1.97 (2.21)
ENV DANGER	Indicator of job hazard perception of workers. 1 = If worker's job exposes him to environmental problems or unhealthy conditions at workplace, 0 = if his job doesn't expose him to environmental problems or unhealthy conditions.	0.61 (0.48)
• Personal characteristics of worker		
EXPERIENCE	Work experience (in years)	17.85 (11.15)
PRIMARY	1 = If the worker has completed primary education (i.e. spent 5 years in school), 0 = otherwise.	0.22 (0.41)
SECONDARY	1 = If the worker has completed secondary education (i.e. spent 10 years in school), 0 = otherwise.	0.29 (0.45)
HS	1 = If the worker has completed higher secondary education (i.e. spent 12 years in school), 0 = otherwise.	0.31 (0.46)
GRADUATE	1 = If the worker is a graduate or has a college degree (i.e. spent 15 years in school), 0 = otherwise.	0.06 (0.23)
SC	1 = If the worker belongs to the Schedule Caste, 0 = if the worker belongs to other castes.	0.16 (0.37)
MIGRANT	1 = If the worker is a migrant, 0= if the worker's native is Gujarat.	0.56 (0.49)
DEPENDENTS	The number of dependents (children and elderly) of the worker.	0.86 (0.34)

(*Continued*)

Table 4.1 (Continued)

Variable	*Description*	*Mean & standard deviation*
INCOME OF OTHERS	Income of other family members of the worker.	5928.51 (10241.18)
OWNS LAND	1 = If the worker owns land, 0 = if he doesn't own any land.	0.62 (0.48)
OWNS HOUSE	1 = If the worker owns house, 0= if he doesn't own any house.	0.55 (0.497)
OWNS VEHICLE	1 = If the worker owns any motor vehicle, 0 = if he doesn't own any vehicle.	0.65 (0.47)
• **Firm Characteristic**		
WSIZE	Total number of workers currently employed in the factory where the worker works.	699 (1245.19)
• **Job characteristics**		
JOB TYPE	1 = if worker's job is permanent, 0 = if the work is contractual or temporary.	0.73 (0.43)
SECU	1 = If the worker's job is secured, 0= otherwise.	0.60 (0.48)
TRAINING	1= If the worker completed job training in the same factory where he is a full-time worker now, 0 = if worker completed job training elsewhere.	0.42 (0.49)
UNION	1 = If worker is a union member, 0 = if the worker is not a union member.	0.07 (0.26)
OT	1 = If worker's job requires him to work overtime, 0= otherwise.	0.77 (0.41)
PHW	1 = If worker's job requires physical hard work, 0 = doesn't require hard work.	0.45 (0.49)

(Continued)

Table 4.1 (Continued)

Variable	*Description*	*Mean & standard deviation*
MENT	1 = If worker's job requires mental work (if worker must engage in any mathematical calculations or measurements in their work), 0 = doesn't require any mental work.	0.47 (0.50)
DEC	1 = If decision-making is a part of worker's job, 0 = worker doesn't need to make any decision.	0.51 (0.50)
FAST	1 = If worker's job requires him to work fast, 0 = otherwise.	0.23 (0.42)
NOMIS	1 = If worker's job requires him to be very careful, 0 = otherwise.	0.85 (0.35)
HECTIC	1 = If worker's job is hectic, 0 = otherwise.	0.41 (0.49)
PHCOND	1 = If the working condition is pleasant (i.e. if workplace is clean, has proper ventilation, and space to work, enough lighting, facilities of drinking water and toilets), 0 = if working conditions is poor.	0.89 (0.30)
• **Job designations**		
CONTRACTOR	1 = If worker is a contractor, 0 = otherwise.	0.03 (0.18)
SUPER	1 = If the worker is a supervisor, 0= otherwise.	0.07 (0.26)
FITTER	1 = If the worker is a fitter (does assembly, installation, repair, and maintenance of machineries), 0 = otherwise.	0.14 (0.35)
TECH	1 = If the worker is a technician, 0 = otherwise.	0.06 (0.24)
ASSIST	1 = If the worker is an assistant or helper, 0 = otherwise.	0.12 (0.33)

(*Continued*)

Table 4.1 (Continued)

Variable	*Description*	*Mean & standard deviation*
• Industrial region/division (location of factories)		
DIV 1	1 = If the worker belongs to a factory located in industrial division 1 of Ahmedabad district, 0 = otherwise.	0.26 (0.44)
DIV 2	1 = If the worker belongs to a factory located in industrial division 2 of Ahmedabad district, 0 =otherwise.	0.20 (0.40)
DIV 3	1 = If the worker belongs to a factory located in industrial division 3 of Ahmedabad district, 0 =otherwise.	0.33 (0.47)

Source: Author's calculation based on primary data collected from factory workers at Ahmedabad (Majumder & Madheswaran, 2018, 2022).

schedule caste (lower social group). 56 per cent of the workers are migrants from other Indian states, while the remaining workers in the sample are natives of Gujarat. On average, workers in the sample have one dependent member (children and elderly parent) in their family. The average income of other family members of a worker is INR 5928.51 per month. About 62 per cent of the workers in the sample own house, 55 per cent of them own land, and 65 per cent of them own vehicle (i.e. motorbikes, auto-rickshaws, or cars).

The variable WSIZE indicates the number of workers employed in the factory in which the respondent works. The average employee strength of the factories that were visited during primary survey is 699.

Job characteristics are captured through dummy variables reflecting the nature of employment and the worker's union status. Approximately 73 per cent of the workers in the sample were employed in permanent positions. However, only 60 per cent of these workers consider their job to be secured. Most workers begin their career in factories as apprentices. After acquiring job-specific skills over time, they are employed as permanent workers in the same factory where they received their training. It is observed that 42 per cent of the workers in the sample have obtained job training from the same factory in which they are currently employed. Only 7 per cent of the workers are union members. A large majority of workers in the sample (77 per cent) worked overtime in order to receive additional wage compensation. 45 per cent of the workers are engaged in jobs that require them to undertake physically hard work, like loading and unloading of finished products or stacking raw materials in the storeroom, et cetera. Forty-seven per cent of the workers reported that their job requires mental work like mathematical calculations or taking measurements during their work. While 51 per cent of the workers must make on-the-job decisions, 23 per cent of them are engaged in jobs that require them to work fast (e.g. assembly line workers). About 85 per cent of the sampled workers stated that their jobs necessitated careful and attentive work to avoid mistakes. Only 41 per cent of the workers reported their job to be hectic. Another important aspect of any job is the work environment, which affects not only workers' health but also their productivity. These factors comprise cleanliness at the workplace, proper ventilation, adequate working space, appropriate lighting, and the availability of drinking water and toilet facilities. Therefore, the workers in the sample were asked whether their work conditions were pleasant or not. Eighty-nine per cent of the workers in the sample reported their work conditions to be pleasant. If employers provide better amenities at workplace and good work environment, then workers may be willing to accept slightly lower wages from the employers.

The job designation of the workers is captured through five dummy variables. In the sample of workers used in this study, 34 per cent are contractors, 7 per cent are supervisors, 14 per cent are fitters, 6 per cent are technicians, and 12 per cent are assistants. While 27 per cent of the workers belong to the other job designations, which have been taken as the base category.

The final set of dummy variables pertains to the three region dummies. About 26 per cent of the workers in the sample belong to the factories located in industrial division 1, while 20 per cent of them belong to factories located in industrial division 2. On the other hand, 30 per cent of the workers belong to factories from industrial division 3, and 24 per cent are from factories located in industrial division 4 (which is the base category).

4.5 Descriptive analysis of survey data

Given the description of the variables, this section presents a simple analysis of the primary data. Table 4.2 shows the distribution of the workers in the sample by their job experience. It also shows the after-tax hourly wage of the workers by their experience level. A highest proportion of workers in the sample have an experience of six to ten years. These workers earn an average after-tax hourly wage of INR 38.89. On the other hand, the lowest proportion of workers has an experience of 41 years and above. They earn an average wage of INR 39.86 per hour. Figure 4.2 shows the relationship between worker's experience level and income. It is observed that the hourly wage of a worker increases with the increase in his job experience. However, their earnings start to decline slowly after attaining a peak at experience level of 26–30 years. Therefore, an inverted U-shaped relation is observed between worker's wage and his job experience.

Table 4.2 Distribution of average hourly wage by experience of the workers

Range of experience	*Percentage of sample*	*Average hourly wage*
0–5	11.6	33.73
6–10	20.0	38.89
11–15	15.8	42.96
16–20	13.7	45.76
21–25	15.6	47.85
26–30	7.4	48.90
31–35	7.4	46.71
36–40	5.8	42.0
41 and above	2.6	39.86
For full sample	100	42.96

Source: Author's calculation based on primary data collected from factory workers at Ahmedabad (Majumder & Madheswaran, 2018).

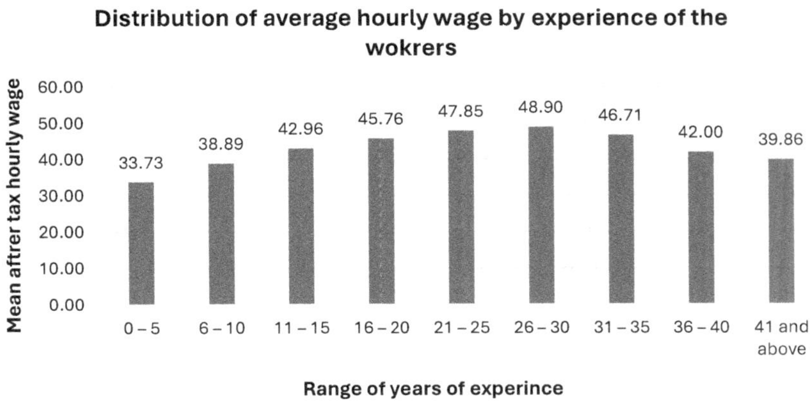

Figure 4.2 Relationship between average hourly wage and experience of the workers.

Source: Author's calculation based on primary data collected from factory workers at Ahmedabad (Majumder, 2019).

Given the relation between worker's wage and experience level, Table 4.3 shows the distribution of the hourly earnings of workers by their education level. In this study, there are five categories of education level, which depend on the years of schooling completed by the workers. On average, an illiterate worker in the sample earns an after-tax hourly wage of INR 35.96. On the other hand, a worker who has completed his graduation earns an average after-tax hourly wage of INR 47.5. As observed from Figure 4.3, the hourly wage of the workers increases with an increase in their education level. An average worker in the sample has attained 8.4 years of schooling.

Some of the personal characteristics, like the education level and experience, vary by the job designation of the workers, and this is shown in Table 4.4. It is observed that contractors in the sample have an average experience of 15.6 years, 8.5 years of schooling, and earn an average hourly wage of INR 50. Supervisors in the sample have an average experience of 20.4 years and earn an average wage of INR 46 per hour. They have the highest years of experience and highest level of education from among all the job designations. On average, fitters have job experience of 18.8 years, complete 8.7 years of education and earn an average wage of INR 42.8 per hour. On the other hand, technicians have an average of 18.7 years of experience and 8.64 years of education, and they earn an average hourly wage of INR 45. Assistants have an average experience of 16.1 years, complete 6 years of schooling, and earn an average wage of INR 38 per hour. Other job

Table 4.3 Distribution of average hourly wage of workers by their level of education

Level of education	*Years of schooling*	*Percentage of sample*	*Average hourly wage*
Illiterate	0	0.12	35.96
Primary	5	0.22	39.81
Secondary	10	0.29	44.9
Higher secondary	12	0.31	46.63
Graduate	15	0.06	47.5
For full sample	8.4	100	42.96

Source: **Author's calculation based on primary data collected from factory workers at Ahmedabad.**

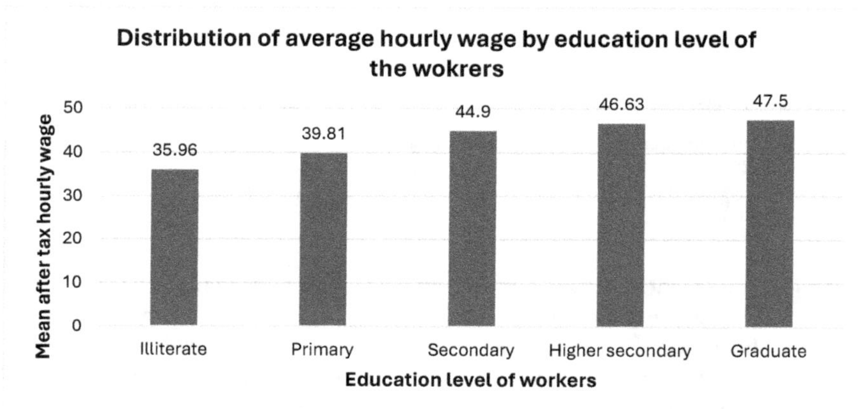

Figure 4.3 Relationship between average hourly wage and level of education of the workers.

Source: Author's calculation based on primary data collected from factory workers at Ahmedabad (Majumder, 2019).

Table 4.4 Distribution of personal characteristics of workers by their job designations

Job designation	*Average experience*	*Average years of education*	*Average hourly wage*
Contractor	15.60	8.50	50
Supervisor	20.48	10.33	46
Fitter	18.89	8.70	42.8
Technician	18.70	8.64	45
Assistant	16.01	6.00	38
Others	17.10	8.20	36
Full sample average	17.80	8.40	42.96

Source: Author's calculation based on primary data collected from factory workers at Ahmedabad.

designations (which are the base category for dummy variables on job designation) have an average experience of 17.1 years, have completed 8.2 years of education, and earn an average wage of INR 36 per hour.

Information on personal and job-related characteristics was collected through a primary survey of workers across four industrial divisions in Ahmedabad. It will be interesting to examine how the parameters like wage, job-related fatal risk, injury risk, job hazard perception, and personal and job characteristics of workers vary among the industrial divisions. Division-wise information on workers' personal and employment characteristics is reported in Tables 4.5–4.7.

Table 4.5 shows the distribution of workers in the sample across the four industrial divisions of Ahmedabad. It also presents the division-wise distribution of job risks and wages of the workers. The workers in the sample have been randomly chosen from across each industrial division. However, as observed from Table 4.5, majority of the workers are from division 3, which

Table 4.5 Division-wise information on wages and distribution of workers in the sample from each division

Division	*No. in the sample*	*Average hourly wage*	*Average probability of fatal risk per one lakh workers*	*Average probability of injury risk per 1000 workers*	*Job hazard perception (in percentage)*
DIVISION 1	113	47.84	21.72	1.97	64
DIVISION 2	89	42.82	19.00	1.56	62.8
DIVISION 3	144	45.99	16.94	2.68	61
DIVISION 4	84	35.19	21.04	1.23	56.9
For full sample	430	42.96	19.67	1.85	61

Source: Author's calculation based on primary data collected from factory workers at Ahmedabad.

Table 4.6 Division-wise information on personal characteristics of workers in the sample

Division	*Illiterate*	*Primary*	*Secondary*	*Higher secondary*	*Graduate*	*SC*	*Migrant*
	(Figures are in percentage)						
DIVISION 1	10	29	27	28	6	21	48
DIVISION 2	8	22	25	37	8	16	58
DIVISION 3	10	20	37	29	4	14	62
DIVISION 4	20	17	27	30	6	17	18
For full sample	12	22	29	31	6	16	56

Source: Majumder and Madheswaran (2018).

Table 4.7 Division-wise information on job characteristics of workers in the sample

Division	*Physical hard work*	*Over time*	*Job security*	*Mental work*	*Carefulness*	*Fast*	*Decision*	*Hectic*	*Conditions of work*
	(Figures are in percentage)								
DIVISION 1	52	68	56	48	84	19	49	44	92
DIVISION 2	43	72	55	54	84	23	60	41	92
DIVISION 3	33	87	76	51	83	30	55	34	90
DIVISION 4	52	81	57	39	89	24	40	45	82
For full sample	45	77	61	48	85	24	51	41	89

Source: Majumder and Madheswaran (2018) and Author's calculation based on primary data collected from factory workers at Ahmedabad.

has an average hourly wage of INR 45.99. On the other hand, workers in division 1 earn highest average hourly wage of INR 47.84 and face highest fatal risk per one lakh workers. On the contrary, the workers in division 4 earn the lowest average hourly wage of INR 35.19 amongst the four industrial divisions but face high risk of death, that is, like division 1. This result is quite surprising because workers engaged in risky jobs are expected to earn more. However, the injury risk is lowest for division 4, and only 56.9 per cent of workers in this division perceive that their job exposes them to environmental problems or unhealthy conditions. This may be the reason for the workers of division 4 to accept lower wages. A further examination of this issue has been undertaken in the following chapter.

Tables 4.6 and 4.7 provide division-wise information on the personal and work characteristics of the workers in the sample. Table 4.6 presents division-wise information on workers' personal characteristics, including education level, caste status, and migrant status. Approximately 12 per cent of workers in the overall sample were illiterate. The highest share of illiterate workers was observed in factories located in division 4, while division 2 recorded the lowest proportion of illiterate workers. The proportion of workers with primary education is highest in division 1, while the proportion of workers attaining secondary education is highest in division 3. The proportion of workers attaining higher secondary education and graduation is highest in division 2. Division 1 has the highest proportion of workers belonging to the Scheduled Caste (SC), while division 3 has the lowest proportion of SC workers. About 56 per cent of the workers in the sample are migrants out of which majority of them belong to division 3. Division 4 has the lowest proportion of migrant workers.

Job-related characteristics of workers across the four industrial divisions are reported in Table 4.7. Majority of workers who engage in physically hard work belong to divisions 1 and 4. Overtime work is quite high for workers from all the divisions. It is highest for workers from division 3. Job security is highest for workers in division 3 compared to the workers from other industrial divisions. A highest proportion of workers from division 2 engage in mental work. Highest proportion of workers from division 4 reported that they need to very focused on their work to prevent the possibility of injury. A comparatively small proportion of workers from all the divisions are engaged in jobs that require them to work fast. Majority of the workers in the sample who make job decisions belong to division 2. Highest proportion of workers from division 4 reported their job to be hectic. About 90 per cent of the workers from all the divisions (except division 4) reported their working conditions to be pleasant.

4.6 Pre-estimation analysis for functional form selection

It is necessary to determine a suitable functional form before the estimation of hedonic wage equation is undertaken. In doing so, two methods have been used in this study. The first one involves normal probability plots of residuals, while the second one involves Box-Cox transformation analysis.

4.6.1 Normal probability plots for determining appropriate functional form

One of the major assumptions of OLS method is that the disturbances (i.e. the error term) should be normally distributed. A normal probability plot (NPP) of the residuals is used to assess whether the assumption of normally distributed error terms is reasonable. When the data follow a normal distribution with mean μ and variance σ^2, a plot of the theoretical normal percentiles against the observed sample percentiles should display an approximately linear pattern. Given the concern regarding the normality of the error terms, an NPP of the residuals is constructed. If the resulting plot appears roughly linear, the error terms are assumed to follow a normal distribution.

The hedonic wage equation has been estimated in three possible forms, that is, linear form, semi-logarithmic form, and inverse form, and the residuals from each of the estimated equations have been plotted. Figures 4.4, 4.5, and 4.6 show the plots for the residuals of the three forms of the estimated hedonic wage equation. For all the specifications, the independent variables used are job risk measures (FATAL and INJURY); dummies for education level of workers, experience, and squared of experience; dummy for union membership, job type and training; dummies on migrant status and social class; workers size in factories; dummies for work characteristics (PHW, SECU, MENT, and FAST); and dummies for job designations and industrial divisions of Ahmedabad. The dependent variable used in each specification is the same, that is, the after-tax hourly wage of the worker. However, the

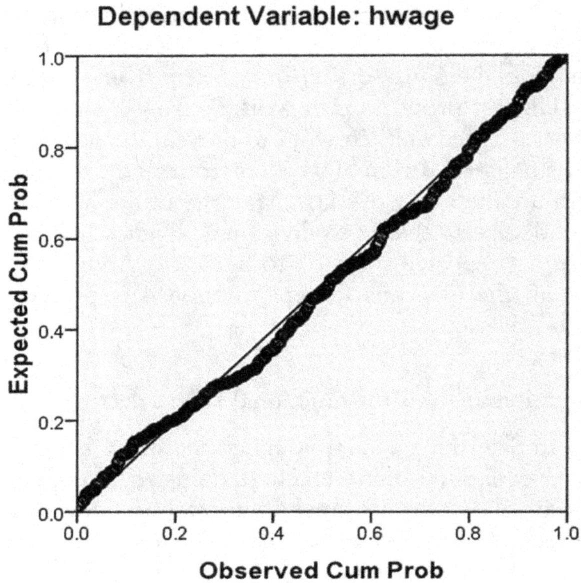

Figure 4.4 Normal probability plot of hedonic wage regression in linear form.
Source: Author's own creation from analysis of data (Majumder, 2019).

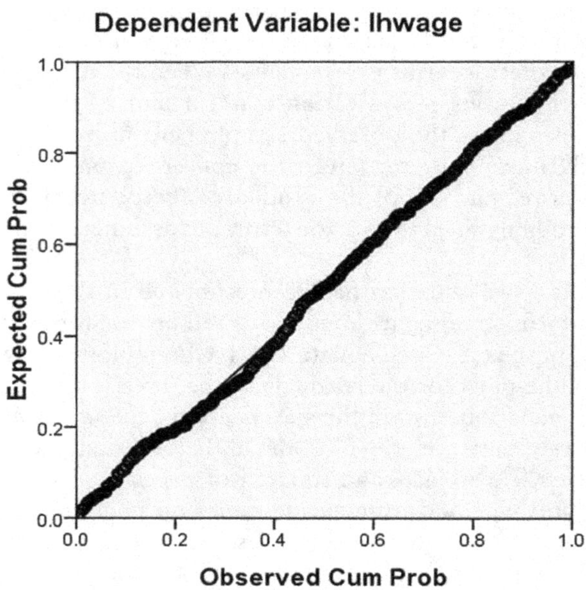

Figure 4.5 Normal probability plot of hedonic wage regression in inverse form.
Source: Author's own creation from analysis of data (Majumder, 2019).

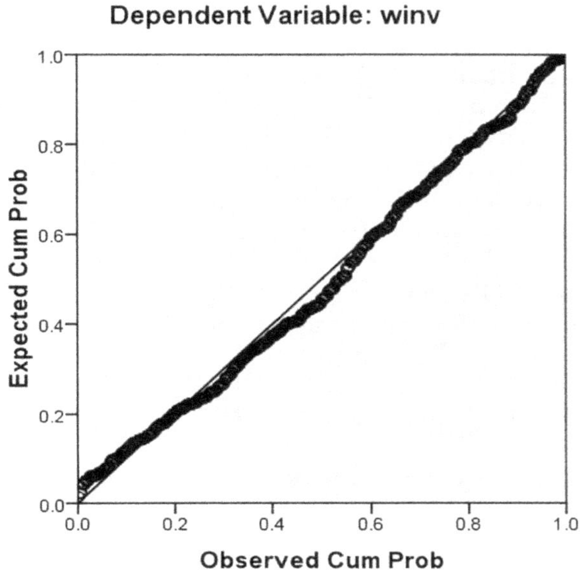

Figure 4.6 Normal probability plot of hedonic wage regression in semi-logarithmic form.
Source: Author's own creation from analysis of data (Majumder, 2019).

dependent variable takes different forms (i.e. linear form, semi-logarithmic form, and inverse form) for each specification.

The linear and inverse specifications both produce residuals that are not normally distributed, indicating that OLS estimation under these forms may be inappropriate or yield biased results. In contrast, the semi-logarithmic specification generates normally distributed residuals, making it the appropriate functional form for estimating the hedonic wage equation.

4.6.2 *Box-Cox transformation for determining appropriate functional form*

The functional form analysis using NPPs provides a rough idea about the suitable functional form for estimating hedonic wage equation. A flexible functional form analysis has been done using the Box-Cox transformation to further ascertain the appropriate functional form.

Under the Box-Cox framework, the following wage equation is estimated using the maximum likelihood method.

$$\frac{w_i^{\lambda} - 1}{\lambda} = \alpha + \beta_1 p_i + \beta_2 q_i + \sum{}_k \gamma_k X_{ki} + \epsilon_i \tag{4.9}$$

It is assumed that the parameter λ takes a value that ensures the model satisfies the assumptions of normality, homoscedasticity, and linearity in the regression framework. The parameter λ is estimated by maximising the log-likelihood function and is restricted to lie between −1 and +1. When λ approaches −1, an inverse functional form is appropriate; when λ approaches zero, a semi-logarithmic specification is indicated; and when λ approaches one, a linear form is preferred. The results of the Box-Cox transformation analysis are reported in Table 4A in Appendix 4A of this chapter. Based on the mean square error (MSE), the semi-logarithmic specification is identified as the most suitable functional form for estimating the hedonic wage equation. Accordingly, the semi-logarithmic wage equation is specified as follows.

$$LnWAGE = \alpha + \beta_1 FATAL + \beta_2 INJURY + \sum_k \gamma_k X_{ki} + \epsilon_i \tag{4.10}$$

Here, X_{ki} includes a set of explanatory variables capturing human capital characteristics, such as the worker's level of education; firm-related attributes, including firm size and private sector status; and individual characteristics of workers, such as age, place of origin, religion, social class, and occupation.

4.7 Estimation and results of hedonic wage equation

Table 4.8 reports the estimates of the semi-logarithmic hedonic wage equation (4.10) under three different specifications. The first specification includes only fatal and injury job risks, along with other independent variables. This equation is estimated using OLS method, and it yields the VSL and VSI estimates. Specification (2) includes only the subjective risk measure along with other independent variables and yields the value of danger. The last specification corrects the selectivity bias using Garen's modified selectivity bias-correction procedure and presents the bias-corrected estimates of VSL and VSI. All the specifications have been examined for heteroscedasticity and multicollinearity.

4.7.1 Discussion on result of specifications (1) and (2)

As predicted by the theoretical model, the results from specification (1) indicate that risk variables have a positive and statistically significant effect on workers' wages. This suggests that workers in the sample receive positive CWDs for exposure to fatal and non-fatal job risks. The annual CWD for job-related fatal risk is estimated to be INR 446, and that for injury risk is INR 1,673. This implies that, on average, a worker in the sample is paid INR 446 annually for an increase in job-related fatal risk by a very small probability of 0.000001 (i.e. 1/100,000) and INR 1,673 annually for an increase in job-related injury risk by a small probability of 0.001 (i.e. 1/1,000). Scaling

Table 4.8 Results of estimation of hedonic wage equation

Variables	*(1)*	*(2)*	*(3)*
Constant	3.269* (57.33)	3.360* (60.30)	3.282* (52.97)
FATAL	0.0048* (4.73)		0.0038* (3.57)
INJURY	0.01800* (3.75)		0.046** (1.77)
ENV DANGER		0.046* (2.25)	
EXP	0.011* (3.46)	0.011* (3.51)	0.011* (3.47)
EXP^2	-0.0001*(-1.99)	-0.0001* (-2.13)	-0.0001* (-2.05)
PRIMARY	0.131* (3.51)	0.147* (3.82)	0.124* (3.35)
SECONDARY	0.114* (3.17)	0.126* (3.40)	0.112* (3.13)
HS	0.208* (4.34)	0.174* (4.75)	0.168* (4.79)
GRADUATE	0.170* (3.33)	0.186* (3.53)	0.179* (3.51)
SC	-0.055* (-2.60)	-0.076 (-2.82)	-0.064* (-2.45)
MIGRANT	-0.065* (-2.48)	-0.059* (-2.73)	-0.045* (-1.99)
UNION	0.050 (1.22)	0.088* (2.12)	0.007 (0.15)
SIZE	-0.025 (-1.15)	-0.032 (-1.38)	-0.041** (-1.79)
JOBTYPE	0.051* (2.03)	0.067* (2.57)	0.041*** (1.61)
TRAINING	-0.031 (-1.45)	-0.038** (-1.77)	-0.019 (-0.79)
PHW	-0.041** (-1.93)	-0.053* (-2.43)	-0.035*** (-1.63)
SECU	0.015 (0.66)	0.015 (0.65)	0.030 (1.05)
MENT	0.037** (1.82)	0.048* (2.32)	0.026 (1.19)
FAST	-0.057* (-2.47)	-0.064* (-2.69)	-0.058* (-2.53)
CONTRACTOR	0.294* (5.04)	0.334* (5.59)	0.243* (3.91)
SUPERVISOR	0.133* (3.47)	0.137* (3.46)	0.135* (3.53)
FITTER	0.096* (3.33)	0.103* (3.43)	0.078* (2.44)
TECH	0.078** (1.94)	0.091* (2.21)	0.064 (1.54)
ASSIST	-0.109* (-3.51)	-0.109* (-3.42)	-0.118* (-3.71)
DIV 1	0.246* (8.17)	0.251* (8.09)	0.202* (5.67)
DIV 2	0.134* (4.26)	0.121* (3.74)	0.111* (3.43)
DIV 3	0.203* (6.79)	0.193* (6.45)	0.174* (4.83)
$I_{RESIDUAL}$			0.249*** (1.63)
FATAL × $I_{RESIDUAL}$			-0.019* (-2.82)
INJURY × $I_{RESIDUAL}$			-0.025 (-0.70)
N	427	427	427
R-squared	0.55	0.52	0.56
F-Statistics	19.43	17.81	17.96
VSL	4,46,91,254 (INR 44.69 million or $0.66 million)		3,58,58,231 (INR 35.85 million or $0.53 million)
VSI	16,70,285 (INR 1.67 million or $0.024 million)		43,07,061 (INR 4.30 million or $0.064 million)
Value of Danger		4,358	

Source: Author's own calculation (Majumder & Madheswaran, 2018).

Note: t-values are given in parentheses, (Exchange rate: 1 USD = INR 88.07, Reserve Bank of India 2016–2017).

* 1 per cent level of significance
** 5 per cent level of significance
*** 10 per cent level of significance

up the annualized CWD for individual workers to one lakh workers, we obtain the baseline estimates of the VSL and VSI from specification (1) which are INR 44.69 million (USD 0.66 million, 2016USD) and INR 1.67 million (USD 0.024 million, 2016USD), respectively.

The second specification, reported in column (2), includes ENVDANGER as the sole risk variable along with other wage determinants. The self-reported job risk measure exhibits a positive and statistically significant effect on workers' wages. Workers who perceive their jobs as dangerous earn an annual wage premium of INR 4,358 (USD 64.97). This estimate is calculated by multiplying the coefficient of the ENVDANGER variable by the workers' average wage and annual hours of work. The implied value of danger is substantially lower than the estimated VSI, which may be attributed to workers' limited awareness of the actual risks associated with their jobs.

The other independent variables have expected sign as per economic theory. A worker's wage rises significantly with experience up to a certain point, after which it begins to decline. Higher the education level of a worker higher are the wage earnings. Migrant workers and workers belonging to lower social group are paid significantly lower wages compared to other workers in the sample. Union workers earn higher wages as union membership improves bargaining power of workers. This result also indicate that union workers are made aware of their job risks by the union and hence they can demand higher wages for riskier jobs. While the UNION variable is statistically significant in specification (2), it is not significant in specification (1). The total number of workers working in a factory (i.e. size of a factory) does not affect the wage of the workers significantly. The workers who are engaged in permanent jobs earn significantly higher compared to workers engaged in contractual jobs. Workers who received job training in the same factory where they are currently employed earn comparatively less than other workers in the sample. While this variable is significant at 5 per cent level for specification (2), it is insignificant for specification (1). For both specifications, workers engaged in jobs that require mental work are paid more, while workers engaged in jobs that require hard physical work are paid significantly lower wages. Contrary to the expectation, job security is observed to have no significant influence on worker's wage. Workers engaged in jobs that require them to work fast (e.g. workers engaged in sorting or packaging goods) earn significantly lower than other workers in the sample. Contractors, supervisors, fitters, and technicians earn significantly higher wages compared with workers in other job categories. In contrast, assistants receive significantly lower earnings than workers in other designations. In addition, workers employed in factories located in industrial divisions 1, 2, and 3 earn significantly higher wages than those working in industrial division 4.

4.7.2 *Discussion on results of bias-corrected regression (specification 3)*

The issue of selectivity bias and the method of addressing this bias using two-stage modified selectivity bias technique proposed by Garen (1988) has already been discussed in detail under Section 4.3.3. This section discusses the bias-corrected results that have been presented in Table 4.8 under specification (3).

The first stage regression following Garen's method, involves estimating the job risk equations using OLS method (presented in Table 4B, Appendix 4B). Since two types of job risks, i.e. both fatal and non-fatal job risks are included in the estimation of the basic hedonic equation, the first stage will comprise of a pair of job risk equations. The dependent variables that are used in the first-stage regressions are the inverse normal cumulative density functions of fatal and injury risk. The job risk measures used in this study are in natural units, which lie between zero and one. An inverse normal transformation allow the job risk variables to take any value between minus infinity and a positive random variable (Arabsheibani and Marin, 2000).

Equations (4.6) and (4.7), that is, the job risk equations, are estimated at the first stage. All the independent variables that have been used to estimate the basic hedonic wage equation are included in the estimation of the job risk equations as well. The main hypothesis that is being tested in the first-stage regression is that a worker's choice of job risk depends not only on his personal characteristics but also on his assets and other income sources. Therefore, asset indicator variables (like the income of worker's family members and worker's ownership of motor vehicle) are included as independent variables in job risk equations. Besides, a measure of worker's risk aversion (dependent family members) is also included in the first-stage regression. As per the theory of choice of risk, higher the assets and secondary income sources of a worker, lower will be the job risks undertaken by him. If workers have dependent children and elderly parents they may engage in safer jobs.

In the second stage, equation (4.8) is estimated. The predicted residuals ($\hat{\eta}$ and $\hat{\mu}$) obtained from first-stage equations are included as independent variables in second-stage regression. The predicted residuals are also interacted with the job-risk variables to examine the effect of unobserved worker heterogeneity. However, the predicted residual obtained from fatal risk equation and its interaction with the job risks are found to be insignificant. Therefore, only the predicted residual from injury risk equation (denoted as $I_{RESIDUAL}$) and its interaction with job risks are retained in the 2nd stage regression. The term $I_{RESIDUAL}$ has a positive influence on worker's wage, which implies that there exists a positive association between wages and unobserved factors affecting injury risk. However, this variable is significant only at 10 per cent level. The result shows that the interaction between predicted residual from injury risk equation and fatal risk is significant. This suggests that φ_2 have important effects on returns to injury risk. Since this term is negative, it implies that workers engaged in safer jobs have unexpectedly large values of φ_2. A large value of φ_2 in turn causes the income effect to dominate the substitution effect. This result is consistent with safety being a normal good. The interaction term $\mathbf{INJURY \times I_{RESIDUAL}}$ has a negative sign; however, it is insignificant. This result implies that workers engaged in jobs that are on average riskier tend to earn lower premium for injury risk. This is because the income effect causes workers with low returns to injury risk to choose riskier jobs. Overall, the results suggest that unobserved worker heterogeneity leads to substantial bias in the estimation of the wage premium for fatal and injury risks.

The bias-corrected results show the true relationship between job risk choice on worker's wage taking into account the endogenous relationship between these two variables. Both the job risk variables are found to be positive and significant for specification (3). However, the coefficient of the fatal risk variable obtained from the bias corrected specification (3) is smaller as compared to baseline specification (1). This result indicates that the baseline estimates of VSL had an upward bias, and this bias has been corrected by addressing the endogeneity issue. On the other hand, the coefficient of the injury risk variable obtained from bias corrected specification (3) is larger than the baseline specification (1) indicating the baseline VSI estimate had a downward bias. Thus, on correction of the bias, the VSI increased. The estimated VSL from bias corrected specification (3) is INR 35.8 million ($0.53 million), while the VSI is INR 4.30 million ($0.064 million). This implies that a worker should be paid INR 358 annually for an increase in death risk by 1/100,000 and INR 4,307 for an increase in injury risk by 1/1,000. On comparing the VSL and VSI estimates from baseline and bias corrected specifications, it is observed that the VSL estimate has gone down by INR 8.83 million ($0.13 million) while the VSI has gone up by INR 2.63 million ($0.038 million) after correction of selectivity bias.

All the other independent variables behave in similar fashion as observed in specification (1). However, there are a few exceptions. The variable on size of workers in factories was earlier insignificant, which has become significant at 5 per cent level in specification (3). This result implies, as worker size increases in factories, employers are more likely to pay lower wages to workers. On the other hand, two variables on job characteristics, that is, MENT and TECH, have become insignificant in specification (3).

4.8 Examining the wealth effect

It was mentioned earlier in Section 4.3.2. that workers with greater wealth and higher earnings are less inclined to engage in risky occupations. To examine the phenomenon of this wealth effect, a logistic regression is estimated, and the results on marginal effects of each variable are presented in Table 4.9. The dependent variable used in this regression is the subjective job risk measure (**ENVDANGER**). The independent variables used in this regression are dummy variables such as training, union status, hectic, carefulness in doing job, job designations, and indicators of worker's wealth or assets. As proxy for worker's assets, two variables, namely **OWNLAND** (i.e. ownership of land) and **OWNHOUSE** (i.e. ownership of house), have been used. Since each worker has a different job risk perception, the effect of worker's wealth on his choice of job risk is more effectively captured by using the subjective job risk measure.

The result of the logistic regression yields the marginal effects. For logistic regression with binary explanatory variables, marginal effects measure discrete changes, that is how the predicted probabilities change as the binary explanatory variable changes from 0 to 1, holding all other variables at their means. For a categorical explanatory variable, say X_k, the marginal effects are given as follows.

$$\textbf{Marginal Effect } X_k = Pr(Y = 1 \mid \mathbf{X}, X_k = 1) - Pr(Y = 1 \mid \mathbf{X}, X_k = 0)$$

The variables TRAINING, UNION, HECTIC, NOMIS, CONTRACTOR, FITTER, OWN LOAND, and OWN HOUSE are significant in this regression. The marginal effects for the variable TRAINING indicate that, holding all other variables at their means, the predicted probability of perceiving one's

Table 4.9 Logistic regression for examining wealth effect of workers

Variables	*Mean value*	*Marginal effects*
EXPERIENCE	17.85	–0.0004 (–0.18)
TRAINING	0.42	–0.100* (–1.95)
UNION	0.07	0.182** (1.83)
HECTIC	0.40	0.160* (2.94)
NOMIS	0.85	0.150* (2.11)
CONTRACTOR	0.03	0.454* (2.39)
SUPERVISOR	0.07	0.032 (0.36)
FITTER	0.14	0.170* (2.14)
TECHNICIAN	0.06	0.035 (0.35)
ASSISTANT	0.12	0.014 (0.18)
OWN LAND	0.62	–0.185* (–3.37)
OWN HOUSE	0.55	–0.086** (–1.56)
N	427	

* Figures in parentheses are z scores.

* 1 per cent level of significance

**5 per cent level of significance

***10 per cent level of significance

job to be risky is 10 per cent lower for a worker who has undergone training in the same factory where he is currently employed compared to other workers in the sample. The predicted probability of perceiving one's job to be risky is 18 per cent higher for union workers. This result supports the hypothesis that union workers are better aware of their job risks than non-union workers. The predicted probability of perceiving one's job to be risky is 16 per cent higher for a worker who does hectic job and 15 per cent higher for workers engaged in jobs that necessitate them to be careful. Predicted probability of perceiving one's job to be risky is 45 per cent higher for contractors leading them to demand higher wages from employers. The information obtained during the primary survey indicated that, contractors usually engage in safe jobs like hiring and managing contractual workers on behalf of employers. However, from time to time, contractors may have to operate machines during the absence or shortage of any contractual workers, which increases the likelihood of getting injured (since they may be inexperienced in operate machines). Fitters perceive their job to be riskier than others. This may be because they are engaged in maintenance and repair of heavy machines, and any error on their part may cause them injury or even death. As expected, the wealth indicator variables, ownership of land and ownership of house, are significant and have negative signs. Considering the overall influence of the wealth indicator variables, it can be inferred that wealthier workers tend to select safer jobs, suggesting the presence of a wealth effect among the workers in the sample.

4.9 Implications of benefit transfer for VSL

The earlier sections of this chapter showed how VSL is estimated independently using data on a sample of workers from an Indian city. Many developing countries do not have such kinds of studies on VSL. In the absence of independent VSL studies, policymakers use an alternative approach called the Benefit Transfer Methodology BTM to estimate VSL for developing countries. However, decades of research indicate that BTM underestimates VSL. Therefore, this section intends at examining whether BTM yields underestimated VSL for this study. The next few paragraphs show the process of estimation of VSL using BTM. Finally, the estimate of VSL obtained using BTM is compared with the VSL that has been estimated earlier in this chapter using hedonic wage approach.

The BTM allows VSL estimates from developed countries to be adapted for developing countries using a simple formula. Specifically, if country A is a developing country and country B is a developed country, the VSL estimate for country B can be adapted for country A using the following formula.

$$\frac{VSL^A}{Y^A} = \frac{VSL^B}{Y^B} \tag{4.11}$$

Therefore, from (5.7),

$$VSL^A = \frac{VSL^B}{Y^B} \times Y^A$$

In this expression, Y represents the foregone earnings in each country. The equation implies that the ratio of VSL to foregone earnings is assumed to be the same for both countries. However, the validity of the BTM rests on two strong assumptions. The first assumption is that individuals in both countries share identical preferences towards risk. Equation (4.11) has been formed based on this assumption. However, individuals of developed and developing countries have significant differences in job risk preferences. The second assumption is that the income elasticity of VSL is equal to unity. However, the income elasticity of VSL for developing countries is less than one (Simon et al., 1999). These two impractical assumptions are more than enough to justify that BTM would yield biased estimates of VSL, and therefore, conducting independent VSL studies is essential in developing countries. Nevertheless, we have used the above procedure to transfer VSL from the United States to India. Data on foregone earnings were obtained from the World Bank, while VSL estimates for the United States were sourced from the United States Environmental Protection Agency (USEPA). The ratio of the VSL to foregone earnings for the United States (i.e. $\frac{VSL^{U.S.A}}{Y^{U.S.A}}$) is approximately \$154.53 while the value of foregone earnings of India ($i.e., Y^{India}$) is estimated to be \$2047.64 (2016 US dollar). Thus, the extrapolated VSL for India is

$$VSL^{India} = \frac{VSL^{U.S.A}}{Y^{U.S.A}} \times Y^{India} = (154.53 \times 2047.64) = \$0.31 \text{ million (2016 USD)} = \text{INR } 21.39 \text{ million}$$

This extrapolated estimate of VSL (i.e. INR 21.39 million) is much smaller than the bias-corrected estimate of VSL (i.e. INR 35.85 million) obtained earlier in this chapter using the hedonic wage approach. The country-specific characteristics are taken into consideration in independent VSL studies, which BTM fails to capture, yielding underestimated estimate of VSL. Thus, conducting independent VSL studies like the present one yields a precise estimate of VSL.

Given that the BTM yields VSL for India and VSL estimates obtained in this study using hedonic wage approach pertains to a small sample of workers from an Indian city, this comparison exercise gives us a rough idea about the differences in VSL estimates using two different methods.

4.10 Conclusion

This chapter focused on estimation of the value of statistical life and injury of workers in the sample. The key hypothesis that has been tested in this chapter is whether workers in the sample are paid positive wage premium for undertaking job risks. The result of this study strongly supports this hypothesis. The basic estimates of value of statistical life and value of statistical injury are INR 44.69 million ($0.64 million 2016 USD) and INR 1.67 million ($0.02 million 2016 USD), respectively. The selectivity bias-corrected estimates of VSL and VSI are INR 35.8 million ($0.51 million 2016 USD) and INR 4.30 million ($0.06 million 2016 USD), respectively. On correction of the selectivity bias, estimates of VSL declined, while the estimates of VSI increased. Thus, this study provides evidence that workers in the sample are compensated for the job risks that they undertake. Besides, there is a significant wealth effect for the workers in the sample. This implies that worker's wealth influences his choice of job risk in this study.

This study not only offers updated estimates of the VSL for the Indian labour market but also revises the estimation approach. Unlike earlier studies in India, which assumed an annual working time of 2,000 hours without providing clear justification, this analysis adopts a revised estimate of 2,160 annual working hours for the calculation of both VSL and VSI. A detailed justification for the use of this revised figure is provided in endnote.

The final section of this chapter examined the implications of using BTM to estimate VSL. This is a very important exercise since it underscores the need for conducting independent VSL studies in developing countries rather than extrapolating these estimates from developed countries. We have used BTM to extrapolate the VSL for India from the United States and found that this extrapolation underestimates the VSL for India. The country-specific characteristics are taken into consideration in independent VSL studies, which BTM fails to capture, yielding underestimated estimate of VSL. Thus, conducting independent VSL studies like the present one yields a precise estimate of VSL.

In this chapter, we presented the basic estimates of value of statistical life and injury and further corrected these estimates for selectivity bias. However, this analysis doesn't take into consideration the influence of ex-post compensation benefits provided to workers for job injuries. Therefore, the next chapter analyses the impact of compensation benefits on workers' wages and their VSL estimates.

Note

1 According to the Factories Act (1948), a worker can work up to 9 hours a day, and he/she is entitled to 12 paid leaves in the following year if he works for 240 days in the present calendar year. Therefore, this study assumes that the workers in the sample work 240 days annually. Multiplying 240 days by 9 hours yields the annual work hours to be 2160.

Reference List

Arabsheibani, G. R., & Marin, A. (2000). Stability of estimates of the compensation for danger. *Journal of Risk and Uncertainty*, *20*(3), 247–269. Retrieved August 05, 2016, from https://doi.org/10.1023/A:1007819530588

Bhattacharya, S., Alberini, A., & Cropper, M. L. (2007). The value of mortality risk reductions in Delhi, India. *Journal of Risk and Uncertainty*, *34*, 21–47. Retrieved July 05, 2016, from https://doi.org/10.1007/s11166-006-9002-5

Borjas, G. J. (2013). *Labour economics* (6 ed.). McGraw-Hill. Retrieved February 27, 2015, from https://idealmatrix.ru/conspectus/labor_economics/Labor%20Economics.pdf

Dickens, W. T. (1984). Differences between risk premiums in union and nonunion wages and the case for occupational safety regulation. *American Economic Review*, *74*(2), 320–323

Dionne, G. (1982). Moral hazard and state-dependent utility function. *Journal of Risk and Insurance*, *49*, 405–422.

Garen, J. E. (1988). Compensating wage differentials and endogeneity of job riskiness. *The Review of Economics and Statistics*, *7*(1), 9–16. Retrieved February 27, 2015, from https://ideas.repec.org/a/tpr/restat/v70y1988i1p9-16.html

Labour Bureau, Ministry of Labour and Employment, Government of India. (2022). *The Factories Act, 1948*. Retrieved 20/06/2026

Madheswaran, S. (2007). Measuring the value of statistical life: Estimating compensating wage differentials among workers in India. *Social Indicators Research*, *84*(1), 83–96. Retrieved October 11, 2015, from https://doi.org/10.1007/s11205-006-9076-0

Majumder, A. (2019). *Valuation of statistical life: A study on compensating wage differential* (Doctoral dissertation, University of Mysore).

Majumder, A., & Madheswaran, S. (2018). *Value of statistical life in India: A hedonic wage approach* (ISEC Working Paper No. 407). Retrieved October 31, 2024, from https://www.isec.ac.in/wp-content/uploads/2023/07/WP-407-Agamoni-Majumder-and-Madheswaran-Final.pdf

Majumder, A., & Madheswaran, S. (2020). Compensation for occupational risk and valuation of statistical life. *Social Indicators Research*, *149*, 967–989. Retrieved October 31, 2024, from https://doi.org/10.1007/s11205-020-02269-z

Majumder, A., & Madheswaran, S. (2022). Discounting long-term job-related health risks in the context of Indian workers. *The Indian Journal of Labour Economics*, *65*, 1099–1120. Retrieved October 31, 2024, from https://doi.org/10.1007/s41027-022-00415-4

Mincer, J. A. (1974). Schooling and earnings. In J. A. Mincer (Ed.), *Schooling, experience, and earnings* (pp. 41–63). National Bureau of Economic Research. Retrieved February 27, 2015, from https://www.nber.org/system/files/chapters/c1765/c1765.pdf

Shanmugam, K. R. (2000). Valuations of life and injury risks – Empirical evidence from India. *Environmental and Resource Economics*, *16*, 379–389. Retrieved June 19, 2015, from https://link.springer.com/content/pdf/10.1023/A:1008364502517.pdf

Shanmugam, K. R. (2001). Self-selection bias in the estimates of compensating wage differentials for job risks in India. *Journal of Risk and Uncertainty*, *22*(3), 263–275. Retrieved June 19, 2015, from https://doi.org/10.1023/A:1011135118675

Shanmugam, K. R. (2006). Rate of time preference and the quantity adjusted value of life in India. *Environment and Development Economics*, *11*(5), 569–583. Retrieved June 19, 2015, from https://www.cambridge.org/core/journals/environment-and-development-economics/article/abs/rate-of-time-preference-and-the-quantity-adjusted-value-of-life-in-india/A3BBB3BE8FB8EB5B1BB8B39D3B339854

Shanmugam, K. R. (2011). Discount rate for health benefits and the value of life in India. *Economics Research International*, *2011*, 1–5. Retrieved June 19, 2015, from https://doi.org/10.1155/2011/191425

Shanmugam, K. R., & Madheswaran, S. (2011). The value of statistical life. In A. K. Haque, M. N. Murty, & P. Shyamsundar (Eds.), *Environmental valuation in South Asia* (pp. 413–443). Cambridge University Press. (Accessed hard copy of the book).

Simon, N., Cropper, M., Alberini, A., & Arora, S. (1999). *Valuing mortality reductions in India: A study of compensating wage differentials*. World Bank. Retrieved June 19, 2015, from https://documents1.worldbank.org/curated/en/582261468751139383/pdf/multi-page.pdf

Thaler, R., & Rosen, S. (1976). The value of saving a life: Evidence from the labor market. In N. E. Terleckyj (Ed.), *Household production and consumption* (pp. 265–302). NBER. Retrieved February 27, 2015, from https://www.nber.org/system/files/chapters/c3964/c3964.pdf

Appendix 4A – Box-Cox transformation

Table 4A Box-Cox transformation for hedonic wage equation

Variables	$\lambda = -1$ *(Inverse)*	$\lambda = 0$ *(Semi-log)*	$\lambda = 1$ *(Linear)*
Constant	0.036* (25.17)	3.269* (57.33)	23.563* (9.37)
FATAL	-0.000093* (-3.64)	0.0048* (4.73)	0.2460* (5.48)
INJURY	-0.0004* (-3.60)	0.0180* (3.75)	0.7670* (3.63)
EXP	-0.0003* (-3.68)	0.011* (3.46)	0.454* (3.19)
EXP^2	-0.000004* (-2.27)	-0.0001*(-1.99)	-0.005** (-1.72)
PRIMARY	-0.003* (-3.95)	0.131* (3.51)	4.763* (2.89)
SECONDARY	-0.003* (-3.62)	0.114* (3.17)	4.178* (2.62)
HS	-0.004* (-5.03)	0.208* (4.34)	6.836* (4.36)
GRADUATE	-0.004* (-3.28)	0.170* (3.33)	7.340* (3.24)
MIGRANT	0.001* (2.13)	-0.055* (-2.60)	-2.687* (-2.88)
SC	0.001* (2.83)	-0.065* (-2.48)	-2.476* (-2.14)
UNION	-0.001***(-1.72)	0.050 (1.22)	1.229 (0.68)
SIZE	0.0009 (1.60)	-0.025 (-1.15)	-0.502 (-0.51)
JOB TYPE	0.001* (2.01)	0.051* (2.03)	2.317* (2.06)
TRAINING	0.0007 (1.38)	-0.031 (-1.45)	-1.368 (-1.45)
PHW	0.0009*** (1.68)	-0.041** (-1.93)	-1.895* (-2.01)
SECU	0.0002 (0.41)	0.015 (0.66)	0.954 (0.89)
MENT	-0.0009** (-1.85)	0.0371** (1.82)	1.611** (1.79)
FAST	0.001* (2.47)	-0.057* (-2.47)	-2.398* (-2.35)
CONTRACTOR	-0.004* (3.33)	0.294* (5.04)	17.422* (6.76)
SUPERVISOR	-0.002* (-2.77)	0.133* (3.47)	6.907* (4.08)
FITTER	-0.001* (2.64)	0.096* (3.33)	4.915* (3.84)
TECHNICIAN	-0.001 (-1.53)	0.078** (1.94)	4.064* (2.29)
ASSISTANT	0.003* (4.06)	-0.109* (-3.51)	-3.839* (-2.80)
DIV1	-0.006* (-8.44)	0.246* (8.17)	9.973* (7.49)
DIV 2	-0.003* (-4.39)	0.134* (4.26)	5.526* (3.97)
DIV 3	-0.005* (-6.86)	0.203* (6.79)	8.375* (6.34)
R^2	0.53	0.55	0.56
F	17.90	19.43	19.77
N	427	427	427
ESS	**33047.2**	**29975.73**	**29980.24**

* 1 per cent level of significance, ** 5 per cent level of significance, *** 10 per cent level of significance

Note: t-values are given in parentheses.

Appendix 4B – Estimation of job risk equations (first-stage regression)

Table 4B presents the results of estimation of job risk equations. As mentioned earlier, the dependent variables used in the estimation of equations (4.6) and (4.7) are the inverse normal cumulative distribution function for fatal and injury risk associated with worker's job.

Most independent variables behave according to the economic theory. Union status of worker has a positive and significant relation with fatal as well as injury risk. Dickens (1984) found a similar association between union membership and job risk in his study. Migrant workers face lower risk of work-related injury compared to other workers. Workers in smaller factories have a higher risk of work-related fatality. This indicates that the work conditions are good in larger factories. Workers who have undergone training in the same factory in which they are currently employed face lower risk of injury compared to other workers. Job security has a positive and significant influence on fatal and injury risks. This implies that workers with secured jobs face a significantly higher risk (both fatal and injury risks) in their jobs. Workers engaged in jobs that require mental work face higher injury risk.

Contractors face a higher work-related fatal risk, while fitters face higher injury risks. This result for contractors is contrary to our expectations since a contractor's work is safer compared to other workers. However, during primary survey it was found that contractors often operate machines and do various other jobs if any of the workers employed by them are absent. This makes the contractors vulnerable to job risks compared to those workers who work regularly on certain jobs and hence are more proficient in doing it.

The workers employed in factories from industrial division 2 and division 3 face lower risk of death compared to the workers in the other industrial divisions. On the other hand, workers in division 1 and division 3 face higher risk of injury compared to workers in other divisions. The variable DEPENDENT is an indicator of the degree of risk aversion of workers. It is negative and significant for the fatal job risk equation. This implies that workers who have dependents at home tend to select safer jobs. However, this variable is not significant for the injury risk equation. The asset or wealth indicator variables have VEHICLE and OTHER'S INCOME. Individuals owning vehicles

Table 4B Estimation of job risk equations (first-stage regressions in Garen's modified selection bias technique)

Variables	*Fatal risk equation*	*Injury risk equation*
Constant	-3.511* (-98.91)	-3.154* (-44.83)
EXP	0.001 (0.85)	0.002 (0.53)
EXP^2	-0.00005 (-1.20)	-0.00001 (-0.13)
PRIMARY	0.034 (1.50)	0.022 (0.49)
SECONDARY	0.021 (0.97)	0.012 (0.29)
HS	0.017 (0.78)	0.014 (0.33)
GRADUATE	0.032 (1.02)	0.039 (0.63)
SC	-0.024 (-1.51)	0.018 (0.58)
MIGRANT	0.008 (0.64)	-0.048** (1.87)
UNION	0.083* (3.30)	0.191* (3.82)
SIZE	-0.044* (-3.17)	0.034 (1.23)
JOBTYPE	-0.025 (-1.60)	-0.040 (-1.30)
TRAINING	-0.006 (-0.48)	-0.068* (-2.60)
PHW	-0.017 (-1.33)	-0.030 (-1.14)
SECU	0.054* (3.62)	0.085* (2.87)
MENT	0.008 (0.70)	0.060* (2.40)
FAST	-0.015 (-1.08)	0.006 (0.22)
CONTRACTOR	0.075* (2.09)	0.056 (0.79)
SUPERVISOR	0.026 (1.09)	-0.039 (-0.84)
FITTER	0.023 (1.28)	0.079* (2.23)
TECH	0.010 (0.40)	0.049 (1.00)
ASSIST	-0.003 (-0.18)	0.050 (1.31)
DIV 1	-0.023 (-1.23)	0.148* (3.94)
DIV 2	-0.036** (-1.87)	0.051 (1.33)
DIV 3	-0.083* (-4.59)	0.159* (4.44)
DEPENDENTS	-0.036** (-1.88)	-0.049 (-1.30)
LOG OF OTHERS INCOME	0.001 (0.74)	-0.005* (-1.93)
HAS VEHICLE	-0.032* (-2.39)	0.041 (1.55)
N	427	427
R^2	0.21	0.1413
F statistics	3.96	3.60

* *1 per cent level of significance,* ** *5 per cent level of significance*
Note: t-values are given in parentheses.

tend to select jobs that have significantly lower risk of death. The impact of vehicle ownership on injury risk is positive, but it is insignificant. On the other hand, income of the other family members has a positive but insignificant impact on fatal job risk. In case of injury risk, it has a significantly negative impact. The overall result for the job risk equations is consistent with the fact that safety is a normal good. Therefore, wealthier workers tend to select safer jobs.

Appendix 4C – Survey questionnaire

INDUSTRIAL DIVISION **DATE**

I	II	III	IV

[0] Identification of the sample		
Sector *(put a tick beside appropriate answer)*	Public	Private
NIC Code *(1)*		
Name of the company		
Address of the company (name of the place)		

Code (1) **15:** Manufacture of Food Products and Beverages, **17:** Manufacture of textiles, **20:** Manufacture of Wood and Products Wood and Cork, **21:** Manufacture of Paper and Paper Products, **23:** Manufacture of Cock Refined Petro Products and Nuclear Fuel, **24:** Manufacture of chemical and chemical products, **25:** Manufacture of Rubber and Plastics Products, **26:** Manufacture of Other Non-Metallic Mineral Products, **27:** Manufacture of Basic Metals, **28:** Manufacture of Fabricated Metal Products, **29:** Manufacture of machinery and equipment, **31:** Manufacture of Electrical Machinery and Apparatus, **35:** Manufacture of Transport Equipment.

[1] Household demographic information	
Name of the respondent *(Optional)*	
Native:	Marital status *(3)*:
Age *(in years)*:	Religion *(4)*:
Education *(2)*:	Social Group *(5)*:

Household members							
	Sex *(put a tick beside appropriate answer)*		**Age** *(in years)*	**Marital status** *(3)*	**Education** *(2)*	**Is the person working anywhere?** *(put a tick beside appropriate answer)*	
Wife	F					Y	N
Children							
1	M	F				Y	N
2	M	F				Y	N
3	M	F				Y	N
4	M	F				Y	N
Father	M					Y	N
Mother	F					Y	N
Others	M	F				Y	N
	M	F				Y	N

*Code (2): **Education*** (**completed**)*:* **01**-illiterate, **02**-primary, **03**-secondary, **04**-higher secondary, **05**-graduate.

*Code (3): **Marital Status:*** **01**-married, **02**-unmarried, **03**-widowed, **04**-seperated.

*Code (4): **Religion:*** **01**-Hindu, **02**-Muslim, **03**-others.

*Code (5): **Social group:*** **01**-Scheduled caste, **02**-Scheduled tribe, **03**-others.

[2] **Job characteristics of the respondent** (just put tick beside appropriate answer)		
Name/Designation of the job:		
Supervisor (If yes, then how many workers are working under you?)		No of workers:
Assistant		
Operates machinery		
Technical work		
Other (if other, then mention the job name)		

<table>
<tr><td colspan="5">Type of job (just put tick beside appropriate answer)</td></tr>
<tr><td colspan="3">Full-time/Permanent</td><td colspan="2"></td></tr>
<tr><td colspan="3">Part-time/Contract</td><td colspan="2"></td></tr>
<tr><td colspan="3">How long have you been working in the present job? (in years)</td><td colspan="2"></td></tr>
<tr><td colspan="3">What is your daily wage rate? (mention amount in Rupees)</td><td colspan="2"></td></tr>
<tr><td colspan="3">How many hours do you work in a day?</td><td colspan="2"></td></tr>
<tr><td colspan="3">How many days have you worked last week?</td><td colspan="2"></td></tr>
<tr><td colspan="3">Does your job need you to work overtime?</td><td>Yes</td><td>No</td></tr>
<tr><td rowspan="2">If Yes, then</td><td>How many hours do you have to work?</td><td colspan="2">Per Day:</td><td>Per Week:</td></tr>
<tr><td>Amount paid for overtime work: (mention amount in Rupees)</td><td>Per hour:</td><td>Per day:</td><td>Per Week:</td></tr>
<tr><td colspan="3">Does your job need you to undergo any training?</td><td>Yes</td><td>No</td></tr>
<tr><td colspan="3">Does your job need you to work fast?</td><td>Yes</td><td>No</td></tr>
<tr><td colspan="3">Does your job need you to make any decision about a task?</td><td>Yes</td><td>No</td></tr>
</table>

[3] Previous job details (if any)						
No.	**Name of previous job**	**Duration**	**Year of joining**	**Year of leaving**	**Wage per day when left**	**Reason for leaving (optional)**
1.						
2.						
3.						

[4] Employment status of the family members					
Working family member	**Name of the job**	**Name of the firm where employed**	**Years of working in the job**	**Monthly wage (in Rupees)**	**Age at which started working**

[5] Family assets and asset income				
Are you living in your own house? *(put a tick beside appropriate answer)*			Y	N
If Yes, then what is the value of the house (*mention approximate value in Rupees*)				
If no, then what is the rent of the house (*mention amount in Rupees per month*)				
What is the distance from house to work site?				
No.	Name of the asset *(put a tick beside appropriate answer)*	Approximate value of the asset (*in Rupees*)	Nature of income (*if it gives income*)	Annual income from the asset (*in Rupees*)
1.	Land ☐			
2.	Other properties ☐ ***Mention the name of the asset***			
3.	Two-wheeler ☐			
4.	Car ☐			
5.	Auto ☐			

[6] Details about the working conditions *(put a tick beside appropriate answer)*			
Does your job require you to exert hard physical work?		Y	N
If yes then,			
1. Do you need to lift 60 kg (*sometimes/once a week/daily*)?		Y	N
2. Is your work physically demanding in ways not covered by heavy lifting?		Y	N
3. Does physical activity at work cause daily sweating?		Y	N
4. Is carefulness important in your work?		Y	N
Do you feel that your work? *(Put a tick beside appropriate answer).*			
(i) Exposes you to constant loud noise:	sometimes	often	always
(ii) Exposes you to gas, dust, or smoke:	sometimes	often	always
(iii) Exposes you to foul odour/smell:	sometimes	often	always
(iv) Exposes you to strong shakes or vibrations:	sometimes	often	always

(v) Expose you to heat:	sometimes	often	always
(vi) Expose you to chemicals:	sometimes	often	always
(vii) Exposes you to environmental problems:	sometimes	often	always
If you think that your job exposes you to environmental problems, then give details of the problems you face: *(You can list up to 5 problems, like skin irritation or allergy, breathing trouble, burning sensation in eyes, and other work-related ill effects on worker's health)* *Note*: **Effects will vary from one industry to another so please ask the workers to describe the problems.**	1. 2. 3. 4. 5.		

Do you feel that the job is so stressful that it is: *(put a tick beside appropriate answer)*		
(i) Mentally demanding/stressful:	Y	N
(ii) Hectic:	Y	N
Do you feel that the present job has: *(put a tick beside appropriate answer)*		
(i) Pleasant physical surroundings	Y	N
(ii) Good job security	Y	N
[7] **Accidents and injuries** *(put a tick beside appropriate answer)*		
1. Did any worker in your factory die due to accident in past one year?	Y	N
2. Did any worker die due to any disease in past one year?	Y	N
If yes: then mention the disease		
3. Did any accident occur to you in past one year?	Y	N

If yes, then answer the following questions:			
Nature of accident (non-fatal injury)	Number of accidents	Reasons for the occurrence	Man-days lost
Temporary injury:			
Permanent injury:			
Did you get any compensation from the employees?		Y	N

If yes, then mention the type of compensation that was paid *(6)*	In case of temporary injury **(6, i):** ***(Give details in case of option D)***	
	In case of permanent injury **(6, i):**	

Sick leaves and allowances *(put a tick beside appropriate answer)*			
1. How many days of leave is given in a year?	**CL:**	**PL:**	**Total:**
2. Are you allowed to avail sick leave days with full pay? **(over and above CL & PL)**	Y		N
Role of union			
(a) Is there any union or association in your factory?	Y		N
(b) Are you a union member?	Y		N
Union membership fees paid per month ***(in Rupees)***			
(c) Does the union help workers in addressing work-related issues/problems?	Y		N
(d) While joining the job did union tell you about the perils associated with your job?	Y		N
Ask the following question if the person faced any job injury in the past			
Did the union help you to get compensation for your accident?	Y		N

Code (6, i): **In case of temporary injury – A:** Compensation according to ESI program, **B:** Leave with pay during period of recovery (in case of contract/non-beneficiaries of ESI program), **C:** Treatment cost borne by employers (in case of contract/non-beneficiaries of ESI program), **D:** Others ***(if answer is option D, then give details)***

Code (6, ii): **In case of permanent injury – a:** Lump sum amount, **b:** Give employment to eligible family member

[8] Insurance benefits & social security		
Are you a taxpayer?	Y	N
If yes, give following details		
Name of tax	Tax amount per year	

Give details on labour social security scheme					
Sr. No.	Type of scheme *(put tick beside schemes that are available)*		Value (in Rupees)	Duration	Premium share of yours (in Rupees)
1	State Employee Insurance program	☐			
2	Pension	☐			
3	Gratuity	☐			
4	Healthcare Expenses	☐			
5	Other benefits (like following)				
	Soap	☐			
	Uniform	☐			
	Clouse	☐			
	Boots	☐			
	Mask	☐			

[9] **Worker's personal characteristics** *(put a tick beside appropriate answer)*		
1. What was the reason for choosing the present job?	(a) More salary: ☐ (b) Less competitive: ☐ (c) Job security: ☐ (d) Other (Specify): ☐	
2. Are you satisfied with the present job? (If not, then provide reason)	Y	N
	(Reason):	
3. Are you thinking of finding new job?	Y	N
4. Have you applied for any alternative job?	Y	N
If yes, give details:		
5. What is the reason for leaving present job? *(give details)*		
6. What is the name of the job applied?		
7. Do you plan to quit your job during this year?	Y	N
8. Are you getting bonus?	Y	N
If yes, how much did you get last year? *(amount in Rupees)*		

5 Interplay amongst workers' compensation benefit, wages, and VSL estimates

5.1 Introduction

Workers employed in hazardous occupations receive compensation either before the risks are realised (i.e. ex-ante compensation) or after an injury occurs (i.e. ex-post compensation). Ex-ante compensation takes the form of a compensating wage differential, while ex-post compensation consists of insurance or compensation benefits provided to workers in the event of work-related injuries (Majumder & Madheswaran, 2018c, 2020). The importance of these two forms of compensation varies according to the extent to which workers seek to insure themselves against income losses arising from job-related injuries (Viscusi & Moore, 1987). However, the compensation benefits are not uniform. The benefit levels vary with the wage level of workers and according to the government mandates. In India, the caps on benefits, minimum benefit levels, and the duration of benefits under different compensation programmes vary by workers' wage levels, the nature of job-related injury, and workers' age. These differences suggest that compensation benefits form a key part of workers' overall remuneration. Accordingly, this chapter provides a detailed discussion on Indian compensation benefit programmes (Majumder & Madheswaran, 2020).

Workers' compensation is found to affect the compensation package in risky occupations through two main channels. The first observation is on the relationship between the ex-ante and ex-post compensation. If higher ex-post compensation is given to workers, then they are ready to accept comparatively lower ex-ante compensation (Viscusi & Moore, 1987). Since the ex-ante compensation is a component of worker's wage, any variation in this component would affect the wage. In this case, a higher compensation benefit may lower the amount paid as compensating wage differential and hence lead to a decline in the overall wage received by a worker for risky jobs. Risky jobs usually pay higher wages to compensate workers for risk, while compensation benefits can reduce the need for such wage premiums because both serve a similar purpose. However, wages are unlikely to fall by much, since workers are unlikely to accept risky jobs that offer little wage compensation even when injury benefits are high. The size of the wage reduction

DOI: 10.4324/9781003628262-5

depends on how attractive the compensation benefits are to workers (Majumder & Madheswaran, 2020). A study by Viscusi and Moore (1989) found that increase in compensation benefits reduces workers' wages as well as job-related fatal risks. On the other hand, studies like Chelius and Smith (1987), Ruser (1985), Butler and Worral (1985), and Krueger (1989) found that moral hazard arises if rates of compensation benefit are increased. When workers can receive higher benefits after an injury under compensation programmes, they may have weaker incentives to avoid work-related accidents. As a result, the number of injury claims is likely to increase (Majumder & Madheswaran, 2020).

Another important finding is that failing to account for workers' compensation benefits results in biased estimates of VSL and VSI. Viscusi and Moore (1987) found that inclusion of worker's compensation in the estimation of hedonic wage equation boosted the coefficient of wage–risk trade-off. On the other hand, Meng and Smith (1999) found that wage–risk trade-off decreased with the inclusion of the compensation variable. As a result, estimates of VSL may be biased either upward or downward across different studies. Viscusi and Moore (1987) are a pioneering study which examined and established these two phenomena. Their analysis, however, considered only compensation for temporary disability. The present study builds on this approach by analysing workers' compensation benefits for three categories of outcomes: temporary disability, permanent total disability (PTD), and death.

Shanmugam and Madheswaran (2011) is the only Indian study that examined the impact of temporary disability on VSI of workers in the sample. However, the analysis that they undertook in their study was preliminary. Against this background, the study adds to the VSL literature in India by closely analysing the role of workers' compensation benefits in shaping wages and in estimating the VSL and VSI. The chapter has three main objectives: first, to examine the relationship between workers' wages and compensation benefits; second, to determine the optimal trade-off between compensation benefits and worker's wage; and third, to estimate VSL and VSI after incorporating compensation benefit variables into the hedonic wage equation. The subsequent sections outline the theoretical framework, describe the data and variables, present the empirical model, report the estimation of the compensation-adjusted hedonic wage equation, and discuss the results.

5.2 Overview of workers' compensation benefits in India

The analysis in this study is based on two important Indian legislations that govern compensation for work-related fatal and non-fatal injuries, namely, the Employees' State Insurance (ESI) Act, 1948, and the Workmen's Compensation Act, 1923. The key provisions of these laws are outlined below.

The Employees' State Insurance Act, 1948, establishes a social insurance programme for workers in the organised sector. This programme aims to provide income security and medical support in situations such as sickness, maternity, various forms of disability, and death resulting from occupational injuries. It also covers medical care for workers and their dependents. The Act has undergone several amendments over time to expand its coverage and revise contribution rates, eligibility criteria, and benefit structures. These amendments have addressed issues such as geographical extension, coverage of establishments and occupations, and the level of contributions by employers, employees, and state governments. This study relies on the compensation rates specified in the 2010 amendment to the ESI Act, under which workers earning a monthly income of up to INR 15,000 are eligible for benefits. Since it is a need-based programme, workers have to register themselves and make monthly contributions towards the programme. The programme is mainly financed by the contributions from employers and workers. A registered worker has to contribute 1.75 per cent of his/her monthly wage, and the employer has to contribute 4.75 per cent of worker's monthly wage towards the programme. Besides, the state government shares 12.5 per cent of the expenditure on provision of medical care. The ESI Act offers compensation for both temporary and permanent forms of disability. The rules governing compensation vary according to the severity of the injury and the number of workdays lost. Benefits are paid based on a schedule of standard benefit rates that correspond to workers' average daily wages (see Table 5A.1 in the Appendix for the benefit rate schedule under the ESI scheme). Sickness benefits amount to 60 per cent of a worker's average daily wage and are available for up to 91 days across two consecutive benefit periods. In the case of temporary disability, workers receive compensation equal to 75 per cent of their average daily wage, which is equivalent to 150 per cent of the standard benefit rate. Benefits for permanent disability are revised from time to time and indexed to changes in the cost of living, and eligible workers receive these benefits for life. In the event of a work-related death, dependants' benefits are paid to the worker's spouse and children at a rate equal to 75 per cent of the average daily wage (Majumder & Madheswaran, 2020).

The Workmen's Compensation Act, 1923, pays a lump sum compensation to workers who suffer disability or death as a result of work-related injuries. The Act applies to workers employed in hazardous occupations, including factories, mines, construction, plantations, and similar activities. Workers are not required to contribute from their wages to receive benefits under this Act. Instead, employers obtain insurance coverage from insurance companies to meet their compensation obligations in cases of work-related injury or death. Several insurance providers in India, such as United India Insurance Company, offer workers' compensation insurance policies to both small and large firms, with insurance premiums generally linked to employees' wage levels. Workers who are covered under the ESI scheme are not eligible for benefits under this Act. Consequently, the Act primarily covers workers who are not enrolled in the ESI programme. The minimum and maximum compensation amounts for death and disability are revised periodically. The level of compensation payable depends on the type of injury, the worker's average monthly wage, and age-related factors specified under the Act (see Table 5A.2 in the Appendix for the age-related factors). This study uses the compensation rates specified in the 2009 amendment, under which the Act was renamed as the Employees' Compensation Act. In cases of PTD, lump sum compensation is calculated as 60 per cent of the worker's monthly wage multiplied by the relevant age-related factor, subject to a minimum compensation of INR 1,20,000. In the event of death due to work-related injury, compensation is determined as 50 per cent of the worker's monthly wage multiplied by the age-related factor, with a minimum payment of INR 1,40,000. For death-related compensation, the maximum monthly wage considered is capped at INR 8,000, and any income above this limit is treated as INR 8,000 for the purpose of calculating the lump sum compensation (Majumder & Madheswaran, 2018c, 2020).

As noted earlier, many workers do not receive benefits under the ESI scheme because they are unable to make the required monthly contributions from their earnings. In the sample, about 66 per cent of workers are enrolled in the ESI programme. Since a majority of the sampled workers are covered by this scheme, benefit rates under the ESI programme are used to analyse the effect of compensation for temporary disability and dependents' benefits on wages, restricted to workers who are enrolled in the ESI programme. In contrast, benefits under the Employees' Compensation Act apply to all workers employed in factories. Accordingly, benefit rates from the Employees' Compensation Act are used to examine the impact of lump sum compensation for permanent disability and death on wages for the entire sample.

5.3 Compensation-adjusted hedonic wage model

The empirical analysis is designed to assess how wages and compensation benefits are traded off against each other in the total remuneration of workers in risky jobs. The aim here is to find out the efficient rate of substitution between these two components. Thus, in this study, a theoretical model is developed following the work by Viscusi and Moore (1987) to examine the properties of the relationship between worker's wage and compensation benefit. The result derived for this trade-off provides the benchmark in the subsequent empirical analysis for determining whether the benefit levels are optimal.

This model is like the health-state-dependent utility function used earlier in this study (see Chapter 2). The model considers two state-dependent utility functions. The first, denoted as $U_1(x)$, represents utility in the good health state. The second, denoted as $U_2(x)$, represents utility in the ill health state resulting from injury. A rational individual prefers good health to ill health, so $U_1(x) > U_2(x) > 0$. The model also assumes that the marginal utility of consumption is higher in the good health state than in the injured state, implying $U'_1(x) > U'_2(x) > 0$. Marginal utility is positive but diminishing in both states, so $U''_1(x) < 0$ and $U''_2(x) < 0$. Let p denote the probability of being in good health, and $1-p$ the probability of being injured. The worker earns wage w_1 in the good health state and receives compensation w_2 in the injured state. If the government imposes a tax at rate t on earnings, the worker's after-tax income in the good health state becomes $(1-t)w_1$. Using this setup, the study examines the trade-off between the wage w_1 and the compensation benefit w_2 for accepting a job with risk level p. The worker's expected utility (EU) can then be written as follows:

$$EU = (1-p)\times U_x^1(1-t)w_1) + p\times U_x^2(w_2) \tag{5.1}$$

The worker's objective is to maximise expected utility for a given level of job risk. The first-order conditions are derived by differentiating equation (5.1) separately with respect to w_1 and w_2, which yields equations (a) and (b).

$$\delta U/\delta w_1 = (1-p)\times(1-t)\times U_x^1 \tag{a}$$

$$\delta U/\delta w_2 = (p)\times U_x^2 \tag{b}$$

The trade-off between worker's wage and compensation benefit is obtained as follows:

$$\frac{dw_1}{dw_2} = \frac{\delta E/\delta w_2}{\delta E/\delta w_1} = \frac{-(p\times U_x^2)}{(1-p)\times(1-t)U_x^1} \tag{5.2}$$

If there is no job risk, meaning $p=0$, then there is no trade-off between wages and compensation benefits, so $\frac{dw_1}{dw_2}=0$. If workers' earnings are not taxed, compensation is actuarially fair, and the market for compensation insurance is effectively perfect. In this case, income is fully smoothed across the two states, so utility is equalised across both states. Under a perfect compensation insurance market, the trade-off between wages and compensation benefits takes the following form.

$$\frac{dw_1}{dw_2} = \frac{-p}{(1-p)} \tag{5.3}$$

Equation (5.3) implies a negative association between wages and compensation benefits. For example, a trade-off of –0.03 means that a worker is willing to reduce income in the healthy state by 3 paisa in order to obtain one rupee as compensation in the event of injury. The average probability of injury in this study is 0.00197 (see Chapter 3). Using this value in equation (5.3), the implied wage–compensation trade-off is –0.0019. This can be interpreted as the optimal rate at which workers in the sample are willing to substitute wages for compensation benefits. Put differently, workers are prepared to give up 0.19 paisa of income when healthy to secure an additional one rupee of compensation in the injured state.

This substitution, however, is valid only when the compensation insurance market functions perfectly, and workers' earnings are not taxed. Viscusi and Moore (1987) report a rate of substitution of –0.04, which they find to be suboptimal relative to the income levels insured. In reality, compensation insurance markets are imperfect. Administrative costs associated with insurance exist which are denoted by '*a*', and taxes on workers' earnings increase the effective cost of compensation. Under such conditions, a worker must forgo (1+a) rupees of income in the healthy state to receive one rupee of compensation in the injured state. As a result, the wage–compensation trade-off becomes less favourable, as captured by equation (5.4).

$$\frac{w_1}{dw_2} = \frac{-p(1+\mathrm{a})}{(1-p)} \tag{5.4}$$

When compensation benefits are generous, workers may have less incentives to take safety precautions, leading to a higher incidence of reported accidents in order to claim benefits. This creates the possibility of moral hazard. To prevent such outcomes, the socially efficient level of insurance coverage is set lower.

Administrative costs, denoted by 'a', are not directly observed and are typically embedded in the contribution rates paid by workers under compensation schemes. In the context of this study, the ESI programme specifies only the worker contribution rate, which is 1.75 per cent of monthly wages. Since the administrative cost component is not separately identified, it cannot be used to directly estimate the true wage–compensation trade-off. The optimal trade-off derived from equation (5.3) can be calculated using work-related risks for the sample. In contrast, the actual trade-off represented by equation (5.4) is obtained through estimation of the compensation-adjusted hedonic wage equation. The estimated optimal trade-off is then compared with the trade-off implied by the ESI programme.

5.4 Description of data and key variables

In addition to the variables discussed in Chapter 4, the analysis also includes key measures of workers' compensation benefits. The variable pertaining to compensation benefit for temporary disability and dependent's benefit is called the compensation replacement ratio ("$\mathbf{R}_i$"), and it has been constructed using the formula provided by Viscusi and Moore (1987). Given the average daily wage rate of the workers (w_i) and the daily standard benefit rates (b_i) listed in Table 5A.1 (see the Appendix), the replacement ratio (R_i) is calculated as follows:

$$R_i = \frac{b_i}{w_i(1-t_i)} \tag{5.5}$$

The replacement ratio is used as an independent variable while estimating the hedonic wage equation. Because R_i is constructed using the worker's wage, including it directly in the hedonic wage equation, where wage is the dependent variable, creates an endogeneity problem. To address this issue, the replacement ratio is first regressed on all explanatory variables. The predicted value of the replacement ratio, $\hat{R}_i$, obtained from this regression, is then used as an exogenous measure in the wage equation.

Average monthly wages and the corresponding age-specific factors specified under the Employees' Compensation Act were used to construct the variables capturing lump sum compensation for PTD and death (D). Since these compensation measures depend on wages, they are endogenous to the wage equation. To address this concern, the same approach used for the compensation replacement ratio is applied here. Table 5.1 reports the descriptive statistics for the workers' compensation variables.

5.5 Empirical model specification

The standard hedonic wage equation does not account for the interaction between workers' compensating wage differentials and compensation benefits. In the absence of compensation benefits, workers would demand a much higher wage premium to ensure against income losses from job-related injuries. To capture this relationship, the basic hedonic wage equation is modified by incorporating a compensation variable in an interactive form. The resulting compensation-adjusted hedonic wage equation is presented below.

$$LOG\ WAGE = \alpha + \beta_1\ FATAL + \beta_2 INJURY + \beta_3 INJURY \times COMP + \sum_k \gamma_k X_{ki} + \epsilon_i \quad (5.6)$$

Table 5.1 Descriptive statistics for workers' compensation variables

Variable	*Description*	*Mean & standard deviation*	*Expected sign*
R_i	Compensation replacement ratio, $[R_i = \frac{Benefit\ Level}{after\ tax\ daily\ wage}]$	0.46 (0.06)	Negative
PTD_i	Compensation in case of Permanent Total Disability, (PTD_i = 60 per cent of the monthly wage × Relevant factor as per the age of the worker)	4,83,225 (726419.7)	Negative
D_i	Compensation in case of Death (D_i = 50 per cent of the monthly wage × Relevant factor as per the age of the worker)	2,58,785 (366566.9)	Negative

Source: Author's calculation based on primary data collected from factory workers at Ahmedabad (Majumder & Madheswaran, 2020).

Here, ***COMP*** = R_i (Compensation replacement ratio) or PTD_i (Lump sum compensation for Permanent Total Disability) or D_i (Lump sum compensation for death).

Equation (5.6), therefore, includes a compensation variable, denoted as **COMP**, which takes one of three values depending on the type of compensation benefit considered in the estimation of the compensation-adjusted hedonic wage equation. These compensation variables are incorporated into the basic hedonic wage equation in both additive and interactive forms. However, only the results of interactive form are reported in this study since it yielded significant results. The modified hedonic wage equation given by equation (5.6) is estimated to obtain the compensation-adjusted VSL and VSI estimates. The calculation of compensation-adjusted VSL and VSI is like the calculation of basic estimates of VSL and VSI.

The compensation-adjusted wage–risk trade-off associated with injury risk is obtained by taking the partial derivative of equation (5.6) with respect to injury risk.

$$\frac{\partial w}{\partial \, injury} \times \frac{1}{w} = \beta_1 + \beta_3 \times Comp$$

$$or, \qquad \frac{\partial w}{\partial \, injury} = (\beta_1 + \beta_3 \times Comp) \times w$$

VSI is obtained by multiplying the annualised compensation-adjusted wage–risk trade-off for injury risk by one thousand.

Compensation Adjusted VSI $= [(\beta_1 + \beta_3 \times Comp) \times \overline{w}] \times 2160 \times 1{,}000$

= [co-efficient of injury variable + co-efficient of compensation variable x mean compensation benefit) x mean wage of the sample] x annual work hours x scale of injury risk.

In a similar manner, the compensation-adjusted VSL is estimated using a hedonic wage equation that incorporates an interaction term between the compensation benefit variable and fatal job risk.

5.6 Estimation and results of compensation-adjusted hedonic wage model

The hedonic wage equation that includes compensation variables allows the study to test two key hypotheses. The first is that omitting workers' compensation benefits from the hedonic wage framework results in biased estimates of VSL and VSI. The second is that more generous workers' compensation benefits are associated with lower compensating wage differentials. Table 5.2 presents the estimation results from hedonic wage equations that incorporate compensation for temporary disability and dependents' benefits under the 2010 amendment of the ESI programme.

Specification 1 reports the estimate of hedonic wage equation excluding the compensation benefit variable. This specification yields similar results to that of the basic hedonic wage equation presented in the last chapter. It is used here to facilitate comparison between the basic results and the compensation-adjusted results of hedonic wage equation. Since the compensation for dependent's benefit and temporary disability are provided at the same rate to registered workers under the ESI programme (2010 amendment), the compensation replacement ratio represents both types of compensation. Thus, the second specification in Table 5.2 yields the estimate of hedonic wage equation that includes compensation paid to dependents if the worker dies because of job injury (i.e. dependents' benefit). On the other hand, the third specification yields the estimate of hedonic wage equation that includes compensation for temporary disability.

Across all model specifications, job risk variables are positive and statistically significant, indicating that higher levels of job risk are associated with higher wages. Based on the first specification, the estimated VSL is INR 45.23 million (USD 0.67 million, 2016 USD), while the VSI is INR 1.67 million (USD 0.025 million, 2016 USD). These estimates imply that an average worker is willing to forgo INR 452 per year to reduce a fatality risk of 1 in 100,000 and INR 1,673 per year to reduce an injury risk of 1 in 1,000. Consistent with expectations, incorporating compensation benefit variables into the hedonic wage equation leads to a substantial increase in the estimated coefficient on fatal risk, rising from 0.0048 in the first specification to 0.0071 in the second and 0.0072 in the third. A similar pattern is observed for injury risk, with the coefficient increasing from 0.0180 in the first specification to 0.0255 in the second and 0.0232 in the third.

In the second specification, the coefficient on the interaction term between dependents' benefits and the fatality rate suggests that a worker must give up 84 paisa of wage income to receive one rupee of compensation in the event of death. This trade-off is considerably larger than the optimal rate of substitution between wages and compensation benefits, which is estimated at 0.19 paisa. The overall effect of death-related compensation on wages is captured by the coefficient $[0.0071 - (0.0084 \times 0.46)] = 0.0032$ which is then used to calculate the VSL. Based on this specification, the estimated VSL is INR 30.27 million (USD 0.45 million, 2016 USD), while the estimated VSI is INR 2.36 million (USD 0.035 million, 2016 USD). The resulting VSL estimate is lower than the baseline VSL obtained from the first specification. It clearly indicates that failure to include compensation variable in estimation of hedonic wage equation yields biased estimate of VSL. In this case, the bias was upward, which resolved after inclusion of the compensation variable. Shanmugam and Madheswaran (2011) obtained similar results for VSI estimate, which decreased from INR 4,876 to INR 3,286 after inclusion of an interaction between compensation benefit and injury risk variable. On the other hand, the estimate

Table 5.2 Hedonic wage estimates incorporating ESI (2010) benefits for temporary disability and dependents

Variables	*OLS estimates (1)*	*Compensation adjusted estimates*	
		(2)	*(3)*
Constant	3.195* (50.25)	3.2024* (56.81)	3.2120* (55.97)
FATAL	0.0048* (4.84)	0.0071* (7.49)	0.0072* (7.53)
INJURY	0.0180* (3.76)	0.0255* (5.12)	0.0232* (4.41)
FATAL × $\widehat{R_i}$		−0.0084** (−1.90)	
INJURY × $\widehat{R_i}$			−0.0050** (−1.86)
EXP	0.0119 * (3.75)	0.0179* (6.11)	0.0177* (6.05)
EXP^2	−0.0001* (−2.23)	−0.0002* (−4.51)	−0.0002* (−4.42)
PRIMARY	0.1316* (3.51)	0.1078* (3.25)	0.1058* (3.19)
SECONDARY	0.1115* (3.08)	0.0781* (2.54)	0.0776* (2.52)
HS	0.1658* (4.65)	0.1212* (3.83)	0.1229* (3.88)
GRADUATE	0.1629* (3.16)	0.2288* (5.04)	0 .2279* (5.02)
SC	−0.0623* (−2.36)	−0.0693* (−2.90)	−0.0695* (−2.91)
MIGRANT	−0.0616* (−2.86)	−0.0450* (−2.20)	−0.0463* (−2.26)
UNION	0.0622*** (1.58)	0.1488 (1.51)	0.1465 (1.49)
JOBTYPE	0.0614* (2.56)	0.1113* (4.38)	0.1106* (4.35)
TRAINING	−0.0284 (−1.34)	−0.0434* (−2.09)	−0.0438* (−2.10)
PHW	−0.0421* (−1.99)	−0.0729* (−3.53)	−0.0801* (−3.88)
OT	0.0221 (0.89)	0.0567* (2.31)	0.0576* (2.35)
PHCOND	0.0253 (−0.78)	−0.0663* (−2.10)	−0.0716* (−2.26)
MENT	0.0377** (1.85)	0.0785* (3.99)	0.0760* (3.85)
DEC	0.0241 (1.13)	0.0578* (2.85)	0.0577* (2.85)
FAST	−0.0562* (−2.42)	−0.0266 (−1.16)	−0.0261 (−1.14)
CONTRACTOR	0.2937* (4.99)	0.3239* (3.86)	0.3105* (3.68)
SUPERVISOR	0.1265* (3.27)	0.1024* (2.98)	0.1050* (3.05)
FITTER	0.0984* (3.39)	0.0974* (3.51)	0.1018* (3.64)
TECH	0.0813** (2.01)	−0.0284 (−0.76)	−0.0347 (−0.91)
ASSIST	−0.0991* (−3.13)	−0.0847* (−2.87)	−0.0779* (−2.65)
DIV 1	0.2470* (8.05)	0.2884* (10.73)	0.2915* (10.81)
DIV 2	0.1295* (4.05)	0.1076* (3.43)	0.1107* (3.53)
DIV 3	0.1976* (6.52)	0.1295* (4.57)	0.1315* (4.64)
N	426	426	426
R-squared	0.5592	0.5678	0.5629
F-Statistics	18.70	31.24	31.23
VSL	45,230,384 (INR 45.23 million or $0.67 million)		66,829,023 (INR 66.82 million or $0.99 million)
VSL obtained after inclusion of worker's compensation		30,270,943 (INR 30.27 million or $0.45 million)	
VSI	1,673,542 (INR 1.67 million or $0.025 million)	2,369,568 (INR 2.36 million or $0.035 million)	
Compensation adjusted VSI			1,941,426 (INR 1.94 million or $0.028 million)

Source: Author's estimation based on primary data collected from factory workers at Ahmedabad (Majumder & Madheswaran, 2020).

Note: t-values are given in parentheses (Exchange rate: 1 USD = INR 67.07, Reserve Bank of India, February 2016).

* 1% level of significance, ** 5% level of significance, *** 10% level of significance

of VSI for the second specification increased as compared to the first specification. In this case, the bias in VSI was downward, which was resolved after the inclusion of the compensation variable in hedonic wage equation.

In the third specification, introducing the interaction term increases the estimated value of statistical life to INR 66.82 million and the value of a statistical injury to INR 1.94 million. The estimated coefficient implies that an additional one rupee of injury compensation is associated with a reduction of 50 paisa in wages. This trade-off is significantly higher than the optimal trade-off between wages and compensation benefits. These results suggest that the compensation benefits available to workers in the sample are below the optimal level, given the income being insured. Providing exceedingly high compensation benefits could encourage moral hazard, as workers may reduce safety efforts, leading to a higher rate of accidents and compensation claims. Thus, compensation benefits are, therefore, maintained at sub-optimal levels.

The remaining explanatory variables show expected patterns across the specifications. Human capital factors, such as work experience and educational attainment, have a positive effect on wages. In contrast, migrant workers and workers belonging to scheduled castes earn significantly lower wages. Union membership does not have a significant impact on wages, which may be explained by the low level of union participation in the sample, with only 7 per cent of workers reporting union affiliation. During the primary survey, respondents indicated that unions in their factories are either inactive or no longer present, making low union participation predictable. In addition, permanent workers earn significantly higher wages than contractual workers.

In the compensation-adjusted specifications, prior job training in the same factory is found to have a negative effect on wages. This finding runs counter to expectations, as trained workers are generally expected to earn higher wages. Most variables capturing job characteristics have a statistically significant impact on earnings. Workers engaged in physically demanding tasks in the sample are primarily involved in loading and unloading activities. Since such work requires relatively low skill levels, these workers earn significantly lower wages than others.

Improved working conditions are associated with higher productivity and better workplace safety. As a result, when employers provide safer and more pleasant working environments, they may offer lower wages. Workers who perform overtime receive significantly higher pay. Similarly, jobs that involve decision-making responsibilities and mental effort are associated with higher wages. Contractors and supervisors earn more than assistants, and workers across all industrial divisions receive significantly higher wages compared to those in division.

Table 5.3 presents the estimation results of the hedonic wage equation that incorporates lump sum compensation for permanent disability and death under the Employees' Compensation Act, 2009.

After incorporating lump sum compensation benefits, the job-risk coefficients increase across all specifications, from specification 4 through specification 7.

Table 5.3 Hedonic wage estimates incorporating ESI (2010) benefits for permanent disability and death

Variables	*OLS estimates*	*Compensation adjusted estimates*			
	(1)	*(4)*	*(5)*	*(6)*	*(7)*
Constant	3.195*	3.2705*	3.2474*	3.2293*	3.2260*
	(50.25)	(59.04)	(56.75)	(55.69)	(55.98)
FATAL	0.0048*	0.0057*	0.0071*	0.0068*	0.0071*
	(4.84)	(6.08)	(7.55)	(7.03)	(7.54)
INJURY	0.0180*	0.0261*	0.0202*	0.0263*	0.0229*
	(3.76)	(5.54)	(3.97)	(5.34)	(4.48)
FATAL × $\widehat{PTD_i}$		4.06e-09*			
		(6.59)			
INJURY × $\widehat{PTD_i}$			1.96e-08*		
			(4.14)		
FATAL× $\widehat{D_i}$				3.74e-09*	
				(2.54)	
INJURY× $\widehat{D_i}$					2.90e-08*
					(2.63)
EXP	0.0119*	0.0161*	0.0164*	0.0171*	0.0174*
	(3.75)	(5.74)	(5.66)	(5.85)	(5.96)
EXP^2	-0.0001*	-0.0002*	-0.0002*	-0.0002*	-0.0002*
	(–2.23)	(–4.08)	(–3.95)	(–4.26)	(–4.29)
PRIMARY	0.1316*	0.1051*	0.1029*	0.1055*	0.1034*
	(3.51)	(3.33)	(3.16)	(3.19)	(3.13)
SECONDARY	0.1115*	0.0741*	0.0812*	0.0719*	0.0812*
	(3.08)	(2.53)	(2.69)	(2.34)	(2.66)
HS	0.1658*	0.1140*	0.1294*	0.1173*	0.1247*
	(4.65)	(3.77)	(4.16)	(3.71)	(3.96)
GRADUATE	0.1629*	0.2091*	0.2287*	0.2197*	0.2263*
	(3.16)	(4.82)	(5.12)	(4.85)	(5.01)
SC	-0.0623*	-0.0589*	-0.0665*	-0.0653*	-0.0661*
	(–2.36)	(–2.58)	(–2.83)	(–2.74)	(–2.77)
MIGRANT	-0.0616*	-0.0384**	-0.0483*	-0.0435*	-0.0465*
	(–2.86)	(–1.96)	(–2.40)	(–2.13)	(–2.28)
UNION	0.0622***	0.1761**	0.1565***	0.1566***	0.1527
	(1.58)	(1.88)	(1.62)	(1.60)	(1.56)
JOBTYPE	0.0614*	0.0989*	0.1084*	0.1077*	0.1110*
	(2.56)	(4.08)	(4.34)	(4.26)	(4.39)
TRAINING	-0.0284	-0.0472*	-0.0452*	-0.0429*	-0.0444*
	(–1.34)	(–2.38)	(–2.20)	(–2.07)	(–2.14)
PHW	-0.0421*	-0.0626*	-0.0828*	-0.0729*	-0.0811*
	(–1.99)	(–3.17)	(–4.09)	(–3.55)	(–3.95)
OT	0.0221	0.0227	0.0386***	0.0469**	0.0486*
	(0.89)	(0.95)	(1.57)	(1.89)	(1.97)
PHCOND	0.0253	-0.0691*	-0.0836*	-0.0708*	-0.0783*
	(0.78)	(–2.30)	(–2.67)	(–2.25)	(–2.46)
MENT	0.0377**	0.0656*	0.0757*	0.0744*	-0.0771*
	(1.85)	(3.48)	(3.91)	(3.78)	(–3.93)
DEC	0.0241	0.0401*	0.0603*	0.0520*	0.0574*
	(1.13)	(2.07)	(3.03)	(2.57)	(2.85)

(*Continued*)

Table 5.3 (Continued)

Variables	*OLS estimates (1)*	*Compensation adjusted estimates*			
		(4)	*(5)*	*(6)*	*(7)*
FAST	-0.0562* (-2.42)	-0.0391** (-1.77)	-0.0284 (-1.26)	-0.0289 (-1.26)	-0.0257 (-1.12)
CONTRACTOR	0.2937* (4.99)	0.3949* (4.88)	0.3525* (4.25)	0.3479* (4.13)	0.3376* (4.03)
SUPERVI-SOR	0.1265* (3.27)	0.1006* (3.06)	0.1209* (3.55)	0.1067* (3.11)	0.1153* (3.34)
FITTER	0.0984* (3.39)	0.0995* (3.75)	0.0962* (3.52)	0.1018* (3.67)	0.1006* (3.63)
TECH	0.0813** (2.01)	-0.0165 (-0.47)	-0.0223 (-0.62)	-0.0153 (-0.42)	-0.0185 (-0.51)
ASSIST	-0.0991* (-3.13)	-0.0849* (-3.03)	-0.0725* (-2.51)	-0.0787* (-2.69)	-0.0746* (-2.54)
DIV 1	0.2470* (8.05)	0.2640* (10.20)	0.2752* (10.35)	0.2784* (10.30)	0.2800* (10.40)
DIV 2	0.1295* (4.05)	0.0892* (2.97)	0.1065* (3.45)	0.0976* (3.09)	0.1075* (3.44)
DIV 3	0.1976* (6.52)	0.1503* (5.52)	0.1412* (5.04)	0.1320* (4.67)	0.1331* (4.71)
N	426	426	426	426	426
R-squared	0.5592	0.5607	0.5594	0.5600	0.5597
F-Statistics	18.70	35.76	32.78	31.56	31.62
VSL	45,230,384 (INR 45.23 million or $0.67 million)		65,903,871 (INR 65.90 million or $0.98 million)		66,625,805 (INR 66.62 million or $0.99 million)
VSL obtained after inclusion of worker's compensation		71,240,400 (INR 71.24 million or $1.06 million)		72,112,302 (INR 72.11 million or $1.07 million)	
VSI	1,673,542 (INR 1.67 million or $0.025 million)	2,428,538 (INR 2.42 million or $0.036 million)		2,446,587 (INR 2.44 million or $0.036 million)	
Compensation adjusted VSI			2,761,605 (INR 2.76 million or $0.042 million)		2,825,229 (INR 2.82 million or $0.042 million)

Source: Author's estimation based on primary data collected from factory workers at Ahmedabad (Majumder & Madheswaran, 2020).

Note: t-values are given in parentheses (Exchange rate: 1 USD = INR 67.07, Reserve Bank of India, February 2016).

* 1% level of significance, ** 5% level of significance, *** 10% level of significance

The estimated values of a statistical life for the compensation-adjusted models range from INR 65.90 million (USD 0.98 million, 2016 USD) to INR 72.11 million (USD 1.02 million). Similarly, the estimated values of a statistical injury range between INR 2.42 million (USD 0.036 million) and INR 2.82 million (USD 0.042 million). These estimates are higher than the baseline VSL and VSI obtained from specification 1. Overall, the findings clearly indicate that omitting workers' compensation benefits leads to biased estimates of both VSL and VSI.

Specifications 4 and 5 capture the effect of lump sum compensation for PTD through the interaction terms. Similarly, Specifications 6 and 7 examine the inclusion of lump sum compensation for death. As shown in Table 5.3, the coefficients on these interaction terms are positive but very small in magnitude, indicating that the degree of substitution between compensation benefits and wages is negligible. This suggests that higher lump sum compensation for permanent disability or death is associated with higher wage demands rather than lower wages. Consequently, the second hypothesis is not supported for compensation related to permanent disability and death. A possible explanation for this is that PTD results in a complete loss of earning capacity for the remainder of a worker's life, while death eliminates income entirely. The risks associated with these outcomes are therefore much greater than those linked to temporary disability. Under such circumstances, higher compensation benefits alone may be insufficient, and workers may require both higher wages and higher compensation to accept these risks.

5.7 Conclusion

This chapter examines how workers' compensation benefits influence wages and wage premiums associated with job-related risk. To address this issue, the analysis draws on two compensation schemes. The Employees' State Insurance Act, based on the 2010 amendment, is used to study the impact of compensation for temporary disability and dependents' benefits on wages, while the Employees' Compensation Act, incorporating the 2009 amendment, is used to assess the effect of compensation for permanent disability and death on wages. The trade-off between compensation benefits and wages is analysed within a health-state-dependent utility framework. The findings show a significant negative trade-off between wages and compensation for temporary disability. In contrast, the trade-off between compensation for permanent disability and wages is positive but very small in magnitude.

The results also demonstrate that omitting workers' compensation variables from the hedonic wage equation leads to biased estimates of the value of statistical life and injury. In addition, the study estimates the optimal trade-off between wages and compensation benefits. The findings suggest that the temporary disability compensation programme is less than optimal from an insurance perspective. Nevertheless, such suboptimal compensation levels may be justified, as overly generous benefits can give rise to moral hazard.

This study differs from existing VSL research in India by offering a detailed examination of workers' compensation. It provides, for the first time, estimates of the rate of substitution between compensation benefits and wages using data from an Indian city and evaluates whether existing compensation levels are adequate for workers. The results offer important insights into the design and functioning of government workers' compensation programmes in India.

Thus far, the analysis has relied on a static framework to estimate compensating wage differentials, as well as VSL and VSI for the sampled workers. The following chapter extends the analysis by estimating the discount rates workers apply to intertemporal risks of death.

Reference List

Butler, R. J., & Worrall, J. D. (1985). Work injury compensation and the duration of nonwork spells. *The Economic Journal*, *95*(379), 714–724. Retrieved April 05, 2018, from https://ideas.repec.org/a/ecj/econjl/v95y1985i379p714-24.html

Chelius, J. R., & Smith, R. S. (1987). Firm size and regulatory compliance costs: The case of workers' compensation insurance. *Journal of Policy Analysis and Management*, *6*(2), 193–206. Retrieved March 29, 2018, from https://www.jstor.org/stable/3324515

The Employees State Insurance Act. (1948). *Benefits*. Retrieved September 20, 2018, from https://www.esic.nic.in/attachments/actfile/a4be21587177569bb213b8254b83148e.pdf

Krueger, A. B. (1989). *Incentive effects of worker's compensation insurance* (Working Paper No. 3089). National Bureau of Economic Research. Retrieved April 05, 2018, from https://ideas.repec.org/p/nbr/nberwo/3089.html

Majumder, A., Madheswaran, S. (2018). *Role of worker's compensation benefit in estimating value of statistical life* (ISEC Working Paper No. 423). https://www.isec.ac.in/wp-content/uploads/2023/07/WP-423-Agamoni-Majumder-and-Madheswaran_2-Final.pdf

Majumder, A., & Madheswaran, S. (2020). Compensation for occupational risk and valuation of statistical life. *Social Indicators Research: An International and Interdisciplinary Journal for Quality-of-Life Measurement*, *149*(3), 967–989.

Meng, R., & Smith, D. A. (1999). The impact of workers' compensation on wage premiums for job hazards. *Applied Economics*, *31*(9), 1101–1108. Retrieved April 05, 2018, from https://ideas.repec.org/a/taf/applec/v31y1999i9p1101-1108.html

Reserve Bank of India. (n.d.). *Reference rate archive*. Reference Exchange rate date: 1/02/2016. https://www.rbi.org.in/scripts/referenceratearchive.aspx

Ruser, J. W. (1985). Workers' compensation insurance, experience-rating, and occupational injuries. *The RAND Journal of Economics*, *16*(4), 487–503. Retrieved April 05, 2018, from https://ideas.repec.org/a/rje/randje/v16y1985iwinterp487-503.html

Shanmugam, K. R., & Madheswaran, S. (2011). The value of statistical life. In A. K. Haque, M. N. Murty, & P. Shyamsundar (Eds.), *Environmental valuation in South Asia* (pp. 413–443). Cambridge University Press. (Accessed hard copy of the book).

Viscusi, W. K., & Moore, M. J. (1987). Worker's compensation: Wage effects, benefit inadequacies, and the value of health losses. *The Review of Economics and Statistics*, *69*(2), 249–261. Retrieved March 29, 2018, from https://www.jstor.org/stable/1927232

Viscusi, W. K., & Moore, M. J. (1989). Rates of time preference and valuations of the duration of life. *Journal of Public Economics*, *38*, 297–317. Retrieved March 29, 2018, from https://ideas.repec.org/a/eee/pubeco/v38y1989i3p297-317.html

Workmen's Compensation Act. (1923). Retrieved August 08, 2018, from https://labour.gov.in/sites/default/files/TheWorkmenAct1923(1).pdf

Appendices

Appendix 5A

Table 5A.1 Benefit rates under ESI (2010)

Sr. No	*Worker's average daily wage (in Rs.)*	*Daily standard benefit rates (in Rs.)*	*Sr. No*	*Worker's average daily wage (in Rs.)*	*Daily standard benefit rates (in Rs.)*
1	≤ 27	14	22	176 – 185	93
2	28 – 31	16	23	186 – 195	98
3	32 – 35	18	24	196 – 205	103
4	36 – 39	20	25	206 – 215	108
5	40 – 47	24	26	216 – 225	113
6	48 – 55	28	27	226 – 235	118
7	56 – 59	30	28	236 – 249	125
8	60 – 63	32	29	250 – 259	130
9	64 – 71	36	30	260 – 269	135
10	72 – 75	38	31	270 – 279	140
11	76 – 79	40	32	280 – 289	145
12	80 – 87	44	33	290 – 299	150
13	88 – 95	48	34	300 – 309	155
14	96 – 105	53	35	310 – 319	160
15	106 – 115	58	36	320 – 329	165
16	116 – 125	63	37	330 – 339	170
17	126 – 135	68	38	340 – 349	175
18	136 – 145	73	39	350 – 359	180
19	146 – 155	78	40	360 – 369	185
20	156 – 165	83	41	370 – 379	190
21	166 – 175	88	42	380 – 389	195

Source: Employee's State Insurance (ESI) Programme, 2010 (Majumder & Madheswaran, 2020).

Table 5A.2 Age and compensation factors for permanent total disability under ESI (2009)

Age	*Factor*	*Age*	*Factor*	*Age*	*Factor*	*Age*	*Factor*
16	228.54	29	209.92	42	178.49	55	135.56
17	227.49	30	207.98	43	175.54	56	131.95
18	226.38	31	205.95	44	172.52	57	128.33
19	225.22	32	203.85	45	169.44	58	124.7
20	224	33	201.66	46	166.29	59	121.05
21	222.71	34	199.4	47	163.07	60	117.41
22	221.37	35	197.06	48	159.8	61	113.77
23	219.95	36	194.64	49	156.47	62	110.14
24	218.47	37	192.14	50	153.09	63	106.52
25	216.91	38	189.56	51	149.67	64	102.93
26	215.28	39	186.9	52	146.2	> 65	99.37
27	213.57	40	184.17	53	142.68		
28	211.79	41	181.37	54	139.13		

Source: Employees Compensation Act (2009 amendment) (Majumder & Madheswaran, 2018).

6 Discounting long-term job-related health risks for Indian workers

6.1 Introduction

Many health outcomes occur with a time lag hence it is essential to examine the the trade-off between worker's wage and the health/life risks arising from working in a hazardous job over a long time horizon. For example, developing country workers from chemical factories exposed to toxic fumes in their daily work often ignore the long term consequences this exposure may have on their lung health and continue working without safety gears and low pay. The questions that arises here are: will the wage-risk trade-off be different when workers realize that the job risks not only affect them in the current period rather have a lingering impact on their health and life? If they do realize this, are they ready to trade good health in the future for current income gains? In order to answer these complex questions, the concept of "discounting" is very crucial. More specifically, the focus is on discounting future health consequences (in the form of benefits or costs) which will be explored in details in this chapter. Another aim of this chapter is to identify the discount rate of the workers in the sample that can be used to compare the present income benefits against future health costs.

From a safety perspective, an example of delayed health impact is visible from, installing airbags in cars that would save numerous lives over the long run. Similarly, there are many environmental policies that yield health benefits over long time periods. In such situations, individuals need to decide on incurring expenses on safety measures at current period so that they can obtain benefits at some future period. It becomes very important to weigh the present costs against the future benefits because such a decision involves the allocation of limited financial resources over different time periods. The value of future benefits can be converted into monetary terms at the present period by discounting them at some rate of interest. This is done to compare the future benefits with the present costs and take decisions accordingly.

An individual will choose to delay gratification only when there is a possibility of receiving higher reward by waiting. For example, a person who wishes to buy a car saves money in a bank account. By saving this money in a bank, he is also earning interest on the amount of money he saved. The interest earned on his savings can be used to gain additional utility in the form of

DOI: 10.4324/9781003628262-6

consumption of additional goods in the future. Thus, discount rates indicate the amount of future utility that an individual would require for waiting. This illustrates the concept of time preference. Time preference is defined as "the amount of future utility that is equivalent to the current utility of consuming a good or service" (Lawless et al., 2013, p. 2). In this context, it is important to distinguish between the individual rate of time preferences and society's rate of time preferences while making decisions on public policies. The individual time preferences pertain to the private decisions of an individual (such as deferring consumption), and the social time preferences pertain to society's preferences for the well-being of others (Lawless et al., 2013). This study focuses on the individual rate of time preference of the workers in the sample.

The rate of time preference plays an important role in "shaping public policy, explaining psychological decision making, and uncovering motivations behind seemingly irrational health behaviour" (Lawless et al., 2013, p. 2). The use of time preference in policy decisions of developing countries is quite different from that of developed countries. Time preference can explain why developing countries allocate their limited resources to specific programmes. In this context, Lawless et al. (2013) give the example of the AIDS pandemic in East Africa, which has been a huge policy challenge in the developing world. The two strategies that can be used to prevent this disease are: creation of a vaccine for this disease and distribution of contraceptives like condoms. Even though the latter strategy was readily enforced, the first strategy never received much attention because the government has a high social rate of time preference. Development of cancer vaccines could have saved numerous lives over the long term; however, it would have required a huge investment by the country in research and development of the vaccine. It has been observed that governments of developing countries have high social discount rates, and therefore, they are unwilling to invest large number of resources for the prevention of such health outcomes. On the other hand, governments of developed countries have low social discount rates and are more likely to invest in the prevention of such diseases. Investment in health research improves the health outcomes across various income levels in developed countries as compared to developing countries. Thus, "understanding the interplaying psychological factors that contribute to changes in time preference is essential for establishing appropriate public policy" (Lawless et al., 2013, p. 7).

There are numerous studies that examine the relationship between an individual's rate of time preference and educational attainment, consumption, income, and health outcomes. Samuelson (1937) laid the foundation for studies on intertemporal decision-making. Later in 1964, Becker developed the theory of investment in human capital, and Grossman (1972) applied this theory to health. The theory of human capital posits that individuals who are less willing to invest in their future have higher discount rates compared to individuals who are more oriented towards the future (Mincer, 1958; Becker, 1964). This indicates that individuals with high discount rates would invest less in improving human capital (such as education and skill development) compared to individuals with low discount rates who are willing to delay their rewards. Grossman (1972) found an inverse relationship between the decision to invest in health and an individual's rate of time preference. Viscusi (1979) observed that workers who have low discount rates prefer delayed benefits of investment in education and health. There are many studies that have found a negative association between educational attainment and individual rate of time preference. The possible reasons for such a relationship were provided by Becker and Mulligan (1997). According to them, schooling focuses the attention of students on the future. Therefore, "through repeated practice at problem solving, schooling helps children learn the art of scenario simulation. Thus, educated people should be more productive at reducing the remoteness of future pleasures" (Becker & Mulligan, 1997). A study by Bickel et al. (1999) found that individuals with high discount rate are more likely to smoke. However, Fuchs (1982) found that smoking and rate of time preference are weakly related. A study by Borghans and Golsteyn (2006) found that individuals with high discount rate have high body mass index (BMI). This may be because of the fact that such individuals are impatient, and they tend to make decisions that involve immediate gratification (i.e. they value candy, fast food, and other things that provide instant satisfaction). Della and Paserman (2005) found that individuals having high discount rates accept a lower reservation wage compared to individuals having low discount rates. Stephens and Krupka (2006) found that households which have a low rate of time preference gather more assets. A study by Golsteyn et al. (2013) examined the relationship between rate of time preferences in childhood and social and economic outcomes in the long run. They used Swedish longitudinal dataset on 11,907 children and followed them throughout their lives. It was found that individuals with low rate of time preference have successful school career and comparatively higher income. On the other hand, individuals with high rate of time preference were found to have "lower incomes at middle age, more days in unemployment, higher risk of obesity and teen-age motherhood" (Golsteyn et al., 2013, p. 16).

The discussion in the earlier paragraphs indicates that many individuals place less value on the future health benefits compared to the present costs. But the question that remains is "how much more highly should current, as opposed to future effects be weighted?" (Viscusi, 1995, p. 125). The choice of discount rates is a debatable issue. In this context, the options are to use a zero-discount rate, opportunity cost of capital, and the interest rate on low-risk bonds (Shanmugam, 2006). Using a zero-discount rate implies weighing present and future events at par. Investing in future health benefits is an alternative to investing money in some project with substantial amount of returns (e.g. keeping money in a bank account); therefore, opportunity cost of capital can possibly be used. However, capital markets are not perfect, and therefore, they may not fully reflect the collective interest of a society in transferring certain resources to future. Low-risk investment, such as government bonds, yields safe returns, and it is close to the interest rate that a society would assign to transfer the scarce resources across generations (Viscusi, 1995). Thus, the issue of choice of discount rate is resolved empirically by researchers. Studies generally estimate discount rate for health outcomes using various methods and then compare those with the existing market rate of interest (Shanmugam, 2006).

Workers engaged in risky jobs demand additional wage payment because certain level of fatal and injury risk is associated with their job. Therefore, traditional compensating wage differential studies examine the impact of fatality and injury risks on worker's wage. Moore and Viscusi (1988) is a pioneering study which extended this idea and examined the effect of duration of life at risk on worker's wage. Thereby, they utilised the discounted expected life years approach and estimated the implicit discount rate of the workers that ranged between 10 and 12 per cent. The corresponding implicit value per statistical life was estimated to be $175,000. Once again, Moore and Viscusi (1990a) estimated the implicit rate of time preference for health risk using life cycle approach. They found the real discount rate to be 2 per cent, which was much lower compared to their previous study. However, this rate was at par with the real rate of return to capital prevailing during the study period. Another study by Viscusi and Moore (1989) used a multi-period Markov model to estimate the rate of time preference of individuals. They found that highly educated workers assign lower discount rates for future health benefits. This implied that educated individuals assign higher weight to the future benefits compared to the present, and, therefore, they assign lower discount rates for future benefits. The rate of time preference of the workers in their study was estimated to be 11 per cent. In 1990, Moore and Viscusi undertook another study in which they utilised five models to estimate the discount rates. Their study yielded a range of discount rates between 1 and 14 per cent. The discounted life years approach yielded discount rate of 9.6 to 12.2 per cent, the basic Markov chain model yielded discount rate of 10.7 per cent, and the life cycle model yielded discount rate of 1.6 to 2 per cent. In this study, they used three new versions of the Markov model. The "structural Markov model with market locus restriction" and the "Integrated structural Markov model" yielded discount rate of 1 per cent, while the "Integrated structural Markov model with bequest" yielded a discount rate of 14.2 per cent.

In the Indian context, Shanmugam (2006) was the first study that estimated the quantity-adjusted value of life using the discounted expected life years approach. He estimated the implicit discount rate to range between 7.6 and 7.9 per cent. These discount rates were found to be close to the financial market interest rate on debt to private creditors but lower than the bank interest rate prevailing during the study period. In 2011, Shanmugam used the life-cycle model to estimate the real discount rate for the workers in the sample. The discount rates ranged between 2.4 and 5.1 per cent. The estimated discount rates were found to be similar to the real rate of external debt during 1990. A slightly different method was used by Pender (1996) to estimate the discount rate of individuals. He used choice experiment method to examine the implication of credit market models of discount rates for individuals from two Indian villages. An experimental setup was used in which farmers were asked to choose from a set of eight alternatives. Each alternative included a choice of obtaining a certain quantity of rice in the current period or a different quantity of rice in the future period (e.g. receiving 10 kg of rice in the month of December this year or receiving 15 kg of rice in the month of August next year). The choice of farmers indicated how they weighed current period over the future period. For all the experimental groups, he found the discount rate to be comparatively higher than the maximum interest rates paid on outstanding loans by most of the respondents. Another study by Kula (2004) estimated the social rate of time preference for India to be 5.2 per cent.

This chapter intends to determine the and discount rate of workers for long-term health impacts. Labour market data from this study has been used to measure the implicit rates of time preference that individuals reveal through their willingness to incur risks associated with their jobs. Three approaches have been utilised to estimate the discount rates. The first one is the discounted expected life year approach that has been developed by Moore and Viscusi (1988). The second approach is structured life-cycle models that have been used by Moore and Viscusi (1990a). The third approach is the multi-period Markov model that has been proposed by Moore and Viscusi (1989). The chapter begins by exploring the mathematical models that have been used for estimating discount rates of workers in the sample. The empirical analysis of the models and results are presented in the following sections.

6.2 Approaches for estimation of discount rate

Estimation of rate of time preference for long-term health outcomes is accomplished using information on labour market decisions. The next few sub-sections present the models that have been used to estimate the discount rate of workers in the sample.

6.2.1 *Discounted expected life years approach*

A typical hedonic wage equation focuses on risks that may immediately alter the health status of a worker, depending on their choice of job risk in the current period. However, there are many latent health risks that are "far removed in time from the exposure to the risk". Therefore, a basic hedonic wage equation doesn't consider the variation in the quantity and quality of life among individuals. A young person loses comparatively higher amount of lifetime utility than an older person if any fatality occurs. Thus, age plays an important role in determining an individual's job risk preferences. Thaler and Rosen (1976) and Viscusi (1979) attempted to resolve this issue by introducing an interaction term between an individual's age and fatal job risk into the hedonic wage equation. However, their approach failed to account for differences in life expectancy, the rate of time preference of individuals, and changes in life expectancy as an individual age (Shanmugam, 2006). Therefore, the discounted expected life years approach was used. In this approach, information on worker's age and his expected remaining life years (**Ti**) are used to calculate his expected remaining life at risk. This is given as follows:

$$\textbf{Discounted remaining life} = \frac{\left[1-\exp\left(-r\times T_i\right)\right]}{r} \qquad (6.1)$$

Here, "r" is the real rate of time preference. The discounted remaining life is then weighed by probability of fatal risk to obtain the expected life years lost,

$$\textbf{Expected life years lost }(\textbf{ELYL}) = \textbf{Discounted remaining life} \times \textbf{ Fatal risk}_{\text{i}}$$

To examine the influence of change in expected remaining lifetime on worker's wage, the basic hedonic wage equation is modified by incorporating the ELYL as an independent variable. Thus, the fatal job risk measure is replaced with ELYL variable. Estimation of this modified hedonic wage equation yields the real rates of time preference of the workers in the sample.

6.2.2 *Life-cycle approach*

The life-cycle model assumes that all the years of an individual's life are equally valued, and any job risk would only reduce the duration of life. The conceptual model is based on a simple setup in which we consider that an individual faces only two states. In state 1, the individual is healthy, and he earns a wage "w". The wage of the worker increases with the increase in the job risk level "p". Therefore, utility under healthy state can be denoted as $\mathbf{U}^1(\mathbf{w}(\mathbf{p}))$. In state 2, the worker dies due to injury, and his utility is considered to be zero. A worker's time horizon equals his expected remaining lifetime, "$\mathrm{T_i}$" which decreases with an increase in "p" such that $\mathbf{T}_\mathrm{p} < 0$. If this worker discounts his future utility at a real rate of "r", then the expected discounted lifetime utility with "T" years of remaining life can be calculated as

$$V = \int_0^{T_p} U^1(w(p))e^{rt}\,dt$$

For simplicity, if we assume the job risk to be constant at a level "p" and the worker works in his job till he dies, then he will maximise his expected discounted lifetime utility given the wage,

$$\max_p V = \frac{1}{r}\left(1 - e^{-rT(p)}\right) \times U\left(w(p)\right)$$

The first order condition is

$$V_p = \frac{1}{r}\left(1 - e^{-rT(p)}\right)U_w\frac{\delta w}{\delta p} + \frac{\delta T}{\delta p}Ue^{-rT(p)} = 0 \quad (6.2)$$

Re-arranging equation (6.2), we get

$$\frac{\delta_w}{\delta_p} = r\frac{\delta TU}{\delta\, pU_w}(e^{-rT(p)} - 1)^{-1}. \quad (6.3)$$

Equation (6.3) shows the wage–risk trade-off between worker's current earning and job risk, which depends on the expected remaining life years "T", the discount rate "r" and trade-off between longevity and risk $\left[\frac{\delta T}{\delta p}\right]$. Taking logarithms on both sides of equation (6.3) yields the following expression:

$$ln\frac{\delta T}{\delta p} = \alpha - rT + \epsilon. \tag{6.4}$$

In this expression ϵ is the error term which captures the error in approximation, that is,

$$ln\left(e^{-rT(p)} - 1\right)^{-1} \approx rT$$

In case of small values of "r" and "T", the errors will be small. Estimation of equation (6.4) yields the real discount rate "r", which will be taken up in later section.

6.2.3 *Multi-period Markov decision model*

This model focuses on the issue of duration of life and estimates individual preferences with respect to years of life. It is a unique approach which "incorporates the theoretical structure of multi-period job risk problem" Viscusi and Moore (1989). This model acknowledges the multi-period nature of job risk and the effect of fatal risk on worker's time horizon. It is quite complicated to include the influences of many factors, such as changes in job risk, earnings capacity, and savings over an individual's life cycle, the role of bequest, and capital market imperfections, in an empirical framework. The theoretical framework used in this model is same as life-cycle model in which an individual is assumed to face only two states (good health state and death state). The aim of the worker is to maximise his discounted expected lifetime utility, which takes the form of a time-invariant Markov decision problem

$$\max_{p_j} V = (1-p)U(w(p_j)) + \beta(1-p)^2 U(w(p_j)) + \ldots\ldots\ldots + \beta^{(t-1)}(1-p)^t U(w(p_j)) \tag{6.5}$$

In equation (6.5), the utility in the death state is normalised to zero with no loss of generality. On the other hand, the utility derived from surviving in period "t" is weighted by a discount factor $\beta^{(t-1)}$ and the probability of living for at least "t" periods, which is denoted as $(1-p)^t$. It is assumed that the worker initially selects a lifetime risk "p" which remains constant over time (i.e. time invariant). This model provides an optimal solution under an infinite time horizon, given that the risks and rewards are time invariant. Re-arranging equation (6.5) yields equation (6.6).

$$\max_{p_j} V = (1-p)U(w(p_j))\sum_{t=1}^{\infty}[\beta(1-p)]^{(t-1)} \tag{6.6}$$

$$\text{Let } \mathbf{G}(\mathbf{p}) = \sum_{t=1}^{\infty} [\beta(1-p)]^{(t-1)} = \frac{1}{[1-\beta(1-\mathrm{p})]} \tag{6.7}$$

Then equation (6.7) takes the following form

$$\max_{p_j} V = (1-p)U(w(p_j)) \times G(p) = (1-p)U(w(p_j)) \times \frac{1}{[1-\beta(1-\mathrm{p})]} \tag{6.8}$$

Differentiating equation (6.8) with respect to the risk "p" yields the following:

$$\begin{aligned} V_p &= (1-\mathrm{p})G(p) \times U'(w(p_j)) \times \frac{\delta \mathrm{w}}{\delta \mathrm{p}} + U(w(p_j)) \times (1-p) \times G'(p) - \\ &\quad U(w(p_j)) \times G(p) = 0 \end{aligned} \tag{6.9}$$

Solving equation (6.9), yields

$$\frac{\delta \mathrm{w}}{\delta \mathrm{p}} = \frac{\mathrm{U}(\mathrm{w}(\mathrm{p_j})) \times \mathrm{G(p)}}{(1-\mathrm{p}) \times \mathrm{G(p)} \times \mathrm{U'(w(p_j))}} - \frac{\mathrm{U(w(p_j))} \times (1-\mathrm{p}) \times \mathrm{G'(p)}}{(1-\mathrm{p}) \times \mathrm{G(p)} \times \mathrm{U'(w(p_j))}}$$

$$\frac{\delta \mathrm{w}}{\delta \mathrm{p}} = \frac{\mathrm{U}}{\mathrm{U'}} \times \left[\frac{1}{(1-\mathrm{p})} - \frac{\mathrm{G'}}{\mathrm{G}}\right] \tag{6.10}$$

To obtain the expression for **G'(p)**, equation (6.7) is differentiated with respect to "p"

$$\mathrm{G'(p)} = \frac{\beta}{[1-\beta(1-p)]^2} \tag{6.11}$$

Substituting this expression in equation (6.10) yields the following:

$$\frac{\delta \mathrm{w}}{\delta \mathrm{p}} = \frac{\mathrm{U}}{\mathrm{U'}} \times \left[\frac{1}{(1-\mathrm{p})} - \frac{\beta}{[1-\beta(1-p)]^2}\right] \tag{6.12}$$

The first order differential equation (6.12) can be solved if $\left(\frac{\mathrm{U}}{\mathrm{U'}}\right)$ is assumed to be constant. To avoid this additional restriction, a different approach is followed that will be discussed under the empirical estimation section.

6.3 Estimation of discount rates under alternative approaches

In the following sections, discount rate is estimated using three alternative approaches and appropriate econometric specifications. The estimated results are also discussed here.

6.3.1 Estimation of discount rate using discounted expected life years approach

In the Discounted Expected Life Years approach, the basic hedonic wage equation (5.6) is modified by introducing a variable termed as "ELYL" to estimate the quantity-adjusted value of life and the discount rate of workers in the sample.

$$LnW_i = \alpha + \beta_1 \; ELYL_i + \beta_2 INJURY_i + \beta_3 INJURY_i \times WC_i + \sum_k \gamma_k X_{ki} + \epsilon_i \quad (6.13)$$

The dependent variable in this model is the logarithm of the after-tax hourly wage of the workers. The fatal job risk variable used in this equation is **ELYL**, which accounts for the discounted duration of remaining life that is at risk. The weighing of the death risk variable with discounted remaining life years reflects the fact that an individual is concerned not only with the probability of death but also with the discounted duration of life and corresponding lifetime utility at risk. To construct the ELYL variable, the information on expected remaining years of life (i.e. life expectancy) corresponding to the age of the workers in the sample is calculated from the abridged life tables 2011–2015 (Office of the Registrar General & Census Commissioner, India, 2017). The mean life expectancy of the workers in the sample is 42.8 years. ELYL is a non-linear function of the discount rate, and therefore, a non-linear regression method is used to estimate the modified hedonic wage equation.

An alternative measure of job risk, denoted as $ELYL$, has been used in a separate specification. This variable contains an interaction between subjective job risk measure ***"ENVDANGER"***, the fatal job risk measure, and discounted remaining life (i.e. $\text{ELYL1} = \textbf{\textit{Fatal risk}}_i \times \textbf{\textit{DANGER}} \times \textbf{\textit{discounted remaining life}}$). Given that the objective job risk variable used in this study is not differentiated by industry and occupation, an attempt has been made to introduce an element of job-specific variation in the risk levels through the use of this alternative job risk variable. On the other hand, the **INJURY** variable is used in additive form as well as in interaction with the workers' compensation variable (**WC**). The mean value of the WC variable is 0.46.

The discount rate that is obtained from estimation of equations (6.13) is allowed to take any value. It may be even zero if workers do not discount future utility at all, or it may be infinite if they are myopic. The results of the estimation of equation (6.13) have been presented in Table 6.1 under two alternative specifications. The first specification contains the job risk measure ***ELYL*** along with other independent variables, while the second specification contains ***ELYL1*** as the job risk measure.

The key variables of interest are the job risk variables and the discount rate. The injury risk variable has a positive and significant influence on worker's wage implying that wage increases with the increase in the possibility of incurring job injury. The estimated real discount rate for the first specification is 10.6 per cent, while for the second specification, it is 13 per cent. The

Table 6.1 Estimation of hedonic wage equation under the discounted expected life years approach

Variables	*(1)*	*(2)*
Constant	3.21* (74.9)	3.29 (100.8)
ELYL	0.006* (4.2)	
ELYL1		0.005* (4.0)
R (Discount rate)	0.106* (5.02)	0.130* (2.7)
Injury	0.051* (5.5)	0.052* (5.6)
Injury × WC	−0.040* (−2.0)	−0.045* (−2.3)
Experience	0.0080* (4.1)	0.006* (5.0)
Primary	0.193* (5.5)	0.189* (5.5)
Secondary	0.185* (5.5)	0.182* (5.4)
Higher Secondary	0.236* (6.8)	0.231* (6.8)
Graduation	0.279* (4.4)	0.281* (4.3)
SC	−0.086* (−2.8)	−0.088* (−2.9)
Supervisor	0.156* (3.4)	0.172* (3.5)
N	427	427
Adjusted R^2	0.31	0.32
Log Likelihood	15.83	17.36
F Statistic	19.01	19.41
No. of iterations	4	1

Source: Majumder and Madheswaran (2022).

Note: t-values are given in parentheses.

* 1 per cent level of significance

discount rates are highly significant at the 1 per cent level, which implies that workers in the sample assign positive and finite discount rates for future health reasons. These rates are much higher than financial market interest rates.

The implicit value of life is estimated to be (coefficient of ELYL variable from Table 6.1 × mean wage × annual hours of work × 100,000 = 0.006 × 42.96 × 2160 × 100000) INR 55.6 million ($0.83 million, Exchange rate: 1 USD = INR 67.70, Reserve Bank of India, February 2016) and $(0.005 \times 42.96 \times 2160 \times 100000)$ INR 46.3 million ($0.69 million) from specifications 1 and 2, respectively. The corresponding implicit value per additional expected year of life is estimated to be INR 1.29 million ($0.019 million) and INR 1.08 million ($0.016 million). The implicit value per additional expected year of life is calculated by dividing the implicit value of life by the mean expected remaining life years (i.e. life expectancy) (Majumder & Madheswaran, 2022).

The signs of the explanatory variables used in both the specifications are as expected. The injury risk variable is highly significant and has a positive sign. The previous Indian studies did not incorporate the worker's compensation variable during estimation of the modified hedonic wage equation (6.13). As expected, the compensation variable is negative and significant, implying that higher compensation benefits will lead to a lower CWD. The estimated VSI for the two specifications are [(co-efficient of injury variable + co-efficient of compensation variable × mean compensation benefit) × mean wage of the sample] × annual work hours × 1,000 = (0.051 – (0.040 × 0.46)) × 42.96 × 2160 × 1,000] INR 3.02 million ($0.045 million) and [(0.052 – (0.045 × 0.46)) × 42.96 × 2160 × 1,000] INR 2.90 million ($0.043 million), respectively. As the experience and education level of a worker increases, his income increases. Workers belonging to scheduled castes earn comparatively less income than other workers. Income of supervisors is significantly more compared to workers holding other job designations (Majumder & Madheswaran, 2022).

6.3.2 *Estimation of discount rate using life-cycle approach*

In Section 6.2.2, the theoretical model has been developed, and the trade-off between worker's earnings and job risk has been obtained (which depends on the remaining life of the worker and rate of time preference). However, there are certain issues with estimation of equation (6.4) that need to be addressed. The first issue pertains to the endogeneity of the variable "T", which depends on the job risk "p", and the second issue is with the estimation of the equilibrium wage–risk trade-off or the implicit prices $\left(\frac{\delta w}{\delta p}\right)$. These two problems can be resolved at the same time by using a structural hedonic equilibrium model. In this model, the implicit prices are estimated from a first-stage regression of wage on a vector of non-linear functions of job risk and worker's personal characteristics. The estimated coefficient of the job risk variable from the first-stage regression is used to calculate the implicit prices. Once the implicit prices are calculated, it is used as a dependent variable in equation (6.14). To overcome the problem of endogeneity, the two-stage least squares technique has been used to estimate this equation. The instruments used here are the interaction between the fatal risk variable and the location/region dummies.

The first-stage regression takes the form of a basic hedonic wage equation that has been modified to include interaction terms between fatal risk and four region dummies. The job risk measures are incorporated in linear as well as squared form into the interaction terms. These interaction terms indicate that variations in risk level and regions cause variation in the implicit prices. Thus, the first-stage regression is given by equation (6.14)

$$\ln w_i = \beta X_i + \sum_{k=1}^{4} (\gamma_1 R_{ik} p_i + \gamma_2 R_{ik} p_i^2) + v_i \qquad (6.14)$$

In this equation, $\mathbf{R}_i$ are the region dummies that indicate the location of the factories. The implicit prices are calculated by differentiating equation (6.14) with respect to job risk "p"

$$\begin{aligned} \frac{1}{w} \times \frac{\delta w}{\delta p} &= (\gamma_1 R_{ik} + 2\gamma_2 R_{ik} p_i) \\ \frac{\delta w}{\delta p} &= w \times (\gamma_1 R_{ik} + 2\gamma_2 R_{ik} p_i) \end{aligned} \quad (6.15)$$

This equation shows that the implicit prices depend on the region's dummies, the risk level, and worker's wage. The discount rate of the workers is finally obtained from the following equation:

$$ln \frac{\delta w_1}{\delta p_1} = \alpha - rT_i + \varepsilon_i$$

The term "α" is function of discount rate, worker's utility function, and trade-off between longevity and risk. It can be approximated to a vector of variables "**Z**" which includes personal and job characteristics of the workers. However, the observations with negative implicit prices may disappear if logarithmic transformation is taken; therefore, simple wage–risk trade-off or the implicit prices are used as dependent variables so that the equation used to estimate worker's rate of time preference takes the following form:

$$\frac{\delta w_i}{\delta p_i} = \varphi Z_i - r^* T_i + \varepsilon_i \quad (6.16)$$

The discount rate is estimated using the following expression:

$$r = \frac{\delta\, ln\left(\frac{\delta w}{\delta p}\right)}{\delta T} = \frac{1}{\left(\frac{\delta w}{\delta p}\right)} \times \frac{\delta\left(\frac{\delta w}{\delta p}\right)}{\delta T} = r^* \times \frac{1}{\left(\frac{\delta w}{\delta p}\right)}$$

Thus, equation (7.16) is estimated in the second stage.

Table 6.2 shows the results of the first-stage regression for estimation of implicit prices. The dependent variable used for this regression is the logarithm of the after-tax hourly wage of the workers in the sample. The interaction variables between region dummies and fatal risk have expected sign and they are significant for all the regions. Generally, worker's compensating wage differential increases with the increase in the job risk level. However, in this case, these differentials decrease significantly with rise in job risk levels. Except for division 2, for all the other regions, the linear as well as the

Table 6.2 First-stage regression under life-cycle model

Variables	*Coefficient*
Constant	3.3064* (48.5)
Div1*f	0.0250* (4.10)
(Div1*f)^2	−0.0003* (−2.85)
Div2*f	0.0102*** (1.64)
(Div2*f)^2	−5.48E-05 (−1.39)
Div3*f	0.0270* (3.83)
(Div3*f)^2	−0.0004* (−2.59)
Div4*f	0.0113*** (1.87)
(Div4*f)^2	−1.31E-05 (−1.54)
Primary	0.1879* (4.35)
Secondary	0.1992* (4.78)
HS	0.2576* (6.28)
Graduation	0.2446* (4.09)
SC	−0.0903* (−2.95)
N	430
Adjusted R^2	0.42
F Statistics	17.20

Source: Majumder and Madheswaran (2022).

Note: **t-values are given in parentheses.**

* 1 per cent level of significance, *** 10 per cent level of significance

squared interaction between fatal job risks and region dummies is significant. Worker's wage increases with the increase in education level of the worker. On the other hand, workers from lower social group, SC earn lower wages than other workers in the sample. The goodness of fit indicates that the model explains 42 per cent of the variation in the wages of the workers.

The implicit prices (i.e. the wage–risk trade-offs) obtained from estimation of equation (6.14) are used as dependent variable in the second stage regression. The mean value of the estimated implicit price is 0.0175 (Majumder & Madheswaran, 2022). Equation (6.16) is estimated using the two-stage least squares technique and the result is presented in Table 6.3.

This result strongly supports the model of intertemporal choices. The most important variable in this table is the life years lost (LYL) variable, which is significant at 1 per cent level and reduces worker's wage. The coefficient of the LYL variable yields the real discount rate of the workers in the sample, which is 6.71 per cent. This rate is comparatively lower than the discount rates obtained using the discounted expected life year approach. However, this rate of interest is close to the commercial bank interest rate on term deposits during the study period.

Equation (6.16) and Figure 6.1 represents a linear demand curve for longevity. It shows that there is a negative relation between implicit prices for longevity and the quantity demanded (Majumder & Madheswaran, 2022).

Table 6.3 Estimation of implicit price equation under life-cycle model

Variables	*Coefficient*
Constant	1.667* (3.76)
LYL (-r)	- 0.671* (-2.66)
Primary	0.219* (2.01)
Secondary	0.261* (2.51)
HS	0.219*(2.22)
Graduation	0.275*(2.07)
SC	-0.089 (-1.28)
Union	-0.197** (-1.92)
Migrant	-0.137* (-2.07)
Super	0.270* (2.65)
Tech	0.268* (2.54)
N	427
Adjusted R^2	0.083

Source: Majumder and Madheswaran (2022).

* 1 per cent level of significance, ** 5 per cent level of significance
Note: t-values are given in parentheses.

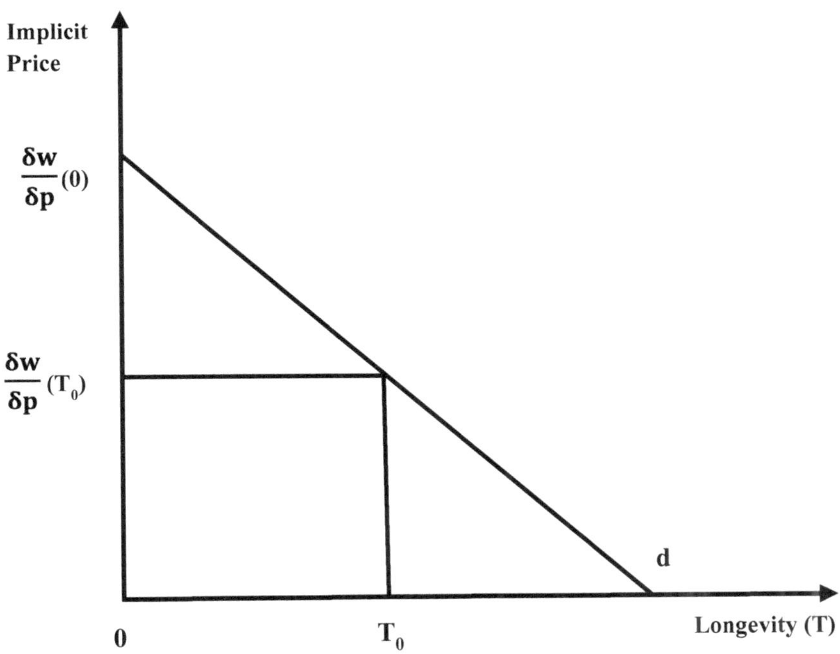

Figure 6.1 Demand curve for longevity.
Source: Majumder and Madheswaran (2022).

The value of longevity can be obtained using willingness-to-pay approach. Therefore, the willingness to pay for longevity (T_0) can be obtained by summing the area under the demand curve for longevity.

$$V(T_0) = T_0\left(\frac{\delta w}{\delta p}\right)(T_0) + 0.5 \times T_0\left(\left(\frac{\delta w}{\delta p}\right)(0) - \left(\frac{\delta w}{\delta p}\right)(T_0)\right)$$

Using the coefficient of the independent variables from Table 6.3 and their mean values, the implicit price when T = 0, that is, $\left(\frac{\delta w}{\delta p}\right)(0)$ is obtained to be 0.150. Therefore, a worker is willing to forego $[V(T_0) = (43) \times (0.1926) + 21.5 \times (0.1509 - 0.1926)] =$ INR 9.17 in hourly wages for a risk exposure of 43 additional years of life. In other words, the worker would require yearly compensation with a present value of approximately INR 19,825 ($305) for risking 43 years of longevity. This willingness to pay is quite large, as it constitutes 2.13 per cent of the annual earnings of the workers in the sample (Majumder & Madheswaran, 2022).

6.3.3 *Estimation of discount rate using multi-period Markov model*

The multi-period Markov model comprises two equations. The first one is the implicit price equation given by equation (6.14). The second equation is given by equation (6.12). However, there is a problem with estimation of this equation. The form of utility function, that is, "U" is not specified in this equation. Therefore, the Markov model assumes an amenable functional form for the utility function in equation (6.12). In doing so, the implicit price equation is expressed in terms of variables for which the information can be obtained from the labour market. There is an unknown constant "β", a parameter "c" that represents the degree of worker's risk aversion and implicit prices in the expression. The implicit prices can be estimated from a first-stage regression, and the estimated implicit prices are then used as an independent variable in estimating equation (6.12). This method is the same as the one followed under the discounted expected life years approach.

An estimable version of equation (6.12) is obtained because "U" represents a constant relative risk aversion utility function which takes the following form:

$$U = a + bw^c$$

In this expression, "a" and "b" are arbitrary constants and "c" is the index of risk aversion of the individual. Without loss of generality, let us consider that $a = (-1/c)$ and $b = (1/c)$, then the expression becomes

$$U = \frac{w^c - 1}{c}$$

The shape of the utility function "U" depends on the parameter **c** and in certain cases it generates linear and semi-logarithmic utility functions. A constant relative risk aversion utility function provides an estimable relation between a function of wage and a function of implicit prices. Therefore, from above definition of "U", the marginal utility is obtained as follows:

$$\mathbf{U}' = \mathbf{w}^{\mathbf{c}-\mathbf{1}},$$

Then,

$$\frac{U}{U'} - \frac{1}{c}(w - w^{1-c})$$

Replacing the above expression in equation (6.12) yields the following:

$$\frac{\delta w_i}{\delta p_j} = \frac{1}{c}(w_i - w_i^{1-c}) \times \left[\frac{1}{(1-\mathrm{p}_i)} - \frac{\beta}{[1-\beta(1-\mathrm{p}_i)]^2}\right] \qquad (6.17)$$

Here, the utility function is individual-specific and therefore "i" is added in the subscript of the parameter's "**w**" and "**p**". Multiplying (6.17) by the term "$\mathbf{cw}^{\mathrm{c}-1}$" and dividing by the term in the brackets yields the following equation:

$$\left[\frac{1}{(1-\mathrm{p}_i)} - \frac{\beta}{[1-\beta(1-p_i)]}\right]^{-1} \times \mathbf{cw}^{\mathrm{c}-1}\frac{\delta w_i}{\delta \mathrm{p}_j} = \mathrm{w}_i^{\,\mathrm{c}} - 1 \qquad (6.18)$$

Since $\frac{\delta w^c}{\delta w} = \mathbf{cw}^{\mathrm{c}-1}$, we can express equation (7.18) in a simpler form

$$\mathrm{w}_{\mathrm{i}}^{\mathrm{c}} = 1 + \left[(1-\mathrm{p}_{\mathrm{i}}) - \beta(1-\mathrm{p}_{\mathrm{i}})^2\right]\frac{\delta w_i^c}{\delta p_j} \qquad (6.19)$$

Since "c" measures the degree of risk aversion of individual, we consider the outcome if "c" takes up different values. If "$\mathbf{c} \to \mathbf{0}$", equation (6.19) will represent a logarithmic utility function for a risk-averse individual

$$\ln \mathrm{w}_{\mathrm{i}}^{\mathrm{c}} = 1 + \left[(1-\mathrm{p}_{\mathrm{i}}) - \beta(1-\mathrm{p}_{\mathrm{i}})^2\right]\frac{\delta \ln w^c}{\delta p_j}$$

If "$\mathbf{c} \to 1$" then for a risk-neutral individual, equation (6.19) will represent the following

$$w_i = 1 + \left[(1-\mathrm{p}_{\mathrm{i}}) - \beta(1-\mathrm{p}_{\mathrm{i}})^2\right]\frac{\delta w_i}{\delta p_j}$$

If a vector of variables (which includes worker's personal and job characteristic) y_{2ki} and an unobservable term ε_{2i} is added, then equation (6.19) becomes

$$\mathrm{w}_{\mathrm{i}}^{\mathrm{c}} = 1 + \left[(1-\mathrm{p}_{\mathrm{i}}) - \beta(1-\mathrm{p}_{\mathrm{i}})^2\right]\frac{\delta w_i^c}{\delta p_j} + \sum_k \alpha_k y_{2ki} + \varepsilon_{2i}$$

For illustrative purposes, let us consider a logarithmic form of the above equation

$$\ln \mathrm{w}_{\mathrm{i}}^{\mathrm{c}} = \left[(1-\mathrm{p}_{\mathrm{i}}) - \beta(1-\mathrm{p}_{\mathrm{i}})^2\right]\frac{\delta \ln w_i^c}{\delta p_j} + \sum_k \alpha_k y_{2ki} + \varepsilon_{2i} \qquad (6.20)$$

Estimating this equation has an issue because the value of "**p**" is so small that the value of $(\mathbf{1}-\mathbf{p_i})$ and $(\mathbf{1}-\mathbf{p_i})^2$ will be indistinguishable. Therefore, to resolve this issue, both the variables are treated to be approximately equal, and the value of the parameter "β" is estimated. Therefore, equation (6.20) takes the following form

$$\ln w_i = \left[(1-\mathrm{p}_{\mathrm{i}})(1-\beta)\right]\frac{\delta \ln w_i}{\delta p_j} + \sum_k \alpha_k y_{2ki} + \varepsilon_{2i} \qquad (6.21)$$

In equation (6.21), the implicit price $\left(\frac{\delta \ln w_i}{\delta p_j}\right)$ is unobservable and therefore another issue arises with its estimation. This issue is resolved by running a first-stage regression of wages on workers' personal and job characteristics and job risk measures. Equation (6.21) represents a structural equation which is identified only if the first-stage regression contains variables that are excluded from the structural equation. The appropriate instruments that can be used in this context are the interaction between region dummies and job risk measures (Viscusi & Moore, 1989). The first-stage regression used here is the same as equation (7.14) used under the life-cycle approach.

Equation (6.21) indicates that all the workers have the same rate of time preference. To show that the discount rate varies among individuals due to variation in the level of education "$\mathbf{S_i}$" among individuals and due to other unobservable effects "ε_{3i}", this equation is rewritten as follows:

$$\ln \mathrm{w}_i = [(\mathbf{1}-\mathrm{p}_{\mathrm{i}}) - (\mathbf{1}-\beta_0)]\frac{\delta \ln w_i}{\delta p_j} + \beta_s S_i(\mathbf{1}-\mathrm{p}_{\mathrm{i}})\frac{\delta \ln w_i}{\delta p_j} + \sum_k a_k y_{2ki} + \varepsilon_i^* \qquad (6.22)$$

Here, the key aim is to estimate the discount rate, which is obtained from the term $[(\mathbf{1}-\beta) = \frac{r}{\mathbf{1}+r}]$ that varies across individuals. However, allowing the discount rates to vary across individuals leads to the problem of heteroscedasticity as

$$\varepsilon_i^* = \varepsilon_{2i} + \varepsilon_{3i}(\mathbf{1}-p_i)\frac{\delta \ln w_i}{\delta p_j}$$

And

$$Vr\left(\varepsilon_i^* = E\left(\varepsilon_i^{*2}\right)\right) = \sigma_2^2 + \sigma_3^2\left[(1-p_i)\frac{\delta \ln w_i}{\delta p_j}\right]^2 + 2\sigma_{23}(1-p_i)\frac{\delta \ln w_i}{\delta p_j}$$

The effect of this type of heteroscedasticity has been accounted for in estimation of the implicit price equation (6.12). To tackle this, two equations are estimated under the Markov decision model. At the first stage, equation (6.14) is estimated. Then the estimated implicit prices obtained from equation (6.14) are used to run equations (6.22), which finally yield the personal rate of time preference of the workers in the sample. Since the implicit prices and the term (1-p) are endogenous, equation (6.22) must be estimated using two-stage least squares. The interaction between regional dummies and fatal risk measures is taken as instruments in this respect.

Table 6.4 presents the result of estimation of the implicit price equation under the Markov decision model. The estimate of $(1-\beta)$ is obtained from the coefficient of the variable containing interaction between implicit price and one minus fatality risk. This coefficient yields the implicit discount rate "r". The impact of the level of education is estimated using the interaction term between years of schooling "S" and the variable $(1-p_i)\frac{\delta \ln w_i}{\delta p_j}$. The other independent variables included are the measures of worker's years of schooling, his social class, his job designation, and union status, which have expected relationship with the dependent variable. Since the education dummies yielded insignificant results, years of schooling have been used as an independent variable in this regression.

The aim of this estimation is to obtain individual discount rate for deferred health outcomes. Therefore, the method of estimating the discount rate is discussed hereafter.

Table 6.4 Estimation of implicit price equation under the Markov decision model

Variables	*Coefficient*
Implicit price $\times$ (1-p) $\times$ $(1\text{-}\beta)_0$	0.2454* (2.41)
Implicit price $\times$ (1-p) $\times$ years of schooling (β_s)	−0.0122** (−1.89)
Years of schooling	0.026** (1.79)
SC	−0.047*(−2.01)
Super	0.170* (3.35)
Union	0.011 (1.04)
N	428
Adjusted R^2	0.37
F	18.06

Source: Majumder and Madheswaran (2022).

Note: t-values are given in parentheses.

* 1 per cent level of significance, ** 5 per cent level of significance

From Table 6.4, the coefficient of the implicit price variable yields the estimate of $(\mathbf{1}-\beta)$ to be equal to $(0.2344–0.0122 \times S)$. The mean year of schooling (S) for the sample of workers is 8.4 (Majumder & Madheswaran, 2022). Therefore, the discount rate is obtained using the following steps:

$$\text{Since, } \left[(\mathbf{1}-\beta) = \frac{r}{\mathbf{1}+r} \right] = 0.2454\text{-}(0.0122 \times 8.4)\text{=}0.14292$$

$$\text{So, } \left[\beta = \left(\mathbf{1} - \frac{r}{\mathbf{1}+r} \right) \right] = (1\text{-}0.14292) = 0.85708$$

$$\text{Therefore, } r = \left(\frac{\mathbf{1}}{\beta} - \mathbf{1} \right) = 16.67$$

The Markov decision model yields the real discount rate of an average worker in the sample, which is 16.6 per cent, and it is highly significant since both interaction variables of implicit price are significant. Unlike the discounted expected life years approach and the life-cycle approach, the Markov model doesn't provide the real rate of time preference of individuals. Therefore, this measure of discount rate is converted into real interest rate by accounting for the inflation rate, which is around 4 per cent (Reserve Bank of India, 2017). Therefore, the real interest rate of 12.6 per cent is higher than the financial market interest rates (Majumder & Madheswaran, 2022).

A Markov model yields a rate of time preference based on the education level of workers. Results indicate that workers with primary level of education have a discount rate of 22.6 per cent (real discount rate is 18.6 per cent), while workers who have completed secondary level of school education have a discount rate of 15.2 per cent (real discount rate is 11.2 per cent). On the other hand, workers who have completed higher secondary and graduation have discount rates of 10.9 and 6.6 per cent (i.e. real discount rates of 6.9 per cent and 2.6 per cent), respectively. Thus, the higher the education level of the worker, the lower is his rate of time preference (Majumder & Madheswaran, 2022). Such relation is observed by many studies (Mincer, 1958; Becker, 1964; Viscusi, 1979; Viscusi & Moore, 1989; Becker & Mulligan, 1997; Golsteyn et al., 2013) which have been discussed in the introduction section of this chapter. In Chapter 4, the analysis of primary data (see Table 4.3, Chapter 4) indicated that the income of the worker increased with their education level. This observation is linked with the discount rate of the individuals. Thus, it can be said that the workers in the sample who are more educated have higher earnings and lower rates of time preference. On the other hand, workers with lower levels of education have lower earnings and higher rate of time preference.

An individual worker is willing to pay (0.5 ×mean implicit price× mean wage × annual hours of work = 0.5 × 0.0175 × 42.96 × 2160) INR 812.8 ($12.10) for a unit reduction in fatality risk. Therefore, 100,000 workers would be jointly willing to pay INR 81.28 million ($1.21 million), which is the estimate of the value of statistical life for discounted life years. This estimate is much higher than the VSL estimates obtained in earlier chapters. However, it corroborates with the estimates of the earlier studies in India that estimated the VSL for discounted life years. Shanmugam (2006) estimated the value per statistical life to range between INR 24.3 ($1.34 million) and INR 26.5 million ($1.47 million), which was much higher than the basic estimates of VSL estimated in his earlier studies using the same sample. Shanmugam (2011) estimated the industrial region-wise VSL that ranged between INR 19.98 ($1.11 million) and INR 30.2 million ($1.67 million) (Majumder & Madheswaran, 2022).

6.4 Conclusion

The rate of time preference for future health outcomes plays an important role in evaluation of health and environmental policies that yield benefits in distant future. For example, the benefits obtained from health policies that aim at reducing the exposure of factory workers to hazardous carcinogens in the workplace should be discounted to make them comparable with the current period benefits and costs. Most researchers and policymakers are hesitant to use financial market interest rates to discount these benefits. Since perfect markets are non-existent for health, financial market interest rates may not be appropriate in this respect. Financial market rates yield a lower bound of the discount rate that is suitable for discounting health outcomes (Moore & Viscusi, 1990b). Therefore, this chapter examined the individual rate of time preference of workers in the sample.

Three alternative approaches have been used to estimate the discount rate for long-term health outcomes. The real individual rate of time preference of workers in the sample for this study ranges between 2.6 and 18.6 per cent. The first model is the discounted expected life year approach, which emphasises the quality of life that is at risk. This approach has yielded a real discount rate of 10.6 and 13 per cent, respectively, from two alternative specifications. These discount rates are higher than financial market interest rates. The second approach used is the life-cycle approach, which captures the changes in life expectancy as an individual age. The real discount rate that is estimated from this approach is 6.71 per cent. This rate is close to the rate of interest on term deposits in banks. The last approach is a multi-period Markov decision model which considers work-related fatal risk to be temporal in nature. This model yields a real discount rate of 12.6 per cent for the full sample. The estimated discount rate is much higher than financial market interest rates (Majumder & Madheswaran, 2022). However, individuals in developing countries are observed to assign higher discount rates for future health outcomes than those in developed countries. While the discount rate used in developing countries ranges between 8 and 15 per cent, the discount rate used by the developed countries ranges between 3 and 7 per cent (Zhuang et al., 2007). The real discount rate obtained from the Markov decision model is consistent with this observation. The Markov model allows researchers to examine how the discount rate varies with the education level of workers. A worker having primary education discounts the future health outcomes at 18.6 per cent, while a graduate discounts it at the rate of 2.6 per cent. Thus, it is observed that individuals with higher levels of education assign lower discount rates for long-term health outcomes compared to individuals with lower levels of education (Majumder & Madheswaran, 2022). This finding is also in line with the findings of the earlier studies (Viscusi, 1979; Viscusi & Moore, 1989) examining the variation of discount rate with education level.

The results of this study indicate that workers in the sample take rational decisions while allocating their resources over time. The overall consistency of the discount rates across models indicates that the findings of this study are robust. However, in many cases, discount rates are found to be much higher than financial market interest rates. This indicates that simply using financial market interest rates to discount future utility of individuals may not be appropriate. Rather, the rates of time preference should be estimated from individual studies. The high discount rates obtained in this study indicate that current and near-term health risks are weighed more heavily compared to distant future health risks. Therefore, workers will require higher wages to take up risky jobs.

Reference list

Becker, G. (1964). *Human capital, a theoretical and empirical analysis with special reference to education*. Columbia University Press. Retrieved December 11, 2018, from https://www.jstor.org/stable/2229541

Becker, G. S., & Mulligan, C. B. (1997). The endogenous determination of time preference. *The Quarterly Journal of Economics*, *112*(3), 729–758. Retrieved June 15, 2015, from http://www.jstor.org/stable/2951254

Bickel, W., Odum, A., & Madden, G. (1999). Impulsivity and cigarette smoking: Delay discounting in current, never, and ex-smokers. *Psychopharmacology*, *146*(4), 447–454. Retrieved December 11, 2018, from https://pubmed.ncbi.nlm.nih.gov/10550495/

Borghans, L., & Golsteyn, B. (2006). Time discounting and the body mass index, evidence from the Netherlands. *Economics and Human Biology*, *4*(1), 39–61. Retrieved August 07, 2018, from https://doi.org/10.1016/j.ehb.2005.10.001

Della, V. S., & Paserman, D. (2005). Job search and impatience. *Journal of Labor Economics*, *23*(2), 527–588. Retrieved February 27, 2015, from https://www.nber.org/papers/w10837

Fuchs, V. R. (1982). Time preference and health: An exploratory study. In *Economic aspects of health* (pp. 93–120). National Bureau of Economic Research, University of Chicago Press. Retrieved December 16, 2018, from https://www.nber.org/system/files/chapters/c6546/c6546.pdf

Golsteyn, B. H., Grönqvist, H., & Lindahl, L. (2013). *Time preferences and lifetime outcomes* (Discussion Paper No. 7165, IZA Institute of Labour Economics).

Retrieved February 27, 2015, from https://www.iza.org/publications/dp/7165/time-preferences-and-lifetime-outcomes

Grossman, M. (1972). On the concept of health capital and the demand for health. *Journal of Political Economy*, *80*(2), 223–255. Retrieved August 05, 2018, from https://www.jstor.org/stable/1830580

Kula, E. (2004). Estimation of a social rate of interest for India. *Journal of Agricultural Economics*, *55*(1), 91–99.

Lawless, L. J., Nayga, R., & Drichoutis, A. (2013). *Time preference and health behaviour: A review* (Paper No. 45382). Munich Personal RePEc Archive (MPRA). Retrieved December 11, 2018, from http://mpra.ub.uni-muenchen.de/45382/

Majumder, A., & Madheswaran, S. (2022). Discounting long-term job-related health risks in the context of Indian workers. *The Indian Journal of Labour Economics*, *65*, 1099–1120. Retrieved February 27, 2015, from https://doi.org/10.1007/s41027-022-00415-4

Mincer, J. (1958). Investment in human capital and personal income distribution. *Journal of Political Economy*, *66*(4), 281–302. Retrieved June 15, 2015, from https://www.jstor.org/stable/1827422

Moore, M., & Viscusi, W. K. (1988). The quantity-adjusted value of life. *Economic Inquiry*, *26*(3), 369–388. Retrieved July 29, 2018, from https://ideas.repec.org/a/oup/ecinqu/v26y1988i3p369-88.html

Moore, M. J., & Viscusi, W. K. (1989). Rates of time preference and valuations of the duration of life. *Journal of Public Economics*, *38*, 297–317.

Moore, M., & Viscusi, W. K. (1990a). Discounting environmental health risks: New evidence and policy implications. *Journal of Environmental Economics and Management*, *18*(2), S51–S62. Retrieved August 05, 2018, from https://doi.org/10.1016/0095-0696(90)90037-Y

Moore, M., & Viscusi, W. K. (1990b). Models for estimating discount rates for long-term health risks using labor market. *Journal of Risk and Uncertainty*, *3*(4), 381–401. Retrieved August 05, 2018, from https://doi.org/10.1007/BF00353348

Office of the Registrar General & Census Commissioner, India. (2017). *SRS based life table 2011–15*. Ministry of Home Affairs, Government of India. Retrieved September 03, 2018, from https://censusindia.gov.in/nada/index.php/catalog/42514/download/46140/SRS-Abridged_Life_Tables_2011-2015.pdf

Pender, J. L. (1996). Discount rates and credit markets: Theory and evidence from rural India. *Journal of Development Economics*, *50*(2), 257–296.

Reserve Bank of India. (2017). *Results of the survey of professional forecasters on macroeconomic indicators – Round 44*. Retrieved February 06, 2019, from https://rbi.org.in/Scripts/PublicationsView.aspx?id=17433

Reserve Bank of India. (n.d.). *Reference rate archive*. Reference Exchange rate date: 1/02/2016. https://www.rbi.org.in/scripts/referenceratearchive.aspx

Samuelson, P. A. (1937). A note on measurement of utility. *The Review of Economic Studies*, *4*(2), 155–161. Retrieved December 11, 2018, from https://doi.org/10.2307/2967612

Shanmugam, K. R. (2006). Rate of time preference and the quantity adjusted value of life in India. *Environment and Development Economics*, *11*(5), 569–583. Retrieved June 19, 2015, from https://www.cambridge.org/core/journals/environment-and-development-economics/article/abs/rate-of-time-preference-and-the-quantity-adjusted-value-of-life-in-india/A3BBB3BE8FB8EB5B1BB8B39D3B339854

Shanmugam, K. R. (2011). Discount rate for health benefits and the value of life in India. *Economics Research International, 2011*, 1–5.

Stephens, M., & Krupka, E. (2006). *Subjective discount rates and household behaviour*. Working paper, Department of Economics, University of Michigan.

Thaler, R., & Rosen, S. (1976). The value of saving a life: Evidence from the labor market. In N. E. Terleckyj (Ed.), *Household production and consumption* (pp. 265–302). NBER. Retrieved February 27, 2015, from https://www.nber.org/system/files/chapters/c3964/c3964.pdf

Viscusi, W. K. (1979). *Employment hazards: An investigation of market performance*. Harvard University Press. Retrieved June 15, 2015, from https://www.hup.harvard.edu/books/9780674251762

Viscusi, W. K. (1995). Discounting health effects for medical decisions, valuing healthcare. In S. A. Frank (Ed.), *Valuing health care costs, benefits, and effectiveness of pharmaceuticals and other medical technologies* (pp. 125–147). Cambridge University Press. Retrieved February 27, 2015, from https://doi.org/10.1002/pam.4050150323

Viscusi, W. K., & Moore, M. J. (1989). Rates of time preference and valuations of the duration of life. *Journal of Public Economics*, *38*, 297–317. Retrieved July 29, 2018, from https://ideas.repec.org/a/eee/pubeco/v38y1989i3p297-317.html

Zhuang, Z. L., Lin, T., & De Guzman, F. (2007). *Theory and practice in the choice of social discount rate for cost-benefit analysis: A survey*. Asian Development Bank, Economic and Research Department Working Paper Series, Working Paper No. 94.

7 Conclusion

7.1 Introduction

This chapter summarises the results of the preceding analysis. It begins with a discussion on the major findings of this study which are presented under Section 7.2. Following this, the policy implications of the study are presented under Section 7.3. The last section (i.e. Section 7.4) presents the limitations of this study and suggests a few issues on which further research can be undertaken in the future.

7.2 Discussion of key findings

The principal objective of this study is to estimate the value of statistical life and injury of workers in the sample and to examine the impact of compensation benefits and discounting future health outcomes on the VSL estimates. The major findings of the study are presented under the following sub-sections.

7.2.1 Findings from meta-analysis of VSL studies

Chapter 2 provides an extensive review of VSL studies, which indicates that the estimates of VSL vary substantially across studies and over years. Besides methodological differences and sampling variance, there exist numerous unobserved factors that may cause such variations. Therefore, a meta-analysis of VSL studies has been undertaken to understand the source and nature of these variations. The meta-analysis comprises 30 hedonic-wages-based VSL studies from developed and developing countries. A mixed effects regression model has been used for analysis. The results indicate that unobserved heterogeneity is the primary cause of variation in VSL estimates. The income elasticity of VSL is estimated to be 0.25 (Majumder & Madheswaran, 2016, 2018a). This estimate is like the findings of meta-analyses like De Blaeij et al. (2003), Kluve and Schaffner (2008), Stanley and Doucouliagos (2012).

DOI: 10.4324/9781003628262-7

7.2.2 Findings on compensating wage differentials and VSL in India

The first objective of this study is to estimate worker's compensating wage differential for occupational fatal and non-fatal injuries and to calculate the monetary values of statistical life and injury. The results indicate that workers in the sample earn significant and positive wage differentials for job risks (both fatal and non-fatal job risks). The annual compensating wage differential for job-related fatal risk is estimated to be INR 446, and that for injury risk is INR 1,673. This implies that, on average, a worker in the sample is paid INR 446 annually for an increase in job-related fatal risk by the probability of 0.000001 (i.e. 1/100,000) and INR 1,673 annually for an increase in job-related injury risk by the probability of 0.001 (i.e. 1/1,000). Thus, the basic estimates of value of statistical life and value of statistical injury for this study are INR 44.69 million ($0.64 million) and INR 1.67 million ($0.024 million), respectively. Workers who perceive their job to be risky earn a wage premium of INR 4,358 ($64.97) annually (Majumder & Madheswaran, 2018a).

The results pertaining to other explanatory variables used in the analysis are discussed in this paragraph. Earnings of a worker are observed to increase with experience and increase in level of education. On the other hand, migrant workers and workers belonging to schedule castes are found to earn significantly lower wages compared to other workers in the sample. The workers who are engaged in permanent jobs earn significantly higher compared to workers engaged in contractual jobs. The total number of workers working in a factory (i.e. size of a factory) does not have significant influence on workers' wages. Previous VSL studies in India indicated that union status of workers has a significant and positive impact on their wages. However, this study found that union membership does not affect worker's wages. A possible reason for this may be that only 7 per cent of the workers in the sample are union members. Besides, many workers reported during primary survey that labour unions in their factories either are dysfunctional or do not exist anymore. Therefore, a low union participation is not a surprising trend. Workers engaged in jobs that require mental work earn higher wages than other workers. On the other hand, workers engaged in jobs that require them to work fast or engage in hard physical work earn significantly lower wages than other workers. Workers with job designations like contractors and supervisors earn significantly higher wages compared to assistants and workers with other job designations. Workers employed in factories located in industrial division 4 earn significantly lower wages compared to workers located in other industrial divisions.

The results of this study indicate that endogenous relationship between worker's wage and job risk along with unobserved heterogeneity in worker's characteristics cause substantial bias in estimation of wage premium for fatal and injury risks. They create an upward bias for the VSL estimates and downward bias for VSI estimates. Therefore, on removal of this bias, the estimates of VSL decline while the estimates of VSI increase. The selectivity bias-corrected estimates of VSL and VSI are INR 35.8 million ($0.51 million) and INR 4.30 million ($0.06 million), respectively.

The overall results for the fatal and injury risk equations are consistent with the fact that safety is a normal good. The wealthier workers in the sample tend to select safer jobs. Thus, the influence of worker's wealth on his choice of job risk is significantly visible in this study. The implications of using benefit transfer methodology (BTM) to estimate VSL are also examined in this study. It is found that transferring VSL estimates from the United States to India underestimates the VSL of India. The country-specific characteristics are taken into consideration in independent VSL studies, which BTM fails to capture, yielding underestimated estimate of VSL. Thus, conducting independent VSL studies like the present one yields precise estimate of VSL.

This study not only provides an updated estimate of VSL for Indian labour market but also revises the estimation method. The estimation of VSL in this study is done using a slightly different formula compared to previous studies in India. Usually, the estimated CWD for job risk is annualised by multiplying with annual work hours and finally multiplied with the scale of job risk to obtain VSL and VSI estimates. Earlier VSL studies assumed that workers work for 2,000 hours annually; however, proper justification for this assumption was not provided. Therefore, this study revised the value for annual work hours using information from The Factories Act (1948). According to this Act, a worker can work up to 9 hours per day. Besides, a worker is entitled to 12 paid leaves in the following year if he works for 240 days in the present calendar year. In this study, workers in the sample get at least 12 days of paid leave annually. Therefore, it is assumed that workers in the sample work for 240 days on average. On multiplying 240 days with 9 hours, the total annual work hours are calculated to be 2,160. Thus, the annual hours of work for the workers in the sample are 2,160, and it has been used to obtain the estimates of VSL and VSI for this study.

7.2.3 Findings on the nexus between compensation benefit and VSL

The insurance or compensation benefit that a worker would receive in the event of any work-related injury or death plays a significant role in determining the compensation package for risky jobs (i.e. the wage paid for risky jobs). To examine the influence of worker's compensation benefits on their wage, an interaction between job risk measure and compensation benefit is introduced in hedonic wage equation. In case of temporary disability, it is found that inclusion of this interaction term increased the wage–risk trade-offs for fatal as well as injury risk. On inclusion of interaction between fatal risk measure and compensation benefit the VSL estimate decreased to INR 30.27 million ($0.45 million), while the VSI estimate increased to INR 2.36 million ($0.035 million). On inclusion of interaction between injury risk measure and compensation benefit, the estimates of VSL increased to INR 66.82 million ($0.99 million), and the VSI estimate increased to INR 1.94 million ($0.028 million). On inclusion of the lump sum compensation benefits, the coefficient of job risk variables increased and yielded high estimates of VSL and VSI. The VSL estimates for the lump sum compensation adjusted specifications range between INR 65.90 million ($0.98 million) and INR 72.11 million ($1.02 million). On the other hand, the VSI for the compensation-adjusted specifications ranges between INR 2.42 million ($0.036 million) and INR 2.82 million ($0.042 million). Thus, it is found that exclusion of worker's compensation benefits from estimation of hedonic wage equation yields biased estimates of VSL and VSI (Majumder & Madheswaran, 2018c).

In this study, the optimal rate of trade-off between worker's wage and compensation benefit is calculated, and it is compared with the observed trade-off which is obtained from the estimation of compensation-adjusted hedonic wage equation. The optimal trade-off between workers' wages and compensation benefits is calculated to be 0.19. A negative trade-off is observed between worker's compensation for temporary disability and their wage. Results indicate that a worker has to sacrifice 50 paisa from his monthly wage to obtain an additional one rupee worth of compensation in case of temporary injury. This observed rate of trade-off is much higher than the optimal trade-off. Thus, the worker's compensation levels are sub-optimal given the insurance income levels. However, a sub-optimal rate of substitution is desirable if the government has to control the issue of moral hazard (when the benefits are much higher than the number of contributions made towards compensation programmes, workers tend to be less careful about avoiding work-related injuries, and this would raise the number of insurance claims). On the contrary, a positive trade-off is obtained between lump sum compensation benefit (for permanent disability and death) and worker's wage. This indicates that if a worker is provided with higher lump sum compensation for permanent disability and death, then he will demand higher wage. This may be since any kind of permanent disability leads to complete loss of earning capacity for the rest of the life, and death stops the flow of income altogether. So, the risks associated with these outcomes are much higher than temporary disability. In such a scenario, only providing higher compensation benefit is not enough. Therefore, workers would require higher compensation benefit as well as higher wage in case of permanent total disability and death. Besides, the trade-off values are minuscule so that the substitution between the compensation benefit and worker's wage can be considered to be negligible (Majumder &and Madheswaran, 2018c).

7.2.4 Findings on discount rate for long-term job-related health risks

The final objective of this study pertains to estimation of discount rate of workers in the sample. Three approaches have been used to accomplish this.

The first model is the discounted expected life year approach, which provides a real discount rate of 10.6 and 13 per cent, respectively, from two alternative specifications. These discount rates are higher than financial market interest rates. The second approach is the life-cycle approach, which provides a real discount rate of 6.71 per cent. This rate is close to the interest rate on term deposit in commercial banks. The last approach is a multi-period Markov decision model which provides a real discount rate of 12.6 per cent for the full sample. This model also provides discount rates for workers according to their level of education. A worker having primary education discounts the future health outcomes at 18.6 per cent, while a graduate discounts it at the real rate of 2.6 per cent. Thus, it is observed that the higher the education level of workers, the lower is the discount rate for long-term health outcomes (Majumder & Madheswaran, 2022).

Results show that workers in the sample take rational decisions while allocating their resources over time. The current and near-term period health risks are weighed more heavily compared to distant future health risks. Therefore, workers will require higher wages in order to take up jobs that increase the exposure to risk. Most of the estimated discount rates are close to the financial market interest rates. However, in certain cases, the estimated discount rates are found to be much higher. Thus, the results of this study indicate that using financial market interest rates to discount future utility of individuals is not appropriate. The discount rates are consistent across models, indicating that the findings of this study are robust (Majumder & Madheswaran, 2022).

7.3 Policy implications of the findings

This study attempts to estimate the value of statistical life and injury using information on a sample of workers from manufacturing industries of Ahmedabad, district of Gujarat. The estimated VSL ranges between INR 30.27 million ($0.45 million) and INR 81.11 million ($1.21 million). The estimated VSI, on the other hand, ranges between INR 1.67 million ($0.024 million) and INR 4.30 million ($0.064 million). These results have important implications for the performance of the labour market in India. Though the sample used in this study is not representative of the entire country, it provides an insight into the working of the labour market in India. The result of this study indicates that workers earn positive CWD for taking up risky jobs. In this context, the government can play a major role in providing better information on risks associated with various jobs so that workers can assess the job risk and demand the wage differentials accordingly. To do so, more research on OSH in India should be undertaken by researchers, government agencies and government organisations (Majumder & Madheswaran, 2018b).

This study has important policy implications as well. The VSL and VSI estimates obtained from this study can be used for assessment of existing government policies and projects that aim at mortality risk reduction. It will aid policymakers in framing new policies on environmental safety and health. This study also yields some interesting results that provide an insight into the existing government programmes on worker's compensation in India. Given the extent of analysis of this study, the compensation benefit for temporary disability and dependents' benefit under the ESI programme is found to be adequate for workers in the sample from policy point of view.

As discussed in Chapter 3, availability of secondary data on job risks in India is a major concern for researchers. Most developing countries, including India, do not have adequate data on job risk. An elaborate and precise data on job risks would aid in evidence-based policymaking. In this context, there is an urgent need for laying down of proper guidelines and policies by the government towards improving the scope and coverage of the information collected on work-related deaths and injuries in India. The government should modify the system of reporting of industrial accidents so as to prevent under-reporting of such occurrences. The government needs to appoint more factory inspectors and ensure timely inspection of factories to prevent accidents.

The observations from primary survey indicate that the presence of union in factories is dwindling. Therefore, workers have become vulnerable to employer's dictate. Even though workers are compensated for job risks, they have many other issues that remain unattended. In such a scenario, government intervention may become necessary in near future to protect the interest of workers. Besides, there is a rising trend of informal work at lower pay and unsafe work conditions which should be monitored and brought under policy perspective.

Although regulations on OSH exist in India, it has not yet ratified major ILO conventions (C155 and C161) related to occupational health and safety. The government should actively take some steps to ratify these conventions that are necessary for ensuring safety at workplace. It is high time for the government to shift its policy orientation from economic outcomes to those that emphasise the processes and institutions.

7.4 Limitations of the study and scope for future research

Developed countries have elaborate data on industrial accidents and diseases. In the United States, the Department of Labour, Bureau of Labour Statistics (BLS), collects and compiles information on fatal and non-fatal injuries that are stratified on the basis of industries, occupation, age of workers, cohort, gender, race, migrant status, et cetera. Since such detailed information on job risks is unavailable, research on mortality risk reduction in India is limited. There are many researchable issues that could not be addressed in this study due to paucity of secondary data on job risks. For example, the relation between worker's age and VSL could not be examined because the available secondary data on job risk is not stratified by individual's age. Therefore, in the Indian context, there is much scope for future research in examining the role of worker's age, gender, caste, and migrant status in determining their VSL and VSI. Besides, the presence of segmented labour market in India is yet to be examined.

VSL studies in developed countries use a more precise job risk measure by matching industry-level job risk with the occupation of workers. This matching is done because job risks vary across industries and also by the type of occupation of an individual. A manager and a machine operator do not face the same level of job risk even though they work in the same factory. Therefore, a distinction in job risk level by occupation and industry of a worker is essential to obtain more precise estimate of VSL and avoid the problem of measurement error. However, in India, secondary data on job risk are stratified only by industry and available up to a two-digit industrial classification code. The information on job risk in India is thus inadequate, and analysis of such data is difficult. Most developing countries face similar issues. In such a scenario, researchers use a sample comprising of only blue-collar workers to reduce the impact of measurement error. This problem is more serious for white-collar workers because they encounter a different and much safer work conditions (Garen, 1988). In similar manner, this study attempted to reduce the impact of this problem by using a sample that comprises only blue-collar workers.

At present, institutional coverage in collection of secondary data on job risk is narrow since it doesn't cover the vast unorganised sector and emerging service sector which possess various occupational hazards. Therefore, the information on fatal and non-fatal injuries in these sectors is unavailable. Thus, this study only focuses on the organised sector workers who are employed in registered factories. There is a scope for future research in examining the job risk preferences of workers from unorganised sector.

Finally, the results of this study may not be generalised for all the workers in the state of Gujarat or India since that would require a larger representation of the population. A meaningful policy prescription can be provided only after extensive and in-depth research on mortality risk reduction is undertaken in India. Despite these limitations, the result of the present study provides useful insight into the operation of the labour market and into the choice of occupational risks by workers. The results of this study can aid policymakers, researchers, and international agencies in assessing various health projects in India as well as in other developing countries.

Reference list

De Blaeij, A., Florax, R. J. G. M., Rietveld, P., & Verhoef, E. (2003). The value of statistical life in road safety: A meta-analysis. *Accident Analysis and Prevention*, *35*, 973–986. Retrieved April 25, 2015, from https://doi.org/10.1016/S0001-4575(02)00105-7

Garen, J. E. (1988). Compensating wage differentials and endogeneity of job riskiness. *The Review of Economics and Statistics*, *7*(1), 9–16.

Kluve, J., & Schaffner, S. (2008). The value of life in Europe – A meta-analysis. *Sozialer Fortschritt*, *57*(10–11), 279–287. Retrieved August 05, 2016.

Labour Bureau, Ministry of Labour and Employment, Government of India. (2022). *The Factories Act, 1948*. Retrieved 20/06/2026.

Majumder, A., & Madheswaran, S. (2016). *Value of statistical life: A meta-analysis with mixed effects regression model* (Working Paper No. 362). Institute for Social and Economic Change. Retrieved August 01, 2018, from https://www.isec.ac.in/wp-content/uploads/2023/07/WP-362-Agamoni-Majumder-Final.pdf

Majumder, A., & Madheswaran, S. (2018a). Compensating wage differential and value of statistical life: A meta-analysis. *Indian Journal of Labour Economics*, *60*(4), 527–548. Retrieved June 01, 2018, from https://doi.org/10.1007/s41027-018-0102-y

Majumder, A., & Madheswaran, S. (2018b). *Value of statistical life in India: A hedonic wage approach* (Working Paper No. 407). Institute for Social and Economic Change. Retrieved August 01, 2018, from https://www.isec.ac.in/wp-content/uploads/2023/07/WP-407-Agamoni-Majumder-and-Madheswaran-Final.pdf

Majumder, A., & Madheswaran, S. (2018c). *Role of worker's compensation benefit in estimating value of statistical life* (Working Paper No. 423). Institute for Social and Economic Change. Retrieved August 01, 2018, from https://www.isec.ac.in/wp-content/uploads/2023/07/WP-423-Agamoni-Majumder-and-Madheswaran_2-Final.pdf

Majumder, A., & Madheswaran, S. (2022). Discounting long-term job-related health risks in the context of Indian workers. *The Indian Journal of Labour Economics*, *65*, 1099–1120. Retrieved February 23, 2024, from https://doi.org/10.1007/s41027-022-00415-4

Stanley, T. D., & Doucouliagos, H. (2012). *Meta-regression analysis in economics and business* (1st ed.). Routledge. Retrieved October 07, 2015.

Index

Note: Page numbers in *italic* indicate a figure and page numbers in **bold** indicate a table on the corresponding page.

For Product Safety Concerns and Information please contact our EU
representative GPSR@taylorandfrancis.com
Taylor & Francis Verlag GmbH, Kaufingerstraße 24, 80331 München, Germany

www.ingramcontent.com/pod-product-compliance
Lightning Source LLC
LaVergne TN
LVHW010649300926
849161LV00005B/1071

* 9 7 8 1 0 4 1 0 3 9 2 5 9 *